MW01252930

In this impressive book, *the* great sociological theorist of cognition, Stephen Turner, brings together and critically evaluates the important results in cognitive science of the past quarter century; the book serves both as introduction to the uninitiated and a decisive reconfiguration for those who have been following this history. Social theory will not be the same.

John Levi Martin, University of Chicago

How do our best current theories in the cognitive sciences relate to our best understanding of the social? The answer is not well and not easily. Each domain is tumultuous, teeming with theoretical disagreement and conflict. The chances of bringing them into harmony are slim. Yet in this book, Turner makes a heroic attempt to close these gaps and provide some integration. He recognizes that the task is no picnic; there is no easy way to make sense of the various alternatives. At the very least, acknowledging the deep philosophical issues that must be addressed, this primer—this beginner's guide—sketches a rough lay of the land. In this, Turner's brave attempt answers a great need. Given the magnitude of the challenge, this book is surely just a first step on a much longer adventure. But it is an all-important step!

Daniel D. Hutto, Professor of Philosophical Psychology in the School of Humanities and Social Inquiry, University of Wollongong, Australia

Synthesizing and confronting diverse and cutting edge ideas across an impressive array of disciplines, Stephen Turner shows that interdisciplinary dreams of integrating cognitive science and social theory are a long way from fruition. He argues convincingly that complex social life still resists explanation by combining mainstream or classical neuroscience, computation, and evolution, but Turner also pinpoints tough challenges for alternative approaches based on embodied social interaction. This powerful and unusual critical primer assumes no specific prior knowledge, and should be read by everyone keen to understand mind, action, and society.

John Sutton, Macquarie University, Sydney

COGNITIVE SCIENCE AND THE SOCIAL

A serious encounter between cognitive neuroscience and social science is likely to be challenging, and transformative, for both parties. Although a literature has developed on proposals to integrate neuroscience and social science, these proposals go in divergent directions. None of them has a developed conception of social life. Turner surveys these issues, introduces the basic alternative conceptions both of the mental world and the social world, and shows how, with sufficient modification, they can be fit together in plausible ways.

The book is not a "new theory" of anything, but rather an exploration of the critical issues that relate to the social aspects of cognition which expands the topic from the social neuroscience of immediate interpersonal interaction to the whole range of places where social variation interacts with the cognitive. The focus is on the conceptual problems produced by any attempt to take these issues seriously, and also on the new resources and considerations relevant to doing so. But it is also on the need for a revision of social theoretical concepts in order to utilize these resources. The book points to some conclusions, especially about how the process of what was known as socialization needs to be understood in cognitive science friendly terms.

Stephen P. Turner is Distinguished University Professor at the University of South Florida. He has written on issues of cognitive and social science since the 1980s, incorporating philosophy and science studies in related areas, and publishing two collections of articles on these topics, *Brains/Practices/Relativism* and *Understanding the Tacit*, as well as a number of other articles and chapters. Dr. Turner is the author, co-author, editor, or co-editor of twenty-five other books.

COGNITIVE SCIENCE AND THE SOCIAL

A Primer

Stephen P. Turner

Routledge
Taylor & Francis Group

NEW YORK AND LONDON

First published 2018
by Routledge
711 Third Avenue, New York, NY 10017

and by Routledge
2 Park Square, Milton Park, Abingdon, Oxon OX14 4RN

Routledge is an imprint of the Taylor & Francis Group, an informa business

Library of Congress Cataloging in Publication Data
A catalog record for this book has been requested

ISBN: 978-0-8153-8567-7 (hbk)
ISBN: 978-0-8153-8569-1 (pbk)
ISBN: 978-1-3511-8052-8 (ebk)

Typeset in Bembo
by Taylor & Francis Books

For Eileen

CONTENTS

FOREWORD

In writing this book I have attempted to avoid as many narrowly philosophical problems as possible, and to concentrate on the issues most relevant to social theory and social science more generally. One point of the book is that there is a difference, and that both cognitive science and social science look different when these issues are taken into account. Nevertheless, there are several places in the book where I have had to make "philosophical" comments in the course of bridging topics. I have purposely not provided citations of my own writings in support of these comments. The same holds for comments about the interpretation of classic social thinkers. For the interested (or shocked) reader, papers on both topics are readily accessible on my Academia.edu page, and elsewhere. These are different in character from the present book, oriented to very specific professional literatures, and only marginally relevant to the big-picture, broad-brush account presented in this book. However, the professional literature does radically diverge from the conventional viewpoints on the classics people learn in graduate school, so a warning is justified.

The book is not an introduction to current writing in social science that is either attempting to apply cognitive science or attempting to accommodate cognitive science within social science, so there are few citations of the pioneering figures who are beginning this huge task. Nor is the book a critique of these efforts. I applaud them, and would like to mention, in sociology, where this work is still in its infancy, Piet Strydom, Karen Cerulo, Maurizio Meloni, Omar Lizardo, Dimitri Shalin, Tony Waters, Gabe Ignatow, Wayne Brekhus, Gabe Abend, Stephen Vaisey, Margaret Frye, John Levi Martin, and Alban Bouvier, among many others who are starting careers with an interest in cognitive science. The *Journal for the Theory of Social Behavior* should also be noted for its openness to these topics. The literature in other fields is more extensive. Neuroanthropology is a lively field which has developed much more rapidly and raises important questions, nicely introduced in a volume edited by Daniel H. Lende and Greg Downey, *The Encultured Brain*. Neuroeconomics, especially in the work of Ernst Fehr, has exposed issues with the standard model of rationality, and made remarkable progress in dealing with such problems as the neural basis of punishing free-riders. There is an active presence of neuroscience issues in political science, under the heading of neuropolitics—for example in the work of William Connolly, John Gunnell and Darren Schreiber—and in the application of cognitive science to the study of political behavior for practical purposes, as well as to such topics as deliberation, in the work of Helene Landemore, for another example. There are similar movements in law, ethics, management, religious studies, and many other "social" fields. And there are active and bold attempts at inter-disciplinarity, notably by such people as Felicity Callard and, of course, Dan Sperber, who has been a visionary leader. It is not too much to say that this is the beginning of a revolution.

This book is a prolegomena to these worthy efforts, rather than an introduction. The scholars mentioned above were, by necessity, self-taught about cognitive science, and had to construct a working understanding of the issues on their own. This book is meant to provide a partial substitute: a short-cut to the reader's own self-education, a bridge from actual cognitive science to social theory and social science that does not quite fill the gap, but shows what the issues in the gap are.

Some large acknowledgments are due: to David Eck, who collaborated with me on two handbook articles which were partly incorporated into this text; to Spencer Williams, an aspiring undergraduate neuroscientist who provided some useful reactions; and, as always to Eileen Kahl, who has worked with me for almost a quarter century and has taken up even more editorial burdens for me in the last few years, for which I am very grateful.

Stephen Turner
Pass-a-Grille, Florida

INTRODUCTION

Cognitive Science

A primer was a book, originally a prayer book, used to teach children to read. The term came to be used for books that outlined basic principles. The book that follows is a primer both in the larger metaphorical sense of teaching to read and of outlining principles. But the "principles" of cognitive science themselves turn out to be in conflict; and, significantly, the existing social sciences, which have their own conflicts, do not fit very well with the approaches and problem situations that have emerged in cognitive science. Both domains, social science and cognitive science, have features in common. In each domain there is a vast array of topics and findings. Cognitive neuroscience has an extensive and extremely complex literature, with well-developed approaches that are difficult to relate to one another. Social science has a much longer history, but also one with many perspectives, and little in the way of resolution of the differences between perspectives.

My aim is to fill what I see as a gap between the two domains. The gap is conceptual: the way problems are constructed in the two domains differ; the means of explanation and the fundamental conflicts within the domains differ. But there are good reasons to explore the issues raised by the relations between the two domains. In the first place, the domains overlap. Although much of cognitive science, and especially cognitive neuroscience, is concerned with topics—such as the physical mechanics of perception or the chemistry of Alzheimer's, that are not topics of social science—the topics of concern to social science, such as human action and intentionality, are also of central concern to cognitive science. Nor can social science ignore cognitive science: "social" phenomena route their causality through human minds, and therefore also through brains.

The General Problem

Normally, brains are treated as a "black box" which social scientists need not open. Minds are considered differently: something important, but better left stylized in mathematical models of rational choice that are used to make derivations and predictions, or simply treated in common sense terms—either the terms of the people being studied or those of the academic interpreter. This is in some sense the core of the problem of the gap, and it is a problem with many variations, as we will see. The way we can describe the brain does not mesh well with the way we describe our minds and actions.

There is a systematic reason for this as well: complexity. Cognitive science works with easily segregated processes and breaks them down further, and tries also to build from processes to more complex tasks and capacities. In contrast, social science faces highly complex phenomena with multiple causal processes that can usually be approached only by abstractions that simplify in a way that is incompatible with the way cognitive science simplifies. Collective notions like revolution, or leadership, that involve many people, many dimensions, and many interacting causes can be turned into types, which can then be generalized about. It is not surprising that the results do not mesh.

It would be unlikely that any filling of the gap would result in a neat resolution to the puzzles that arise from this failure to mesh. But it is nevertheless a pressing problem. As more is learned in cognitive neuroscience, the more difficult it is for social science to ignore it. The black box is being opened, and what is being learned is being applied to social life, to action, and to reasoning. The results often do not fit with common sense talk about minds. Understanding the problems of cognitive science is necessary for social science to meet this challenge. But, at the same time, social life is a challenge for cognitive science. Social life contains many phenomena that are puzzling for cognitive science. Why, for example, if our cognitive architecture is not only intricate but largely the same across humanity, is there so much cultural variation and variation in concepts between groups? How does this variation arise, and through what cognitive processes?

The gaps are theoretical, and deep. They are connected with fundamental philosophical issues about mind and body, consciousness, and rationality. But a lot of work has been done filling in these gaps, or illuminating them. Many cognitive scientists have drawn implications from their work for social life and the social sciences, or have done work designed to illuminate issues in the social sciences. There are active fields, such as neuroeconomics and social neuroscience, devoted to reconstructing areas of social science in the light of cognitive science findings and experiments. And there is an active effort by social scientists, much greater in some fields than others, to engage with neuroscience.

Much of this engagement has occurred at the level of the consideration of specific findings. In the case of neuroeconomics and decision theory, for example, the emphasis has been on deviations from rational choice and deviations from pure game theoretical rationality that produce alternative game theoretic outcomes. In the case of politics, there has been an emphasis on the cognitive differences between liberals and conservatives. These are of course worthwhile and important topics—they show the limitations of traditional non-cognitive approaches to these problems, and suggest ways in which social phenomena are rooted in fundamental properties of cognition.

From the point of view of basic cognitive neuroscience, however, they are findings that need to be explained, rather than explanations themselves. Why and how do people come to have conservative or liberal cognitive traits? What sorts of things are these cognitive traits? Are they the product of something that happens in the course of childhood development? Or are there genetic roots, or do they arise in the process of the expression of genes—in epigenetics? Are there simply different human cognitive types, and, if so, what explains the differences? These are questions that cannot be addressed without thinking more fundamentally about the relations between the processes in question, and how the different kinds of processes relate to one another.

Why has this not been done before? To some extent it has, as will be discussed in later chapters: there are a few proposals for integrating the various levels and elements of cognitive science that extend to the social world. But for various reasons, mostly reasons intrinsic to the science itself, social life has been a neglected concern in cognitive neuroscience. Much of the effort in this area has been oriented to practical medical problems, such as Alzheimer's, and to the study of fundamental processes and mechanisms; and much of the literature *on* cognitive science has been concerned with such "philosophical" problems as the nature of consciousness. But the larger problem of cognitive neuroscience, as we will see, has been the problem of integrating its multitudinous findings. They come from different approaches and involve different sciences and technologies, as well as fundamentally different ways of thinking about the brain. The focus of this book, accordingly, is on the conflicts in cognitive science and the conflicts between various considerations central to particular approaches to cognitive neuroscience and the larger domain of "the social," and with the question of how they can be, if not resolved, at least understood.

In doing this, it should be evident the concept of "the social" is also in play. Here we have a long history of dispute within the social sciences. Some conceptions of the social fit better with some approaches to cognitive science than others. Some cognitive scientists have taken account of these issues as well, which gives us a base for discussion. It will not spoil the ending to note that the conception of the social that is most in play in light of cognitive science is the one that has dominated social science since Hobbes: the idea of society as a unity of self-interested, more or less rational individuals, organized under something analogous to a contract. Of course, this image has undergone endless revisions by social theorists and social scientists since Hobbes, but many of its elements remain.

Moreover, this image of society has some important strengths: it can be made to fit with both the model of the mind as a computer and the kind of evolutionary psychology that reads rational choice into early humanity, non-human society, and the evolutionary precursors of humanity. And it has other strengths: it allows for computationally tractable analogies to real-world social phenomena, such as markets and institutions, as well as social norms.

Is there an equally appealing alternative to this account of the social that can now be constructed using the bits of cognitive science that conflict with this model of cognition and the mind and brain? Or is there one which has already been constructed, that can be found in present or historical social science, which fits with the parts of cognitive science that either contest or do not fit with the mind as computer model? Or could it be that a reasonable "mind as computer" model also fails to fit the Hobbesian "social," and that some other model of the social, which is a radical revision of this model, is needed?

The Startling Twist

Social science is divided between quantitative research and "interpretation." Quantitative social science reflects the legacy of a particular response to the problem of mind: behaviorism. Behaviorism treated the mind as a black box, rejected the language of intention, belief, and so forth, and argued that externally obser-vable, operationalizable measures, together with causal analysis, provided the only properly scientific way forward in psychology. The subjective and subjective experience was just that: subjective. It could only be understood objectively in terms of correlates of objective inputs and outputs, the outputs being behavior. This led to a practice across social science of objective measurement of such things as attitudes, in which the notion of attitude became the "objective" responses recorded on a survey instrument which were used to predict behavior or to be themselves the subject of prediction. Because people do not come with operationalizable handles, these "measures" were inevitably abstractions from more complex processes in the mind and brain.

Interpretivism had the same issues, but they arose in a different form: inter-pretation requires handles too. The most accessible handle was discourse, or what people say and how they say it, together with objective cultural objects. If one took these things as the factual basis of interpretation, one could then use the model of "hermeneutics," borrowed from its original source in biblical inter-pretation, and construct interpretations. Interpretivists were insistent on the mindedness of the phenomena they studied, but only approached the mind indirectly, through these public manifestations of mind. And doing this required a theory, which in one way or another was a theory that involved the mind.

In one respect, however, the two sides have something in common. Social science explanations typically involve human action, and influences on human action. One speaks of the effect of social structure, for example, on action. And in doing this one appeals to some sort of model of human action, such as the belief-desire-reason model (what is now jokingly known as Good Old-Fashioned Action Theory, or GOFAT), to make sense of the links between particular social structures, which provide agents with particular reasons, constraints, opportunities, and so forth, and the actions that they take. Interpretivists have in mind intentional action and decoding intentions from their discursive manifestations and forms. Economists and rational-choice and game-theorists also are concerned with reasons and motivations, however abstracted.

It is also the case that other forms of quantitative social science depend, often covertly, on some sense of the human actions that are being summarized in the models that are constructed, and thus, however indirectly, on the intelligibility of the actions that are involved. One cannot, for example, make sense of the fact that highly abstracted, macro-level econometric studies show that the money spent on development aid in Africa has no positive effect on the economies, without thinking about how people act and why to produce this lack of positive results. And to talk about this one needs to talk about the reasons and motivations that people have for what they do—in short, GOFAT. This model of action, is, however, a product of refined common sense, and is not "true": it fails to capture important aspects of human cognition. It implies an acceptance of mental entities such as beliefs and intentions that are themselves problematic, and it is culturally specific (Bittner 2001; Wiredu 1983; Wiredu 1987). Nevertheless it fits very well with our emphatic understanding of others, and with such the famously problematic notion of *Verstehen*; though *why* and how it fits is a question that remains open—as we will see in later chapters.

The findings of social neuroscience point in a startlingly new way in the face of such issues. They establish the idea that the understanding of other minds is a distinctive cognitive capacity rooted in particular brain processes: *Verstehen*, the ugly stepchild of social science, regarded as irretrievably subjective, and which even interpretivist approaches prefer to ignore in favor of the more objective external material of discourse, turns out to be grounded in hard physical realities. Mirror neurons, although their significance is controversial, do seem to play a role in such basic elements of understanding others as identifying the kinds of actions they are performing—our ability to recognize what they are doing from very little data, such as a few points of moving light produced by reflectors on the body parts of people engaging in some sort of action, for example (Tomasello and Carpentier 2005; Loula et al. 2005; Hodges et al. 2006; Blake and Shiffrar 2007). Moreover, our capacity for understanding others is not only central to our social interactions, it is also far from being exhausted by the kinds of things captured by the notion of "reasons" and intentions, or of our conscious experience – the usual things we associate with "minds" as distinct from brains. It involves a great deal that is unconscious or pre-conscious, including inarticulable gut feelings (Sripada 2015).

The existence of these capacities is the source of many perplexing questions. Does their efficacy confirm the folk theory of mind, or any theory of mind, or the "theory" implied by our attempts to articulate our knowledge of other minds? These questions point to another set of questions about the limitations of these capacities. The paradoxical downside to the recognition and neuroscientific grounding of these capacities is this: our understanding of ourselves and our own cognitive processes is especially limited. Introspection is a poor guide to what is going on in our brains. Yet it is introspection that deals with the same material as understanding. Our understanding of others is limited in more or less the same ways that our understanding of ourselves is. We learn the language of mind as it applies to ourselves at the same time we learn its application to others: in this sense the language of mind is itself rooted in social interaction and social experience (Gopnik 1993: 3–4).

But do the limits of our powers of self-understanding and social cognition imply that the world we construct through our social experience, including our expressible feelings and thoughts, is a kind of illusion, a result of evolved selective capacities which may conduce to a kind of social efficacy but exclude self-knowledge of the workings of our own minds? We don't have, for example, introspective access to our perceptual processes: objects in the world are just there for us. Is this the case for the bulk of our mental processes, including those pro-ducing actions, as well? Is the window on the mind provided by introspection, reflection, and the language of the mental, the language of belief, desire, reasons, and so forth, systematically and drastically misleading? Does this not also imply that the real processes involved in social interaction are also, at least partly, inaccessible to us?

Does it also imply that GOFAT or folk psychology might simply be wrong? The language of intention, reason, and desire is already controversial and pro-blematic: reasons seem to be the sorts of things employed in justification, after the fact of action, or prospectively for the purpose of justification, and less significant in explaining action (Mercier and Sperber 2011; Mercier and Sperber 2017). The literature on free will is suggestive here as well: it suggests that intentions become conscious after the determinants of action in the brain are already in place, which raises the question of the causal role of what we are conscious of as intentions (Libet et al. 1983; Libet 1985; Wegner 2002; Malle 2006). But intentions and concepts of action cannot be dismissed easily. On the traditional concept of action, actions that cannot be conceived of by the agent cannot be performed by them. And this ties action back to consciousness and the language of belief and desire, as well as "reasons."

What This Means for "the Social"

Misleading and limited or not, the experience and social experience made possi-ble by the *Verstehen* window is "real." It is a fact that needs to be accounted for, and whose causal role needs to be understood in order to account for "mind" or for the social phenomena that are associated with these experiences. And there is no access to this experience other than through the window itself. And this means that the traditional distinction between interpretive approaches and quantitative "scientific" social science needs to be rethought.

The older way of thinking about the differences between the social sciences as *Geisteswissenschaften* and the sciences themselves as *Naturwissenschaften* assumed that they were different realms, constituted in different ways. "Scientific" social science, from behaviorism on, challenged this division by trying to apply the methods of science, as they reconstructed them, to social life. It was assumed that this would produce continuity with "real" science, and results in the form of real science. The model was "reduction"; the idea was that social science would generate its own laws, and that these could then be restated in terms of the laws of other, established, sciences and, ultimately, be deduced from these laws (Carnap [1934] 2011). *Verstehen* was left out of this model, except as a potential source of "hypotheses" that could be turned into measured variables and tested statistically (Abel 1948). It was thought that this process of hypothesis formulation and testing would generate something more than correlations—something more like real science (Zetterberg 1963).[1]

The underlying thought involved the distinction between objective and subjective: the measures were objective; *Verstehen* or interpretation was subjective. This is what no longer holds. Something—it is unclear exactly what it is and what its limits are—is "known" about the actions and movements of others by some sort of matching of our capacities to act and the objective facts we observe, something that cannot be understood as sheer theoretical inference from the same objective facts but involves our specific bodily capacities and our specific mental processes which enables "mindreading."

One implication of this is that social interaction and "the social" are far more complex phenomena than theories of social cognition in sociology, such as symbolic interactionism and ethnomethodology, ever envisioned; and that the experimental tradition of psychology concerned with social cognition, despite producing findings that a deeper cognitive science needs to explain, itself is quite limited and superficial. This poses the question for social science. If "the social" is no longer the stuff of conscious interaction, but a set of hidden causal processes that go along with and enable it, how are we to understand it?

This is not a new problem. There is a vast social science vocabulary devoted to discussing the tacit underpinnings of social life. Notions like *habitus* are ways of talking about this set of processes. But habitus is not a brain concept. Rather, it is a surrogate for one. Nor does it belong to common sense or folk psychology. It is, like culture, a term that is ambiguous between its individual and collective aspects, as well as between objective and subjective—an ambiguity discussed by Bourdieu himself ([1972] 1977). These are not only not exceptional, they are the norm: the terms typically used in social science and discussions of social life to refer to the mental, such as Clifford Geertz's phrase "the mind full of presuppositions" (1983: 84) or the repeated use of the notion of frames in Charles

Taylor (1989: 26), have exactly the same conceptual properties, and the same issues. They are interpretive devices, taken over from neo-Kantian philosophy. In what sense are they anything more? Can they be analyzed into something more fundamental in terms of which the ambiguities can be resolved? Or should they simply be discarded?

The multi-modal character of understanding—verbal, embodied, symbolic, learned, and innate—complicates the problem. The fact that these modes themselves interact in complex ways adds to the difficulty. Research has shown, for example, that the tense structure of languages correlates with actual future-oriented behavior. Speakers of languages with weak future tenses which use constructions like "It rains tomorrow" were "30 percent more likely to save money, 24 percent more likely to avoid smoking, 29 percent more likely to exercise regularly, and 13 percent less likely to be obese, than speakers of languages with strong future tenses, like English," which uses constructions like "It will rain tomorrow" (Chen 2013: 1, 33).

With this we can see one of the central issues here. The causal relations between the various parts of mental processes, and indeed the brain, are highly diverse and often unexpected. They do not sort into separable units, with separable processes, very easily. Nor does the tradition of psychological experimentation as it has been applied to "social cognition" (Fiske and Taylor 2013) help much: the relationships that can be revealed through the usual kinds of experiments familiar from applied social psychology help establish phenomenon, but they do little to help build up an account of the complex causal interactions that go into actual social life and actual social interactions outside the laboratory.

But what does go into social interaction and social life? Even the simplest social interactions are dauntingly complex, from the point of view of neuroscience and indeed of cognitive psychology. If you meet someone in the street, you engage a vast array of cognitive processes: perception; the capacity for face-recognition; mirror neurons that are part of the system that tells you what they are doing; implicit judgments prior to conscious perception that classify in terms of risk and danger, among other things; memory, especially implicit and inarticulable memory, long term and short term, affects of various kinds associated with the memories that are activated by the new interaction; pattern recognition, usually unconscious, of the nature of the social situation; implicit judgments of relevance, together with habituated responses; the self and self-sustaining processes that are engaged by the patterns; the linguistic capacities that are required to speak and understand speech, as well as all that is part of the conscious process of understanding itself—rationality, reflection, calculation, consciousness of social norms and the attitudes of others, conscious judgments of relevance, and so forth—and the tacit underpinnings of these conscious things.

Of course, social science has not ignored the problems of the conditions of social interaction. There is a whole movement in sociology, originally rooted in the philosophy of George Herbert Mead, which focused on the process of

interaction as the whole of social reality. Herbert Blumer (1969), who system-
atized these ideas and presented them to generations of students, understood that
this approach had radical implications: in his lectures he placed it between
sociology, psychology, and cultural anthropology, and claimed that it subverted
and replaced all of them as autonomous fields. This was a serious attempt to get
the metaphysics of the social right. But it was limited by the doctrine, inherited
from G. H. Mead's late lectures, *The Philosophy of the Present* (1932), that all that
was relevant was that which was "present" in interaction. This was an obscure
but significant limitation: it implied that interaction was closely connected to
mindedness and consciousness, and even led Blumer to deny the relevance of the
concept of culture.

The more conventional approach to the problem of the conditions of social
interaction has involved notions like frames and habitus, which are extensions of
ordinary language. These are aids to interpretation, designed to account for and
describe the tacit substrate of social life in such a way as to enable us to understand and explain other people and their beliefs and conduct—people who have
"frames" we do not share or do not feel to be "natural." Language is a good
example of a frame. But how exactly does it influence behavior, indeed so much
behavior? The usual "frames" answer is that it does so by providing modes of
reasoning that are experienced as normal or natural. The modes of reasoning are
thus causes of the reasons that produce action, which can then be explained by
GOFAT. There is, however, a large problem with these concepts: do they refer
to something that is causally real? (Lizardo 2015).

In the case of strong and weak future tenses, it is difficult to see how fitting this
into GOFAT would work: the *reasons* for saving, smoking, exercising, and the
like are reasons whether or not they are stated in strong-tensed languages. The
two are semantically equivalent. Some other causal path, something other than
the one allowed for by the frame and reasons concepts, is operating here. Yet it
also is a path that has to do with social differences, because the languages themselves are social in the sense that they are sustained and enacted in particular
groups of language users, and change through linguistic interaction, as well as
forming a major part of social interaction.

The Problems

In this book, I will not provide "solutions" to the kinds of issues I have raised
here. They are insoluble, at least in present terms, and perhaps intrinsically insoluble, as is sometimes said of the problem of consciousness itself – which, it is
argued, can't be solved because of our own cognitive limitations (Flanagan 1991;
Flanagan 1992; McGinn 1991; McGinn 2012). Insoluble is not unthinkable. And
"thinkable but not soluble" is familiar territory for social theory. Nor is it different for much of cognitive science. But cognitive science, and especially cognitive
neuroscience, provides constraints, things that theorizing cannot ignore, and also

many more issues that are also constraints, issues whose solution can be put off into the future but which already have an identifiable shape which itself provides constraints.

A short list of these issues and constraints might include the following:

- The things revealed through the *Verstehen* window cannot be ignored: they have some role, however obscure, in the explanation of the things relevant to social theory, such as action.
- It does not work to separate the problems: mind and brain, social and physical, conscious and unconscious, the *Verstehen* window and the objective. There are unexpected causal relations that cut across these distinctions. Although there might be some justification for isolating levels and mechanisms or levels of analysis for the tactical purpose of producing a space in which problems can be defined and solved, social theory does not have this luxury: the relevant causal relations can't be specified in advance, but we already know that there are relationships of importance that cannot be limited to a particular level of analysis or type of cause.
- There is a big problem over what is "social"—the relation between models of individuals and this "social"—and over such things as the physical basis of "collective" facts, if there are such things.
- Cognitive science exposes the inadequacy of many of the clichéd extensions of common sense talk about mind used in social theory and elsewhere, notably notions that are useful for interpretation, such as "frame" ideas. Either these can be given an interpretation in terms of actual cognitive mechanisms or they need to be discarded and replaced. This points to a general issue about the tacit, or what John Searle calls "the Background," which is inaccessible to us but the condition of not only our thought but to such mentalistic objects of our thought as "norms" (Searle 1983; Searle 1991).
- There are many causal relations that simply do not fit with social theory models that are extensions of common sense terms. It is conventional to distinguish emotion, which can be named and discussed, from affect, which is known primarily through its effects – which can be very powerful but which are not accessible, or as accessible, to conscious reflection or introspection. But both matter.
- There is a problem about how far we can extend a language of mind bound to *Verstehen*. What is the status of GOFAT? Is it just a bad but convenient theory? What are the alternatives, if any? Nor is it clear how affect or emotion can fit with this model.
- If concepts like "culture" are problematic, what are the alternatives? If cognitive science considerations provide a kind of test or constraint on social theory, what is in and what is out?
- What is the relation between these issues and such core issues for cognitive science as the problem of consciousness? Is this concept, and perhaps many

other concepts, due for rethinking in light of a better concept of "the social"? Are such things as intersubjectivity, as a recent article puts it, the "solution" rather than "the problem" (Gallagher 2013).

Needless to say, there are many complications here, and no simple answers. But we can get a sense of the landscape of the problems, and grope toward a conception of the social that responds to them. These problems overlap one another and point to other traditional problems: mind and body, the relation of experience to physical facts, the nature of consciousness, and so on. But they have their own significance, and need to be thought of on their own terms, not just as a derivative form of these older problems. Indeed, it is characteristic of deep issues that the solutions to them are likely to be found not by addressing them directly but by attending to aspects of them that are marginal or to the side of the main issue. It is there that one is likely to find novel clues.

Nevertheless, these problems lie on the surface: answering them depends in part on how the more basic cognitive and neurophysiological processes are understood, and what the answers to these problems are. As I have suggested, there is a parallel between social theory and cognitive science in this respect: each involves multiple perspectives and foci which are difficult to integrate and divide into drastically different strategies. Where they differ is here: social theory has come to accept the irreducibility of multiple perspectives, and the impossibility of reconciling them. This leaves some common goals, goals like making sense of the social world, but no common agreement on what counts as a good perspective. This is seen, for better or worse, as a contingent matter, relative to historical circumstance or value commitments such as the project of emancipation. In contrast, cognitive neuroscience is subject to the discipline, at least nominally, of physical realizability; and not merely an abstract realizability in some possible, theoretically defined universe, but in actual physical brains as they are actually known. Being tied to this common criterion makes a difference, though it is not a simple matter to say how this criterion bears on particular claims.

In the next chapter, I will provide a kind of overview of the relevant intellectual landscape in cognitive neuroscience. In the following chapters I will discuss the implications of the issues in cognitive science for a revision of the concept of the social, and of the social realm generally. In the end, I will distinguish concepts of the social in terms of their relation to strands of cognitive science thinking, and show how particular cognitive science ideas apply to familiar social science topics, especially in sociology.

In discussing these questions I am trying to avoid jargon as much as possible, and to avoid the disputes over concepts that make up much of the philosophical literature on these topics. Indeed, my goal is to avoid novelty as much as possible, and to piece together the issues in terms that are already available. There is one important exception to this. I will introduce one term of art: "the *Verstehen* bubble." What this means will only be apparent in later chapters, but the basic idea can be outlined here: there are limits to what is intelligible to us and to what is intelligible to others, to what we can communicate verbally or understand in other ways about one another; and these limits are closely connected to the limits we have in understanding ourselves, in introspecting, and in talking about our mental capacities and their operation. These limits are those of the *Verstehen* bubble. What this amounts to is only going to be clear, or as clear as it can be, after we introduce many other issues. But the point of adopting it is to avoid a few problematic alternative ways of framing the relevant distinction, such as in terms of consciousness, or content, or semantic meaning. The concept of *Verstehen* has an impeccable social science pedigree, and its use here will reflect the fact that this book is a social science and philosophy of social science approach to the issues.

Note

1 In this book I will not attempt to expand on comments about "methodological" issues, and in general will try, though with less success, to avoid extensive discussions of the deep history of the social sciences. There are many sources, in my own writings and in the broader literature, for discussions of the relevant issues, though they are often in terms of a set of problems that is quite distinct from the issues addressed in this book. For the most part, they reflect the older problematic of whether the social sciences can be "sciences" in the sense of having their own laws, or theories, at a special "social" level.

References

Abel, Theodore. (1948). "The Operation Called Verstehen." *American Journal of Sociology* 54(3): 211–218.

Bittner, Rüdiger. (2001). *Doing Things for Reasons.* Oxford: Oxford University Press.

Blumer, Herbert. (1969). *Social Behavior as Symbolic Interaction.* Berkeley, CA: Fybate Lecture Notes.

Bourdieu, Pierre. ([1972] 1977). *Outline of a Theory of Practice*, trans. Richard Nice. Cambridge: Cambridge University Press.

Blake, Randolph and Maggie Shiffrar. (2007). "Perception of Human Motion." *Annual Review of Psychology* 58: 47–73.

Carnap, Rudolph. ([1934] 2011). *The Unity of Science.* New York and Abingdon: Routledge.

Chen, M.Keith. (2013). "The Effect of Language on Economic Behavior: Evidence from Savings Rates, Health Behaviors, and Retirement Assets." *American Economic Review* 103 (2): 690–731.

Fiske, Susan and Shelley Taylor. (2013). *Social Cognition: From Brains to Culture* 2nd edn. London: Sage.

Flanagan, Owen. (1991). *The Science of the Mind.* Cambridge, MA: MIT Press.

Flanagan, Owen (1992). *Consciousness Reconsidered.* Cambridge, MA: MIT Press.

Gallagher, Shaun. (2013). "When the Problem of Intersubjectivity Becomes the Solution." In M. Legerstee, D. Haley, and M. Bornstein (eds.) *The Infant Mind: Origins of the Social Brain*, 48–74. Toronto: Guildford Press.

Geertz, Clifford. 1983. *Local Knowledge: Further Essays in Interpretive Anthropology.* New York: Basic Books.

Gopnik, Alison. (1993). "How We Know Our Minds: The Illusion of First-Person Knowledge of Intentionality." *Behavioral and Brain Sciences* 16: 1–14.

Hodges, Nicola J., Janet L. Starkes, and Clare MacMahon. (2006). "Expert Performance in Sport: A Cognitive Perspective." In K. Anders Ericsson, Neil Charness, Paul Feltovich, and Robert R. Hoffman (eds.) *The Cambridge Handbook of Expertise and Performance*, 471–488. Cambridge: Cambridge University Press.

Libet, B., C. A. Gleason, E. W. Wright, and E. K. Pearl. (1983). "Time of Conscious Intention to Act in Relation to Onset of Cerebral Activity (Readiness-Potential): The Unconscious Initiation of a Freely Voluntary Act." *Brain* 106(3): 623–642.

Libet, Benjamin. (1985). "Unconscious Cerebral Initiative and the Role of Conscious Will in Voluntary Action." *Behavioral and Brain Sciences* 8(4): 529–539.

Lizardo, Omar. (2015). "Culture, Cognition and Embodiment." In James D. Wright (editor-in-chief), *International Encyclopedia of the Social & Behavioral Sciences* 2nd edn, Vol. 5, 576–581. Oxford: Elsevier.

Loula, Fani, Sapna Prasad, Kent Harber, and Maggie Shiffrar. (2005). "Recognizing People from Their Movement." *Journal of Experimental Psychology* 31(1), 210–220.

Malle, Bertram F. (2006). "The Actor–Observer Asymmetry in Attribution: A (Surprising) Meta-Analysis." *Psychological Bulletin* 132(6): 895–919.

McGinn, Colin. (1991). *The Problem of Consciousness: Essays towards a Resolution*. Oxford: Blackwell.

McGinn, Colin (2012). "All Machine and No Ghost?" *New Statesman*, 20 February. www. newstatesman.com/ideas/2012/02/consciousness-mind-brain (accessed 13 June 2017).

Mead, George Herbert. (1932). *The Philosophy of the Present*, ed. Arthur Murphy. Chicago, IL: University of Chicago Press.

Mercier, Hugo and Dan Sperber. (2011). "Why Do Humans Reason? Arguments for an Argumentative Theory." *Behavioral and Brain Sciences* 34: 57–111.

Mercier, Hugo and Dan Sperber 2017. *The Enigma of Reason*. Cambridge, MA: Harvard University Press.

Searle, John. (1983). *Intentionality: An Essay in the Philosophy of Mind*. Cambridge: Cambridge University Press.

Searle, John (1991). "Response: The Background of Intentionality and Action." In E. Lepore and R. Van Gulick (eds.) *John Searle and His Critics*, 289–299. Cambridge, MA: Blackwell.

Sripada, C. (2015). "Acting from the Gut: Responsibility without Awareness." *Journal of Consciousness Studies* 22(7–8): 37–48.

Taylor, Charles. (1989). *Sources of the Self: The Making of Modern Identity*. Cambridge, MA: Harvard University Press.

Tomasello, Michael and Melinda Carpenter. 2005. "Intention Reading and Imitative Learning." In S. Hurley and N. Chater (eds.) *Perspectives on Imitation: From Neuroscience to Social Science* Vol. 1, 134–148. Cambridge, MA: MIT Press.

Wegner, Daniel. (2002). *The Illusion of Conscious Will*. Cambridge, MA: MIT Press.

Wiredu, Kwasi. (1983). "The Akan Concept of Mind." *Ibadan Journal of Humanistic Studies* 3: 113–134.

Wiredu, Kwasi. (1987). "The Concept of Mind with Particular Reference to the Language and Thought of the Akans." In G. Fløistad (ed.), *Contemporary Philosophy: A New Survey. Vol. 5: African Philosophy*, 153–179. Dordrecht: Martinus Nijhoff.

Zetterberg, Hans. (1963). *On Theory and Verification in Sociology* rev. edn. Totowa, NJ: Bedminster Press.

1

PERSPECTIVES ON THE BRAIN AND COGNITION

The Problem Domain

If one begins with the navigational powers of an ant, and infers from them the features that an ant's brain must have in order to do the navigating that can be observed in ant experiments, one arrives, as Roger Gallistel (1989) does, with a picture like this: the brain is made up of "functional" components that perform specific tasks in sequences or in relation to one another. It is a reasonable assumption that these components are not the product of learning, but are innate, inherited, fixed, and the product of extremely long evolution. This gets us a striking picture: that the brain is like a transistor radio with separate functional units that match up to physical processes and spaces, and which can be treated as something like transistors which are the same from person to person and "produced by evolution" to be standardized units. Brain regions do have different significance for the capacity to act, speak, perceive, and so forth. But because there are few cases in which these hypothetical structures match physical localized patterns in the brain, one must allow for a good deal of looseness in the assumed relation between these "functional" components and their physical realization.

If one begins with the problems of computation, recognizing that all models of the cognitive processes in the brain are computational, the issues look like this: what is the structure, or architecture, of the computational processes that allow the brain to do the big things that it unquestionably does – remember, often from the distant past and often with difficulty and error; consciously perform logical reasoning and computation; make intuitive distinctions, decisions, and the like that differ from conscious reasoning; receive perceptual inputs and process them; learn and change responses because of learning, and so forth. The constraints on computational models turn out to be substantial: models that suppose the brain to be a more or less fixed computer turn out to be bad at accounting for learning, for example. Constructing models that fit with the apparent malleability or "plasticity" of the brain is difficult to reconcile with the kinds of fast, routine processing that even infants are capable of. But there are ways of modeling those processes too. And, according to computationalists, there is no alternative: all models of cognitive processes are computational models. So the constraints on the models tell us what the constraints on the computational brain are.

If one begins with concepts and reasoning with concepts, the picture looks like this: the brain processes representations through rules embedded in the brain to produce new representations. Indeed, if the brain is ever engaged in manipulating representations according to rules, it is difficult to see how there could be any "thinking" that does not work in this way, simply because any supposed "other" kind of thinking would need to link, through rules and representations, to every other kind of thinking. There is a social angle to this: it is at least tempting to say that the rules are shared, that communication and mutual understanding are possible because and only because of these shared rules. In order to learn a language understood as a whole set of concepts together with their relations one needs to already be able to think about them; to learn about the rules governing the object of thought "apples" one must already be able to identify the object, and think about it, which amounts to having a concept with logical connections to other concepts – that is, to already have a "Language of Thought" (Fodor 1975).

Another linguistic place to start thinking about the brain involves grammar. And here is a puzzle that any account of the brain's capacities must solve: grammarians who have attempted to construct complete grammars for given languages have failed; but children quickly acquire the ability to speak grammatically. This seems to imply that they already had this ability in some form, such as a universal set of rules of language stored in the brain. If one begins with this problem, one wants a model of the brain as "language ready." But why stop there? Why think that only grammatical rules are innate? One can expand this notion to the idea of the "culture-ready" brain, one that is poised and equipped to acquire a culture. The picture here is this: cultures and languages consist of rules, which follow a template but which vary in content, to a limited extent; the values and parameters need to be plugged into the template, at which point the culture or language can be rapidly acquired, mutual understanding is possible, and social life can proceed.

If one starts with development from infancy or the womb to competent adults, one gets thoughts like this: "Senses, reflexes and learning mechanisms – this is what we start with, and it is quite a lot, when you think about it. If we lacked any of these capabilities at birth, we would probably have trouble surviving" (Epstein 2016: n.p.). But is this enough, or must there be something more? The developmental process provides many clues. We get stages in which capacities appear, usually in order and in particular time frames. These indicate some sort of dependence of one capacity on another. But reconstructing how any of this works is difficult. Capacities seem to come and go – such as the ability to pick up a language, or to imitate faces, or reflexes. And the relation between learning, senses, and reflexes is difficult to disentangle. There is a lot of social learning, or learning through interaction, which may mask more fundamental human capacities that do not depend on learning, but are simply activated at certain developmental stages. An example of this is the appearance of the capacity to reason about the erroneous thinking of other people and to infer what they would do based on their erroneous beliefs. This reasoning requires – or is claimed to require – a "theory of mind," which can't be derived merely empirically, from experience, but also represents a stage of social development.

If one begins with issues of human rationality, one focuses on the mind as a system, but one which is not quite as rational as the formal theory of rationality would have it – does not obey rules like transitivity of preferences, for example – and does strange things with discounting future benefits, probabilities, and so forth. Moreover, it seems that the brain runs at two speeds with two distinct systems: the slow conscious system and the fast unconscious one. The fast one makes systematic errors. But if our ancestors had waited for the slow one to tell them how to act, they would have been eaten by predators. And we ourselves could not function normally if we were to reason our decisions and reactions out explicitly or in the "slow" mode.

If one starts with the biological and chemical processes of the brain, one gets a different picture, and a different set of problems. The brain is regulated and mental processes affected by all sorts of complex chemical interactions and processes. These do not look particularly computer-like. This can be put even more starkly from the point of view of basic brain anatomy and biology:

> here is what we are *not* born with: *information, data, rules, software, knowledge, lexicons, representations, algorithms, programs, models, memories, images, processors, subroutines, encoders, decoders, symbols, or buffers* – design elements that allow digital computers to behave somewhat intelligently. Not only are we not *born* with such things, we also don't *develop* them – ever.
>
> We don't *store* words or the rules that tell us how to manipulate them. We don't create *representations* of visual stimuli, *store* them in a short-term memory buffer, and then *transfer* the representation into a long-term memory device. We don't *retrieve* information or images or words from memory registers. Computers do all of these things, but organisms do not.
>
> (Epstein 2016: n.p.; italics in the original)[1]

With small exceptions, the brain is made up of the same kind of stuff – neurons that connect to other neurons, connect to some and not others, and strengthen their connections as a result of "firing" together so that "neurons that fire together wire together." The physical brain is constantly changing as a result of this, and highly individualized so that each brain's set of connections produces a distinct "signature." Although there is spatial differentiation that reflects difference in functions of parts of the brain – as evidenced by the effects of brain injuries or lesions and, more recently, by mapping techniques that have distinguished a large number of areas of the brain by function, or more precisely by type of neural activity – it is also the case that the brain is malleable, that functions can sometimes be recovered, and that, astonishingly, one can function without much brain at all.

If one assumes that brains and cognitive processes are subject to the same degree of biological variability as physical features of the body, one is forced to ask how this variability relates to variations in cognitive processes. Is human sexual dimorphism deeply consequential, both for embodiment and its cognitive consequences and for cognition itself? Or does the social construction of gender and bodies overwhelm any effects of embodiment and differentials in embodied experience? If embodiment is important, how can differences in embodiment not also be important, and not only for cognition but also for social organization? One need not be a believer in the strong effects on social life of evolved capacities to wonder whether recurrent features of social life, such as hierarchy, are associated with biological variation. But talking about the embodied mind and bodies in general opens the door to and many other questions, such as this: how is normal biological variability consistent with theories that assume elaborate, common, rule-like structures in the brain?

If we start with evolution, we get a new set of considerations. Evolved structures don't just happen: they happen over tremendous time scales, and the more complex, the more time it takes to evolve them. If the brain consists of complex systems made up of small, high-speed, transistor-like elements, each doing a specific job, understanding the brain will depend on understanding the constraints and implications of this basic evolutionary fact. As Tooby and Cosmides write in their classic assault on the conventional social science model:

> Each of the neural automata ... is the carefully crafted product of thousands or millions of generations of natural selection, and each makes its own distinctive contribution to the cognitive model of the world that we individually experience as reality. Because these devices are present in all human minds, much of what they construct is the same for all people, from whatever culture; the representations produced by these universal mechanisms thereby constitute the foundation of our shared reality and our ability to communicate. Yet, because these evolved inference engines operate so automatically, we remain unaware of them and their ceaseless, silent, invisible operations. Oblivious to their existence, we mistake the representations they construct (the color of a leaf, the irony in a tone of voice, the approval of our friends, and so on) for the world itself – a world that reveals itself, unproblematically, through our senses.
>
> (Tooby and Cosmides 1995: xii)

This tells us how to think about the ant's dead reckoning capacity, but it also gives a specific picture of the brain's capacities in general: they are already formed, inherited, and sophisticated; and, because of their place in the complex system that produces such things as images of a leaf, or irony detection, which involve lots of these capacities working together, they are fixed and rigid, but also largely universal. If "culture," the core idea of the standard social science model, matters, it is only a superficial overlay on these universal mechanisms evolved in the distant past, rather than the handful of generations who have had anything like civilized life.

Moreover, it seems that basic brain structure is shared by almost all animals, with the apparent exception of the octopus, which seems terrifically intelligent but has a radically different, decentralized nervous system. Indeed, as Gallistel (2011: 254) argues, thinking itself takes a noun-verb form. As studies of animal intelligence advance, more and more of what was considered uniquely human turns out to appear in other species, including species whose evolutionary trajectory separated from that of humans very early.

But there is a twist here as well. "Evolution" is not a big hand that produces "crafted products" and inserts them into our brains. It operates through genetic transmission. And genetic transmission operates through DNA coding. But the codes do not correspond to crafted products of this kind. And thinking about the genetics of the brain leads to some complicated considerations. Although genes work through "codes" which are chemical sequences in DNA molecules and in other molecules that are involved in the process of development (and this is what is genetically transmitted), there is no simple relationship between genetic content, genotype, and what is actually expressed as the characteristics of the person, the phenotype. Genes do not ordinarily have a one-to-one relation with the overt characteristics of interest to neuroscience.

So evolution provides us with a paradox: much of the human genome is shared with the rest of the animal kingdom; and virtually all of it is shared with the higher primates. Most of what we are, as beings with brains, is also shared. And there is a constant barrage of research on animal cognition that shows that animals, even birds, that are far from us on the evolutionary tree, have remarkable reasoning skills, and that the things that were thought to be unique to human cognition are not unique at all. This line of reasoning suggests that we are heavily determined by our genes in our "psychology," which in evolutionary psychology is taken to include rationality, morality, sexual preferences, and much else.

The relation of genes to their expression points in another direction: there is not only no direct one-to-one relation of genes to properties of interest; there are also intervening processes that govern and provide a great deal of variability in the expression of genes. This is the domain of "epigenetics." Trauma, simple variation in biological conditions, and many other factors have effects on how genes are expressed. The effects of trauma indicate something potentially important: the effects are likely to be socially variable. So we can add some sort of social determination to the process of the expression of genes in the individual developmental process.

If one starts instead with psychological experiments, one gets this: a long list of anomalous findings that beg to be integrated, together with a body of ideas that is not far removed from common sense and the common language of the mental. How do false memories happen? Why do the notions that are central to such conventional pieces of psychology – such as Icek Ajzen's model of intentional action (1991, 2002; Ajzen et al. 2009) – seem to fall apart when they are applied in terms of the notion of consciousness, where it seems that the "intentional" part of decisions become conscious only *after* the relevant traces of activity in the brain have occurred (Libet et al. 1983; Libet 1985; Wegner 2002; Haggard 2012). There is, in short, a gap between the plethora of psychological experiments and the phenomena they establish, described in language that is not far removed from common sense, and the physical processes they should be connected to. Worse, there is a chronic problem about the relation between "cognition in the wild" and what goes on in experiments that are highly contrived and do not incorporate the same contextual elements as ordinary cognition (Hutchins 1995).

There is another starting point: we already have a language of the mental, and the theory of the mind behind it is sometimes derisively called "folk psychology." It has functioned for millennia, or so it would seem. It would be odd if it were "wrong": that there was nothing corresponding to such terms as intention and belief, for example. So it is fair to take it as a first approximation of the true scientific theory of mind, and to see how the concepts of folk psychology are realized in the physical brain, and to leave the details of the answer to this question to the empirical future. There is another reason: we have a brain-based capacity, perhaps based on or utilizing mirror neurons, for the empathic understanding of others. Folk psychology is, in some sense, the language we use to express our understanding of others. Indeed, without this ability to understand others we would be hard pressed to do neuroscience at all: much of it, notably lesion studies, depends on our ability to ask patients questions and to engage in interaction with them; similarly for experiments that require instructions to the subjects, or intelligible responses.

The dependence on folk psychology, or something like it, is pervasive – Daniel Dennett (1987) uses the term "intentional stance," while in this book I will be using *Verstehen*. It can be largely ignored in contexts where the issue is not social interaction or others regarding action itself but such processes as memory, perception, or deficits resulting from lesions or disease. But the closer we get to social science topics, the more difficult it becomes to ignore it. The social sciences do not merely employ these terms incidentally, but incorporate them, or refined forms of them such as "rational choice," into their own theories. A rational choice is something intelligible; the "theory" is a model of a certain kind of intelligible action. This makes them different from normal concepts in science.

Oddly, this dependence on the intelligible extends to the core of cognitive science itself. Dennett defends this by arguing:

> Cognitive science has advanced largely because of the growing clarity and specificity of the sub-personal analyses of the informational contributions

made by sub-systems to larger systems, and what better language to use than the idioms of folk psychology harnessed in diminished ("homuncular") roles?

(Dennett 2016: 6)

The problem is evident in the case of ant navigation: it is difficult to think about what the brain does in terms other than what is understandable to us explicitly. If we see the ant identifying a place it wants to go – orienting itself to the location and correcting the course to get there – it seems to follow that it is using dead reckoning, which is how we would do it explicitly with a protractor and compass. If we see the process as the activation of a dead reckoning "module" which has this capacity, and which manipulates representations of the world in a way analogous to the way sailors navigate with a chart and headings, we do this because we want the process to be understandable, meaning understandable in terms we can explain as intelligible instances of reasoning.

Leaving aside the issue of the status of folk psychology, which is the supposed explanatory "theory" behind the language used to articulate our understanding of other people, and leaving aside the language, we are faced with the fact of understanding itself. What is it? What is it based on? These questions lead to yet another brain – the empathic brain. Here we are apparently faced with two options. We can think of the process of understanding in the following manner: that we develop a theory of mind, which enables us to attribute intentions, beliefs, and so forth, and to discuss them. This theory is a very elaborate, though tacit, scheme of prediction and causal inference that allows us to navigate complex social situations by reducing them to general rules or causal expectations. The other option is to regard understanding as rooted in special empathetic capacities of the brain itself. And there is a basis for this in brain anatomy: the controversial fact of mirror neurons. But rooted in or "involving" mirror neurons is not the same as being explained by them: there is a gap between the physical facts and the things that need to be explained (Gallagher 2009).

If we start with facts about our capacity to emulate others – to sense what they feel, to understand what they are doing with their bodies, to engage with them in joint attention to objects or events in the world – it becomes much more plausible that there is some sort of primary process, not derived from an elaborate tacit computational theory, at work in these capacities. It also becomes more plausible to think that this capacity is essential to and interwoven with the social development of the child in more fundamental ways than the usual "theory of mind" model contemplates.

These kinds of facts point to another set of considerations, and yet another approach to the mind, which begins with a reinterpretation of perception. We are, from this point of view, active, embodied beings with a sensory apparatus and sensory experiences that are part and parcel of motor activities, about what we do with our bodies and how we express them in physical form. Our cognitive processes – the higher ones – start here and build on the base of our sensorimotor system. Even the metaphors that distinguish philosophical viewpoints can be traced to these sensorimotor roots (Lakoff and Johnson 2003). Our understanding of others, similarly, is through a primary capacity to respond to their bodily movements, rather than through some sort of theory in our minds that processes mental representations of others.

This approach, called "enaction," is often grouped with ideas like embedding and ecology, which stress the environment in which perception and activity take place. The basic insights associated with these ideas follow from the idea that cognition is always situated, and that it takes advantage of the environment and makes the environment part of cognition itself. A further development in thinking about the role of the amount is to see the ways in which cognition "extends" into it. A simple act like making a grocery list is cognitive in a banal sense: it is a surrogate for memory. But these surrogates are pervasive. We are embedded in a world in which we rely on others, on their knowledge and opinions, on technologies that replace more cognitively demanding routines, on symbols that replace these routines and are less demanding on memory, and on our bodily powers themselves, such as our ability to physically interact with the world and to interact with people with similar powers for common purposes, such as killing a mastodon or playing tug of war.

Fitting the Parts Together: Physical Realizability, Reduction, and Elimination

This is quite a list of approaches and considerations, and one could add to it. They each trade on important theoretical or empirical considerations. They are also incompatible in various ways. In the rest of this chapter I will focus on the problems that are posed by these incompatibilities, problems which extend to the "social." Is there a way of putting these pieces together, or of putting them together with a familiar sense of the nature of social life and the social constitution of such things as the self? These are questions that have produced a large literature, focused primarily on some specific questions about the status of common sense mentalistic terms, such as belief and desire, and the belief-desire model of action explanation, or GOFAT. This may turn out to be a misleading starting point for discussion. But it is a starting point that is entangled, as we will see, with the idea of the social and issues with the cognitive science approach to social action itself.

The root of the problem is this: it would have been nice if one removed the top of the skull and found intentions, beliefs, logical operators, and the like neatly distinguished and related to one another in the way that they are in ordinary language. Or perhaps other things: perceptions, messengers running between parts of the brain with messages, and a director running the show and making decisions; or even more recherché objects, such as conceptual schemes, assumptions, frames, selves, and so forth. This would be a solution to the problem of physical realizability. But of course there is nothing of the sort to be found there, and that is the rub. There are also no algorithms or modules, and there are no drives and reflexes either. All of these things are inferred from external facts, or are models that purport to mimic features of cognition. But none of them are found in physical form in the brain. Nevertheless, each of them has a more or less established role either in our machinery for talking about cognitive processes or in our commonplace mentalistic language of beliefs and intentions, or in such extensions of this language to terms like "frames" and "assumptions." There is another problem: physical realizability need not mean realizability in the brain itself. It is a common way of thinking that the mind, or the things that are associated with mentalistic concepts or "mental" activities, happen in and through the brain. But this is a prejudice: we don't know "where" the mind is, or what physical things can be mental or serve mental processes, a priori. It is an open question as to what role the body, interactions with the environment, physical and interpersonal, and physical objects play in the processes that correspond to "mental" terms. Worse, this plethora of concepts of the mental prevents us from getting a coherent way of talking about the subject. The concepts are not merely diverse, they often appear to conflict with one another.

There is no easy way to integrate the different approaches to the brain and cognition that I have outlined above, and some of them are starkly opposed to others – so some of them are wrong, or at least partially wrong. Each of them is based on inferences from a limited set of facts to a more general characterization of the brain, or cognition, or the social self. Integrating these perspectives and sorting out their relations, and eliminating what is wrong, is the holy grail of cognitive neuroscience. But thinking about *how* to do it is a problem itself. And thinking about *when* to do it is also a problem: is it better for these approaches to simply continue to develop while more or less ignoring the others until the point that they can, perhaps, come to a point of development and certainty that the issue of the relationship can be settled definitively? Or should thinking on a given topic try to take as much account as possible of other approaches? Or should there be a plan of integration, or at least an active discussion of the problem so that researchers are attuned to and consider the implications for other approaches? The same questions apply to social science: should social scientists be attuned to and consider the results of developing cognitive science as they relate to their topics? Or can they wait indefinitely for a more finished discipline?

Calls for integration, or even the use of cognitive science findings by social science, reflect a lack of development in the direction of integration, and institutional obstacles to it. As one prominent author explains:

> one interesting but unfortunate characteristic of the current social and cognitive sciences is a relative lack of interaction and integration among

disciplines ... Each discipline tends to consider a particular aspect and more or less ignore the rest. They generally do not work together.

(Sun 2012: 6)

Questions about how these fields can be made to fit together are not priorities, because of the internal dynamics and special foci of these fields, which are usually on very specific processes. In the case of cognitive neuroscience, for example, the focus might be on topics such as facial recognition, which is a remarkable and mysterious capacity that can be localized to a great extent. But although facial recognition is obviously a foundation of human social interaction, there is no literature exploring this aspect of this capacity: instead the focus is on understanding the capacity itself as it is realized in the brain. This is the norm: with a few controversial exceptions, such as the discovery of mirror neurons (Rizzolatti 2006; Hickock 2014) and the popularizing writing of Steven Pinker (1997), implications for social science have not been drawn by cognitive scientists. Even the enthusiasts for cooperation admit that "cognitive science offers a few initial, provisional proposals for joining with social science, but it is still in its infancy, and if the theory of evolution is our standard for comparison, cognitive science has very far to go" (Turner 2001: 12).

We can start by taking a step backward, to discuss some big questions that have already been endlessly discussed in the literature, as a way to understand the terms used in discussions of integration and their implications, such as "reduction." As it turns out, even these are different between the cognitive science world and the social science world. In the social science world, one common objection to even considering the issues raised for social science by cognitive science is that these approaches, and especially those of evolutionary psychology and "biology," are "reductionist." This term is not meant in its classical philosophy of science sense, which is either that the laws or the scientific terms of one field are fully, logically, derived from the terms of another field. This is beside the point in this context, and indeed for social science and psychology generally: there simply are no "laws" here. And the terms of the social sciences are not "derivable" from cognitive science terms on the basis of what the older philosophers of science called "correspondence rules." What is meant by being opposed to reductionism, for the social scientist, is normally something different: that the social scientist rejects the alternative explanations of social phenomena provided by another field.

There are good and bad reasons for rejecting alternative explanations from other fields or approaches, and it is worth examining some of them because we will encounter more issues of this kind in later chapters. A bad reason for rejecting an alternative explanation would be this: that one prefers one's favored description of the thing to be explained as a matter of dogma, or rejects other kinds of descriptions for the same reason. There is a traditional prejudice in the social sciences against biological explanations generally, as a result of past associations with the discredited concept of race. But there can also be serious methodological grounds for such preferences, based on the idea of disciplinary autonomy and the idea that disciplines have different explanatory and predictive goals. We will have occasion to discuss some of these ideas, which are especially relevant in the case of economics and neuroeconomics.

One good reason for rejecting the alternative explanation is that the alternatives don't explain what the social science explanations attempt to explain. The alternative explanation typically works by a combination of redescription and selectivity. By selecting as important or essential only those elements at the level to be reduced that can be explained, the provider of the alternative explanation can make an apparently compelling argument. But it is based on sleight of hand: the things being reduced are not the facts as everyone else understands and prioritizes them in explanation; they are a subset of the facts, redescribed in a way that fits the new explanation. This is one complaint commonly made about evolutionary psychology: phenomena like marriage and partner choice are highly variable and complex in sociological, anthropological, and historical reality. All this complexity drops out and is left unexplained by the "evolutionary" account, which invents its own phenomena of marriage and sexual selection to explain.

But there is an ambiguity here. Whether this kind of substitution is good or bad depends on whether one thinks the problem has been correctly described in the first place. If there are good reasons one is attached to the original description, and an acknowledgment that there might be something to the alternative explanation, the issue becomes this: what is the relation between the two descriptions and the two problem definitions? They are in some sense "about" the same thing. Neither is completely "right." Each captures something.

Reductionism, in the classical philosophy of science sense, is an answer to this question: reduction implies that everything important about the reduced domain can be described in a way that allows for it, and the laws governing it, to be accounted for by laws and descriptions in another domain. In the context of cognitive science, this gets extended to the problem of the status of mentalistic terms. The reductionist thinks that these usages can be preserved by showing that they correspond to states of the brain. This kind of reductionism is conservative, and does not pose a challenge to a conventional social science that relies on GOFAT.

For this kind of reductionism in neuroscience, the basic idea is that folk psychology is a kind of generic human theory about motivation held by everyone, and which has to be a more or less close approximation to the truth about minds. As Jerry Fodor puts it (1987: x):

> I have no serious doubt that this theory (what I call "commonsense belief/ desire psychology") is pretty close to being true. My reason for believing this ... is that commonsense belief/desire psychology explains vastly more of the facts about behavior than any of the alternative theories available. It could hardly fail to do so: there are no alternative theories available.

What cognitive neuroscience can contribute, if this is the case, is an account of the physical or computational mechanisms that underlie beliefs, desires, and the like. These may add something to our understanding of the nature of belief and desire, but the additions will not fundamentally change our understanding of the nature of human action or how to explain it. The solution to the problem of different descriptions is to show that they largely correspond.

There is a related thesis, known as eliminativism, which is more radical. Eliminativists take the view that ordinary mental concepts are just bad concepts that need to be replaced with scientific ones, or not replaced at all. The whole collection of concepts in a given domain may fall into this category, along with the explanatory problems that are defined by these terms. There is no presumption, or expectation, for the eliminativist, that the descriptions will correspond. Descriptions on one level can be replaced with descriptions on another level, with no loss from the point of view of the explanation of actual empirical facts, and gains from the point of view of precision, physical realizability, and predictive power (Durand-Lose and Jonoska 2102).

Both of these strategies, reductionism and eliminativism, are responses to the problem of relating different approaches or descriptions – to the larger problem of the integration of the fields and approaches of cognitive science. An optimist would hope that as the approaches mature, something like reductionism would be possible: this would be the conservative solution, which preserves as much as possible of the insights and results of different approaches. The eliminativist thinks otherwise: that some of the approaches will prove to be irrelevant to the best explanations.

At first blush, eliminativism seems particularly unfriendly to social science, which depends on ordinary language concepts to define its problems as well as to supply its theories with concepts. But the alternative, as we will see, poses its own challenges. A few of them might be mentioned here. One is that mentalistic terms vary culturally and between languages, and in ways that make the idea that there is one "folk psychology" underlying overt expression implausible. Some cultures invoke novel mental entities or processes; others conceptualize the mind differently. The idea that these are just variant expressions of some underlying generic folk psychology possessed by all people, which the reductionist needs, seems less plausible than the eliminativist view that they are all unscientific and wrong concepts of mind, however socially useful or culturally ingrained they are.

A second issue, which turns out to be especially significant, is that the model of mind that the reductionist normally seeks to reduce ordinary mental language to is a model that is highly individualistic, in this sense: it accounts for the social capacities of people in terms of their common powers if they had a computer-like mind. The social psychologist John C. Turner has this in mind when he complains that: "Outside of social psychology there are still scientists and philosophers trying to build models of the human mind as if individuals were self-free computing or neurological systems functioning in a social vacuum" (Turner 2004: xii). In short, these models of mind lead to a model of social life and the social that is akin to a rationalistic, Hobbesian social order. Turner takes it that this is inconsistent with what we know about selves; in any case it tells us little about actual social interaction between ordinary people driven by affect, ideas of honor, and the rest of human meaning.

It is important to understand that different models of mind might lead to, or be compatible with, different models of social life. One point should be obvious, however, even at this point: findings such as the discovery that forms of future tense speech influence savings and diet are "social" but do not fit into the Hobbesian model of the social, or the "self-free computing or neurological systems functioning in a social vacuum" described by Turner. Acknowledging the social is disruptive *terra incognito* for much of cognitive science because it introduces causal links that, so to speak, go down from the social into the cognitive and even the physical.

Eliminativism produces its own puzzles for social science. If the basic pictures of mind in the various folk psychologies implied by the divergent languages of the mental are wrong, what is their explanatory role? They may be errors, but they also matter. How does this work? Accounts of fundamental mechanisms, such as connectionism, seem to operate on a completely different level than the concepts of folk psychology. Are these concepts really dispensable, or would dispensing with them simply leave us without the explanatory resources to do social science? Is there a way of salvaging what is needed to do social science, or providing a substitute for these concepts? Do we need an equally radical revision of our notion of the social to go along with our radical rejection of folk psychology? And how could a radical revision fit with basic facts about our social capacities for mutual understanding?

These are very big questions, but we have at least two basic options: one which is conservative in the sense that it preserves as much of our ordinary understanding as possible; and one that revises our ordinary understanding and, along with it, our understanding of society. And there may be other options as well that provide for both a radical revision of our understanding of the social and the preservation of some part of our ordinary understanding of ourselves and others. The concept of integration is an attempt, ironically, to avoid the most radical implications of cognitive science for the social, and the social for cognitive science. It deserves a more detailed discussion.

Gintis's Proposal for Integration

The concept of integration treats each approach as revealing some set of considerations that is independently valid and necessary to take into account in a more inclusive account. But it provides a kind of alternative to directly addressing the issues just raised. It is a solution, however, that recalls St. Augustine's prayer to "Grant me chastity and continence, but not yet." It does not abandon the hope of bringing all of the parts of cognitive neuroscience together eventually. But it provides for an intermediate and more realizable stage. Cognitive *neuro*science as distinct from cognitive science generally is especially concerned with the constraint that models of processes such as computations, that the neuronal system is supposed to implement, should be physically realizable in that system. But this concern can be put off, temporarily and perhaps for a very long time, or mitigated. The means of doing this mitigation is through the concept of levels of analysis. The disparate approaches outlined in the beginning of this chapter can at least in part be regarded as representing multiple levels of analysis, loosely linked to one another, so that each of these forms of analysis can be preserved more or less in the same form, subject to the proviso that, ultimately, there needs to be a physical realization of some kind for the concepts (Boone and Piccinini 2016; Marr 1982).

The "loosely linked" element of the levels of analysis picture, which allows for at least the temporary preservation of each of the separate approaches, avoids the charge of, and the demands of, "reductionism" (because the levels are only *loosely* linked). It also fits nicely with a long tradition in science of thinking of the disciplines of science as more or less autonomous – each having a distinct domain, such as organisms or bodies in motion, with their own "laws" which can be studied independently of other disciplines. And it suggests a solution to the problem of the "social" as well: it is just another level, ultimately linked, but only loosely, to the "lower" levels, and only distantly linked to the ultimate problem of physical realizability.

This is a solution that can also be applied to the broader problem of the relation of cognitive science to such topics as meanings (Turner 2001) and institutions (Sun 2002: 195–6; Menary 2006). This is a very unstable solution, however: as the different levels develop in their own ways, it does not always seem that they are converging, even in the limited way provided for in the concept of levels. The problem is exemplified by the case of rational choice models themselves. One can think of this kind of analysis as a level, and argue that "just as billiards players do not solve differential equations in choosing their shots, so decision makers do not solve Lagrangian equations, even though in both cases we may use optimization models to describe their behavior" (Gintis 2007: 9). For the cognitive *neuro*scientist this is a problem: the billiards players do what they do somehow; and if it is not by solving Lagrangian equations, the goal is to figure out how – and how they do it with actual brains, bodies, and objects. But it is commonly the case that the computational models are unrealizable in actual brains, bodies and objects.

The most studied conflict with social science has involved rational choice and game theory. Given the barely concealed hope, expressed explicitly by Ronald Coase ([1988] 1990: 4–5), that the basic principles of economics would be found to be the product of human evolution, it is not surprising that the starting point for a good deal of empirical work was the question of human rationality. One apparent result of cognitive science research is that the formal models of human agency and reasoning used by the various special sciences are false. Rational choice accounts have been a major target (Ostrom 1991; Ostrom 1998; Ostrom et al. 1992; Andreoni 1995; Fehr et al. 1997; Fehr et al. 1998; Gächter and Fehr 1999; Fehr and Gächter 2000; Fehr and Gächter 2002; Henrich et al. 2005). In the case of such fields as behavioral economics and neuro-economics, for example, research has shown that people are "systematically inconsistent in their choices" and "are prone to act on scanty information even when more could be obtained with relatively little effort" (Ross 2012: 298). But this is a case in which the argument can be made that the different aims of the disciplines make these comparisons irrelevant. In the specific case of the relation of neuro-economics to conventional economics, this point has been made by claiming that economics has its own distinct cognitive values that its models serve, which are different from and conflict with the values of cognitive science (Fumagalli 2014).

Within cognitive science itself, there are plenty of similar conflicts. The place these conflicts play out most dramatically is in relation to computational psychology. If it is implausible that ants do dead reckoning, or that birds and billiard players do Lagrangian transformations, even though the models of their cognitive apparatus require that they do, the whole of these approaches is threatened. These approaches depend on reconstructing mental processes in terms of units that are intelligible to us – that we can model by attributing something like our reasoning to their physical structures. If this intelligibilizing approach is misguided for ants and birds, it is probably also misguided for many human mental processes, and perhaps for all of them.

Integrationist strategies are an attempt to face these issues directly. But when they turn to social science, they tend to do so by a novel form of eliminativism. The leading integrationist proposals assume that there is a need for a long-term cognitive science based "revolution," in which the foundations of social science need to be rethought (cf. Turner 2001; Turner 2002; Turner 2011; Gintis 2007; Gallagher 2013). This is a kind of eliminativism: take away the foundations and the structure disappears as well.

This has not gone unchallenged: the idea of making cognitive science a foundational discipline for the social sciences has been attacked most directly by a "critical neuroscience" movement (Choudhury and Slaby 2012). What are the issues here? There is a concern that neuroscience explanations are more readily granted credence than other equally valid explanations of other kinds (von Scheve 2011; Meloni 2012), on the basis of the "belief that the ontologically most fundamental level of explanation [in this case the neuroscience level] is by default the most appropriate one" (Slaby and Choudhury 2012: 30), or that they contain hidden ideology (Pitts-Taylor 2010). Moreover, the integrationist model faces objections against reductionisms generally. It goes against a common view of the relations between sciences, argued by John Dupré (1995), that scientific fields are like different neighborhoods with different rules and concepts, rather than a hierarchy of domains in which one can be "foundational" with the others arrayed in a series of relations of dependence.

The problem of the relation of cognitive science to social science is thus an area of open contestation. The lessons of cognitive science for social science are often highly schematic and overstated. Nevertheless, social science and cognitive science are often talking about the same things; and neither the idea argued for by John Dupré, that science consists of more or less self-contained neighborhoods that work in different ways and do not fit into a grand scheme (which he calls the disunity of science), nor the older view of the sciences as unified or unifiable – with the social sciences as "resting" on psychology but having their own autonomous laws, found in Comte ([1855] 1896) and Mill (1882) – captures the relationship with cognitive science and the nature of the conflicts within it (Lizardo 2014). Cognitive science challenges not only the theories and explanatory practices of the social sciences; it also challenges the disciplinary divisions themselves, and the idea that disciplines can be autonomous.

These reservations need to be kept in mind: we will hear much more about them in later chapters, and about the alternatives. Nevertheless, the arguments for integration, and the proposals themselves, are revealing, especially about the general conceptual problems with cognitive science approaches to the social. These are most clearly exhibited in the most aggressive and elaborate of these proposals, which comes from Herbert Gintis. It is worth seeing how the proposal works and what prices need to be paid in terms of the revision of other fields in order to make it work. Gintis is especially clear about this need for the revision of other disciplines, and also about some of the issues with his own proposal for such a revolution, so we can use it as an illustration of the issues. He begins with the current scandalous state of the social sciences, and provides a model of what *should be* the state:

> Each of the behavioral disciplines contributes strongly to understanding human behavior. Taken separately and at face value, however, they offer partial, conflicting, and incompatible models. From a scientific point of view, it is scandalous that this situation was tolerated throughout most of the twentieth century. Fortunately, there is currently a strong current of unification, based on both mathematical models and common methodological principles for gathering empirical data on human behavior and human nature.
>
> *(Gintis 2004: 52–3)*

Gintis's basic thought is to work up from the biological:

> Biology plays a role in the behavioral sciences much like that of physics in the natural sciences. Just as physics studies the elementary processes that underlie all natural systems, so biology studies the general characteristics of survivors of the process of natural selection.
>
> *(Gintis 2007: 3)*

This role is explicitly not "reductionist" in the classical philosophy of science sense, however, because:

> one cannot deduce the structure and dynamics of complex life forms from basic biological principles. But, just as physical principles inform model creation in the natural sciences, so must biological principles inform all the behavioral sciences.
>
> *(Gintis 2007: 3)*

This is an important distinction: integration, for Gintis, involves understanding a causal and historical hierarchy that goes from genes, evolutionary processes of the co-development of species and cognition, through cognition itself and the co-development of cognition and culture, though to the explanation of such problems as cultural diversity and cultural change.

The process of co-evolution is illustrated by the case of the honey-bee:

> An excellent example of gene–environment coevolution is the honeybee, in which the origin of its eusociality doubtless lay in the high degree of relatedness fostered by haplodiploidy, but which persists in modern species despite the fact that relatedness in the hive is generally quite low, on account of multiple queen matings, multiple queens, queen deaths, and the like (Gadagkar 1991; Seeley 1997). The social structure of the hive is transmitted epigenetically across generations, and the honeybee genome is an adaptation to the social structure laid down in the distant past.
>
> *(Gintis 2007: 4)*

This sounds like the prelude to the kind of "reductionist" argument that sociologists find offensive. It points in the direction of an alternative explanation of their own facts about social structure, rooted in genetics and epigenetics – i.e., forces governing the expression of genes (an especially relevant issue with bees, whose social structure depends on a division of labor in which genetically identical bees are sharply distinguished in function through differences in the expression of these genes, making them into workers or queens) (Winston 1987). These processes are dramatic: the queen bee and the workers are radically different creatures, physically and in terms of what they do and where they sit in the social structure; and the example hints that the same adaptations, to a social structure laid down in the distant past, are in some yet to be explained sense fundamental to human existence also.

The key biological principle is selection, and the selective process gives us an explanation of the basic feature of the brain that is at the core of his integrationist account: "*The brain evolved because more complex brains, despite their costs, enhanced the fitness of their bearers. Brains, therefore, are ineluctably structured to make, on balance, fitness-enhancing decisions*" (Gintis 2007: 3; emphasis in original)

Decisions and the decision-making brain are, in turn, at the core of human distinctiveness. The human brain shares most of its functions with that of other vertebrate species, including the coordination of movement, maintenance of homeostatic bodily functions, memory, attention, processing of sensory inputs, and elementary learning mechanisms. The distinguishing characteristic of the human brain, however, lies in its extraordinary power as a decision-making mechanism.

A few observations are in order at this point. The first is that "decision-making" is a paradigmatic human intentional action – to act on the basis of a decision is almost the definition of action itself, as ordinarily understood. Do mollusks and ants make decisions? Gintis's proposal integrates the cognitive theory of humans and animals, and biologizes human cognition by showing the similarities between them. By treating the "actions" of animals as the product of decisions, he can then treat animal social structure and interaction in terms of game theory, which he calls "the universal lexicon of life." Gintis attributes strategies, preferences, and rationality to non-humans, and explains the social life of non-humans in these terms. He can treat this as recognizing the biological basis of cognition because biologists also use this language. Nevertheless it is a kind of anthropomorphism to make these attributions, and we can ask what justifies doing so. This turns out to be an important problem running through the entire literature, which we will address in later chapters in terms of the intentionalizing bias.

What justifies treating the doings of animals as rational decision-making? The answer is that this model predicts animal behavior, and therefore is true or justified in the same sense in which any model in science is true or justified. Gintis (2007: 3) understands that there is a large price to be paid to integrate this claim with actually existing psychology, so he argues that standard psychology is simply wrong in its emphases: "psychology, which focuses on the processes that render decision-making possible (attention, logical inference, emotion vs. reason, categorization, relevance) … virtually ignores, and seriously misrepresents decision making itself." He also comments that:

> Psychology has two main branches: cognitive and behavioral. The former defines the brain as an "information-processing organ" and generally argues that humans are relatively poor, irrational, and inconsistent decision makers. The latter is preoccupied with learning mechanisms that humans share with virtually all metazoans (stimulus response, the law of effect, operant conditioning, and the like).
>
> (*Gintis 2007: 3*)

These, presumably, are still relevant to human cognition, but irrelevant to the distinctiveness of cognition that is human.

There is a significant conflict here. Gintis notes that Paul Slovic, one of the leading psychologists of decision-making, asserted, accurately I believe, that:

> "it is now generally recognized among psychologists that utility maximization provides only limited insight into the processes by which decisions are made" ... "People are not logical," psychologists are fond of saying, "they are *psycho*logical."
>
> *(Gintis 2007: 2; quoting Slovic 1995: 365)*

Gintis (2007: 2) rejects this: "I argue precisely the opposite position: people are generally rational, though subject to performance errors."

Each field has to give up something to achieve integration.

> The true power of each discipline's contribution to knowledge will only appear when suitably qualified and deepened by the contribution of the others. For example, the economist's model of rational choice behavior must be qualified by a biological appreciation that preference consistency is the result of strong evolutionary forces, and that where such forces are absent, consistency may be imperfect. Moreover, the notion that preferences are purely self-regarding must be abandoned. For a second example, the sociologist's notion of internalization of norms must be thoroughly integrated into behavioral theory, which must recognize that the ease with which diverse values can be internalized depends on human nature.
>
> *(Gintis 2007: 15–16; citing Pinker 2002; Tooby and Cosmides 1992)*

As to sociology itself, it needs to submit to the core idea of fitness and well-being to explain its central concepts, such as values. Sociology's contribution is to socialization theory and the idea of internalization of norms, which Gintis interprets as follows (2007: 7):

> Internalized norms are followed not because of their epistemic truth value, but because of their moral value. In the language of the BPC model [beliefs, preferences, and constraints], internalized norms are accepted not as instruments towards achieving other ends but rather as arguments in the preference function that the individual maximizes, or are self-imposed constraints. For example, individuals who have internalized the value of "speaking truthfully" will constrain themselves to do so even in some cases where the net payoff to speaking truthfully would otherwise be negative.
>
> The human responsiveness to socialization pressures represents perhaps the most powerful form of epigenetic transmission found in nature. In effect, *human preferences are programmable*, in the same sense that a computer can be programmed to perform a wide variety of tasks. This epigenetic flexibility,

which is an emergent property of the complex human brain, in considerable part accounts for the stunning success of the species *Homo sapiens*. When people internalize a norm, the frequency of its occurrence in the population will be higher than if people follow the norm only instrumentally – that is, only when they perceive it to be in their material self-interest to do so. The increased incidence of altruistic prosocial behaviors permits humans to cooperate effectively in groups (Gintis et al. 2005a).

(Gintis 2007: 7–8; emphasis in original)

Gintis claims also that this powerful force is ignored by the other social sciences, wrongly. But he also appreciates limits to the theory in the face of change: the rate

at which values are acquired and abandoned depends on their contribution to fitness and well-being (Gintis 2003a; [Gintis] 2003b) – there are often rapid, society-wide value changes that cannot be accounted for by socialization theory (Gintis 1975; Wrong 1961).

(Gintis 2007: 16)

If we return to our triad of reduction, elimination, and alternative explanations, we can see that Gintis is employing a mixture of the last two. He claims that the psychologists are wrong, and that their errors removes them from the central role psychology should play in the behavioral sciences, which should be to "take the fitness-enhancing character of the human brain, its capacity to make effective decisions in complex environments, as central" (Gintis 2007: 4). This is a kind of biologization through anthropomorphization.

We can give a name to Gintis's thesis: pervasive rationality. He is determined to read the GOFAT model, which he calls the "beliefs, preferences, and constraints (BPC)" model – which he admits is the rational actor model – into biological evolution and selection. And he points to trends in biology that support this:

The rational actor model is the cornerstone of contemporary economic theory, and in the past few decades it has become equally important in the biological modeling of animal behavior (Alcock 1993; Real 1991; Real and Caraco 1986). Economic and biological theory therefore have a natural affinity: The choice consistency on which the rational actor model of economic theory depends is rendered plausible by biological evolutionary theory, and the optimization techniques pioneered by economic theorists are routinely applied and extended by biologists in modeling the behavior of organisms.

(Gintis 2007: 4)

There is an odd contradiction to the doctrine of pervasive rationality, however: if advanced decision-making capacity with a big brain selected for it is what makes humans special, and that this capacity is what economic theory captures, isn't there something implausible about applying this theory to organisms with small brains? Moreover, what seems to be unique to humans is variation in belief, which needs its own explanation.

> It follows that beliefs are the underdeveloped member of the BPC trilogy. Except for Bayes' rule (Gintis 2000c, Ch. 17), there is no compelling analytical theory of how a rational agent acquires and updates beliefs, although there are many partial theories (Boyer 2001; Jaynes 2003; Kuhn 1962; Polya 1990). Beliefs enter the decision process in several potential ways. First, individuals may not have perfect knowledge concerning how their choices affect their welfare. This is most likely to be the case in an unfamiliar setting, of which the experimental laboratory is often a perfect example. In such cases, when forced to choose, individuals "construct" their preferences on the spot by forming beliefs based on whatever partial information is present at the time of choice (Slovic 1995). Understanding this process of belief formation is a demanding research task.
>
> Second, often the actual actions ... available to an individual will differ from the actual payoffs ... that appear in the individual's preference function. The mapping ... the individual deploys to maximize payoff is a belief system concerning objective reality, and it can differ from the correct mapping ....ic For example, a gambler may want to maximize expected winnings but may believe in the erroneous Law of Small Numbers (Rabin 2002).
>
> Third, there is considerable evidence that beliefs directly affect well-being, so individuals may alter their beliefs as part of their optimization program. Self-serving beliefs, unrealistic expectations, and projection of one's own preferences on others are important examples. The trade-off here is that erroneous beliefs may add to well-being, but acting on these beliefs may lower other payoffs (Benabou [and] Tirole 2002; Bodner [and] Prelec 2002).
>
> *(Gintis 2007: 15)*

Gintis ends up with something like a contradiction, and the contradiction lies at the heart of the problem of culture, to which we will turn in the rest of the chapter. On the one hand, he needs a notion of belief to play the role of the B in his BPC model of action. But he sees that there is a problem about the relation of decision to belief – beliefs are conditions of decisions, but less plausibly treated as the products of decisions. Gintis himself speaks of culture as epigenetic programming; but programming is a condition of belief, and, in some accounts, of learning itself. The alternative would be that the enhancements provided by evolution and the processes he dismisses allow the brain *not* to depend on decision-making, except rarely and under duress. Decision-making is notoriously taxing and time-consuming – the point is that tacit processes have substituted for them, and not that they merely supply preferences. This points to one of the major conflicts to be explored in this book: between models of culture that treat the tacit as a close cousin to what is explicit and those that regard it as fundamentally different.

Does This Sort of Thing Actually Explain Social Life?

The larger questions that this book addresses is how cognitive science bears on the study of social life, and how the study of social life provides problems that cognitive science must accommodate or solve in order to account for the cognitive itself. So it is useful to at least begin with some working images of what social life itself consists of, and what needs to be explained or accommodated. These images themselves, as we would expect, will be controversial: an economist looking at social life will see something different, and perhaps more like what Gintis sees, than a sociologist or anthropologist. But it is worth getting these differences out on the table and discussing the issues that the fact of the differences raise. These issues turn out to be connected to the issues of reductionism we have been discussing.

The same point is made, from the direction of genetics, by Joseph Fracchia and R. C. Lewontin in commenting on an influential evolutionary account of culture and cultural change by Boyd and Richerson, and its appropriation by the sociologist Walter Runciman, who embraces "selectionism" as an account of history. Much of Boyd and Richerson's thinking involves the role of selection on the co-evolution of culture and genes. This strategy runs into a problem about the status of analogies, and the particular analogies in question. For the argument to work, the things being selected through the process of selection must be units of a kind for which both the notion of selection and a notion analogous to "inheritance" make sense. Are there such units? The solution found in the popular science literature is the concept of memes. But they admit that this analogy goes too far: "Cultural transmission does not involve the accurate replication of discrete, gene-like entities" (Henrich et al. 2008: 121). Instead, they argue that culture is made up of mental representations. But this change from memes to representations does not eliminate the need for an account of transmission that substitutes for inheritance, that is to say an account about what gets into people's brains, and how they get there, of the kind that we have been discussing in relation to Fodor and Chomsky. It is evident that there is a problem here: either representations are innate, and therefore not cultural, or they are transmitted through some process that does not resemble genetic inheritance, and does not involve anything like replicators.

So how do they save the strategy of treating culture as a set of representations that can be thought of in population terms and transmitted in a way that can be modeled on biological inheritance and selection? They claim that they "also believe that models which assume discrete replicators that evolve under the influence of natural-selection-*like* forces can be useful. In fact, we think such models are useful *because* of the action of strong cognitive attractors during the social learning" (Henrich et al. 2008: 121; emphasis in the original). There are two problems here. The first, to which we will return, is with the "assume" and the idea that because something can be modeled in a certain way this tells us anything about the substance. They themselves admit that the meme notion is faulty: but the basis for it, as we will see shortly, is the same as theirs, namely that culture *can* be modeled as memes. The second is that the entire argument threatens to collapse into a definitional tautology, in which cognitive attractors are defined as strong because they survive in the process of selection, culture is redefined as the set of representations that survives, and in which "strong" attractors are implicitly defined as those that survive. The redefinition raises the question of what this new formulation has to do with what we normally mean by culture. As Fracchia and Lewontin comment, they "jump from the more modest claim that culture "can be modeled as a system of inheritance," which in their case amounts to redefining it as a system of inheritance, to the categorical affirmation that "culture constitutes a system of inheritance" (Fracchia and Lewontin 2005: 18).

The key problematic term here is "modeled." From Boyd and Richerson's point of view, they are doing what scientists always do: extract and conceptualize elements that can be turned into a formal model that yields predictions. The model is confirmed by the success of the predictions, though it may do other things as well; and even false models can be useful in defining a domain, such as the economy, so that the deviations from reality can themselves be explained. Moreover, from this point of view, this is the only access we have to reality: there is no fixed thing to be explained in advance, and even "data" is something that has to be constructed as a model in order to compare it to the model that is doing the predicting (Suppes [1960] 1962: 24–35).

This is a generic problem: do these abstractions actually explain the real world, or are they just makeshift constructions that "succeed" only according to their own definition of the problem? Are they in a kind of circular relationship with the models of the data such that reality is redefined to fit the model, rather than the model fitting reality? This is the issue that Fracchia and Lewontin have in mind when they comment that:

> The real issue, accordingly, is not whether explanations can be successfully manufactured on the basis of paradigmatic assumptions, but whether the paradigmatic assumptions are appropriate to the object of analysis. The selectionist paradigm requires the reduction of society and culture to inheritance systems that consist of randomly varying, individual units, some of which are selected, and some not; and with society and culture thus reduced to inheritance systems, history can be reduced to "evolution." But these reductions, which are required by the selectionist paradigm, exclude much that is essential to a satisfactory historical explanation – particularly the systemic properties of society and culture and the combination of systemic logic

and contingency. Now as before, therefore, we conclude that while historical phenomena can always be modeled selectionistically, selectionist explanations do no work, nor do they contribute anything new except a misleading vocabulary that anesthetizes history.

(Fracchia and Lewontin 2005: 14)

But this is a tricky argument. They say that "a good deal of paradigmatic myopia is required in order to see in social and cultural history only that which fits into the selectionist paradigm" (Fracchia and Lewontin 2005: 17). But the same comment can be applied to them. How do they know what a satisfactory historical explanation is? They tell us what they think needs to be explained: the systemic properties of society and culture. But where do they get this standard? And isn't this just another problematic model of a messier reality in which, for example, the "systematic properties" are not something inherent in "society" or "the culture," if there even are such things in reality, but are themselves an abstraction. The thing being abstracted from is the behavior of individuals who themselves might be disposed to find consistency in their cognitions, to conformity, and so on. In that case the systematicity would not be a property of "the culture" but rather of individual cognition.

With this we come to another problem of selectivity that is inherited from reductionism and intrinsic to it: approaches that prioritize universal (and usually very vague and general) phenomena such as altruism or rationality are plausible *because* of "paradigmatic myopia." As Gabriel Abend has pointed out, this problem is endemic to standard cognitive science approaches to morality. These approaches, following the standard strategy, have focused on moral universals. To say that there is a universal cognitively structured set of elements of morality, for example, works if one is able to define morality very selectively, and to conclude something like "morality conduces to the common good." But when one gets to actual moral distinctions that people in very diverse social settings make in very different ways, things become more difficult. The universal constructions leave out the important and more nuanced aspects of morality that vary socially, but nevertheless presumably also have deep roots in cognitive processes and emotion: dignity, integrity, humanness, cruelty, pettiness, exploitation, or fanaticism (Abend 2011: 145). It also leaves out most of the moral concepts associated with interdictions: *tabu*, the clean–unclean distinction, and similar distinctions that actually constitute moral universes but which vary radically between societies. These need to be accounted for as cognitive phenomena because they have a cognitive and neuroscience aspect.

But "what needs to be accounted for" is highly elastic, and subject to many provisions. Can reproducing the problem of selectivity be avoided? The domain of things that "need" be explained is not given as something well defined. Indeed, as we will see in later chapters, it is very difficult to distinguish "the social" as a domain, and perhaps futile. But we can get our bearings here to some extent by considering an example of something "social" that would seem to clearly fall into the category of facts that "need" explanation: the things that are tacit or non-explicit that are learned, are conditions for different forms of social interaction or institutions, and that vary socially. Consider a simple act of gift-giving from Merleau-Ponty ([1942] 1963) that is also "[a] specific instance of nonexplicit learning" (Hilferty et al. 1998: 178). As Hilferty et al. summarize it:

> The appropriateness of a gift is highly context dependent. For example, many factors have to be calculated:
>
> a   the age, sex, interests, socio-economic status of the recipient;
> b   the relationship between the giver and the recipient (e.g., parent-child, boss-employee, teacher-student, friends, lovers, ex-lovers, spouses, neighbors, acquaintances, etc.);
> c   the reason for the gift (e.g., birthday, graduation, reconciliation, surprise, reward, thanks, Christmas, family tradition, etc.);
> d   the appropriate amount of money to be spent on the gift;
> e   etc., etc.
>
> Therefore, in order to give a present to the neighbor's ten-year-old daughter on her birthday, all of the above factors (and many more) play a role in choosing the appropriate gift. In this situation, a submachine gun, a car, a ham sandwich, a potato, a copy of Carnap's *Meaning and Necessity*, or leather lingerie would normally be thought of as unsuitable gifts. It is doubtful that a set of explicit rules could be stipulated that generates all and only the appropriate presents for such an occasion, let alone all possible variants.
>   In any event, nobody attempts to teach this type of knowledge formally, and yet it is still learned.
>
> *(Hilferty et al. 1998: 178)*

If this is what "culture" is, or more generally what social competence consists of, it would seem, on the surface, to be not only learned but also to consist of something other than rules, however much one might wish to model them as tacit versions of explicit rules. Nor do they look like transmissible, unitized mental representations.

If the kinds of units cognitive science needs to operate with do not match what we wish to explain in social science, what can cognitive science say about these conditions of social life? Can these apparently different kinds of explanatory objects be made to fit into the standard model? Can an approach like Gintis's be extended to account for facts like this? Or are these not "conditions of social life," but incidental byproducts of deeper processes that the standard model, and a sufficient appreciation of complexity or game theory, can accommodate? Are the differences that characterize the sphere of the social largely the product of accidents operating on stable universal cognitive capacities that are the product of evolution, about which nothing scientific can be said? Or are there forms of cognitive science or approaches that do fit such facts, or fit them better? We can begin with these questions by more fully specifying the standard approach and considering the alternatives, which we will do in the next chapter.

Note

1 For an extensive polemical response to Epstein, see Shallit (2016)

References

Abend, Gabriel. (2011). "Thick Concepts and the Moral Brain." *European Journal of Sociology* 52: 143–172.

Ajzen, Icek, Cornelia Czasch, and Michael G. Flood. (2009). "From Intentions to Behavior: Implementation Intention, Commitment, and Conscientiousness." *Journal of Applied Social Psychology* 39(6): 1356–1372.

Ajzen, Icek. (1991). "The Theory of Planned Behavior." *Organizational Behavior and Human Decision Processes* 50: 179–211.

Ajzen, Icek. (2002). "Perceived Behavioral Control, Self-Efficacy, Locus of Control, and the Theory of Planned Behavior." *Journal of Applied Social Psychology* 32(2002): 665–683.

AlcockJ. (1993). *Animal Behavior: An Evolutionary Approach.* Sunderland, MA: Sinauer.

Andreoni, James. (1995). "Cooperation in Public-Goods Experiments: Kindness or Confusion." *American Economic Review* 85(4): 891–904.

Benabou, R. and J. Tirole. (2002). "Self-Confidence and Personal Motivation." *Quarterly Journal of Economics* 117(3): 871–915.

Bodner, R. and D. Prelec. (2002). "Self-Signaling and Diagnostic Utility in Everyday Decision Making." In I. Brocas and J. D. Carillo (eds.) *Collected Essays in Psychology and Economics,* 105–123. Oxford: Oxford University Press.

Boone, Worth and Gualtiero Piccinini. (2016). "The Cognitive Neuroscience Revolution." *Synthese* 193(5): 1509–1534.

Boyd, Robert and P. J. Richerson. (2000). "Meme Theory Oversimplifies How Culture Changes." *Scientific American* 283(4): 70–71.

Boyer, P. (2001). *Religion Explained: The Human Instincts that Fashion Gods, Spirits and Ancestors.* London: Heinemann.

Choudhury, Suparna and Jan Slaby. (2012). *Critical Neuroscience: A Handbook of the Social and Cultural Contexts of Neuroscience.* Chichester: Wiley-Blackwell.

Coase, Ronald H. ([1988] 1990). *The Firm, the Market, and the Law.* Chicago. IL: University of Chicago Press.

Comte, Auguste. ([1855] 1896). *The Positive Philosophy of Auguste Comte,* 3 vols., trans. and condensed by Harriett Martineau. London: George Bell & Sons.

Dennett, Daniel. (1987). *The Intentional Stance.* Cambridge, MA: MIT Press.

Dennett, Daniel. (2016). "Letter to the Editor." *Times Literary Supplement, 4 November:* 6.

Dupré, John. (1995). *The Disorder of Things: Metaphysical Foundations of the Disunity of Science.* Cambridge, MA: Harvard University Press.

Durand-Lose, Jérôme and Natasa Jonoska. (eds.) (2012). *Unconventional Computation and Natural Computation: 11th International Conference, UCNC 2012, Proceedings.* Dordrecht: Springer.

Epstein, Robert. (2016). "The Empty *Brain*." *Aeon*, 20 May. https://aeon.co/essays/your-brain-does-not-process-information-and-it-is-not-a-computer (accessed 24 March 2017).

Fehr, Ernst and Simon Gächter. (2000). "Cooperation and Punishment in Public Goods Experiments." *American Economic Review* 90(4): 980–994.

Fehr, Ernst and Simon Gächter. (2002). "Altruistic Punishment in Humans." *Nature* 415 (10 January): 137–140.

Fehr, Ernst, Simon Gächter, and Georg Kirchsteiger. (1997). "Reciprocity as a Contract Enforcement Device: Experimental Evidence." *Econometrica* 65: 833–860.

Fehr, Ernst, Erich Kirchler, Andreas Weichbold, and Simon Gächter. (1998). "When Social Norms Overpower Competition: Gift Exchange in Experimental Labor Markets." *Journal of Labor Economics* 16(2): 324–351.

Fodor, Jerry A. (1975). *The Language of Thought*. Cambridge, MA: Harvard University Press.

Fodor, Jerry A. (1987). *Psychosemantics*. Cambridge, MA: MIT Press.

Fracchia, Joseph and R. C. Lewontin. (2005). "The Price of Metaphor" *History and Theory* 44(February): 14–29.

Fumagalli, Roberto. (2014). "Neural Findings and Economic Models: Why Brains have Limited Relevance for Economics." *Philosophy of the Social Sciences* 44(5): 606–629.

Gächter, Simon and Ernst Fehr. (1999). "Collective Action as a Social Exchange." *Journal of Economic Behavior and Organization* 39: 341–369.

Gallagher, Shaun. (2009). "Neural Simulation and Social Cognition." In J. A. Pineda (ed.), *Mirror Neuron Systems*, 355–370. Dordrecht: Springer.

Gallagher, Shaun (2013). "The Socially Extended Mind." *Cognitive Systems Research* 25–26: 4–12.

Gallistel, C. R. (1989). "Animal Cognition: The Representation of Space, Time, and Number." *Annual Review of Psychology* 40: 155–189.

Gallistel, C. R. (2011). "Prelinguistic Thought." *Language Learning and Development* 7: 253–262.

Gintis, Herbert. (1975). "Welfare Economics and Individual Development: A Reply to Talcott Parsons." *Quarterly Journal of Economics* 89(2): 291–302.

Gintis, Herbert. (2000c). *Game Theory Evolving*. Princeton, NJ: Princeton University Press.

Gintis, Herbert. (2003a). "Solving the Puzzle of Human Prosociality." *Rationality and Society* 15(2): 155–187.

Gintis, Herbert. (2003b). "The Hitchhiker's Guide to Altruism: Genes, Culture, and the Internalization of Norms." *Journal of Theoretical Biology* 220(4): 407–418.

Gintis, Herbert. (2004). "Towards a Unity of the Human Behavioral Sciences." *Politics, Philosophy, and Economics* 3(1): 37–57.

Gintis, Herbert (2007). "A Framework for the Unification of the Behavioral Sciences." *Behavioral and Brain Sciences* 30(1): 1–61.

Gintis, Herbert, S. Bowles, R. Boyd, and E. Fehr (eds.) (2005a). *Moral Sentiments and Material Interests: On the Foundations of Cooperation in Economic Life*. Cambridge, MA: MIT Press.

Haggard, Patrick. (2012). "The Neuroethics of Free Will." In Judy Illes and Barbara J. Sahakian (eds.) *The Oxford Handbook of Neuroethics*, 219–226. Oxford: Oxford University Press.

Henrich, Joseph, Robert Boyd, Samuel Bowles, Colin Camerer, Ernst Fehr, Herbert Gintis, Richard McElreath, Michael Alvard, Abigail Barr, Jean Ensminger, Natalie Smith Henrich, Kim Hill, Francisco Gil-White, Michael Gurven, Frank W. Marlowe, John Q. Patton, and David Tracer. (2005). "'Economic Man' in Cross-Cultural

Perspective: Behavioral Experiments in 15 Small-Scale Societies." *Behavioral and Brain Sciences* 28(6): 795–855.

Henrich, Joseph, Robert Boyd, and P. J. Richerson, (2008). "Five Misunderstandings about Cultural Evolution." *Human Nature* 19(2): 119–137.

Hickock, Gregory. (2014). *The Myth of Mirror Neurons: The Real Neuroscience of Communication and Cognition.* New York: Norton.

Hilferty, Joseph, Javier Valenzuela, and Òscar Vilarroya. (1998). "Paradox Lost." *Cognitive Linguistics* 9(2): 175–188.

Hutchins, Edwin. (1995). *Cognition in the Wild.* Cambridge, MA: MIT Press.

Jaynes, E. T. (2003). *Probability Theory: The Logic of Science.* Cambridge: Cambridge University Press.

Kuhn, T. (1962). *The Structure of Scientific Revolutions.* Chicago, IL: University of Chicago Press.

Lakoff, George and Mark Johnson. (2003). *Metaphors We Live By.* Chicago: University of Chicago Press.

Libet, B., C. A. Gleason, E. W. Wright, and E. K. Pearl. (1983). "Time of Conscious Intention to Act in Relation to Onset of Cerebral Activity (Readiness-Potential): The Unconscious Initiation of a Freely Voluntary Act." *Brain* 106(3): 623–642.

Libet, Benjamin. (1985). "Unconscious Cerebral Initiative and the Role of Conscious Will in Voluntary Action." *Behavioral and Brain Sciences* 8(4): 529–539.

Lizardo, Omar. (2014). "Beyond the Comtean Schema: The Sociology of Culture and Cognition versus Cognitive Social Science." *Sociological Forum* 29: 983–989.

Marr, David. (1982). *Vision: A Computational Investigation into the Human Representation and Processing of Visual Information.* New York: Freeman.

Meloni, Maurizio. (2012). "On the Growing Intellectual Authority of Neuroscience for Political and Moral Theory: Sketch for a Genealogy." In F. Vander Valk (ed.) *Essays on Neuroscience and Political Theory: Thinking the Body Politic*, 25–49. London and New York: Routledge.

Menary, Richard. (2006). *Radical Enactivism: Intentionality, Phenomenology and Narrative: Focus on the Philosophy of Daniel D. Hutto.* Amsterdam: John Benjamins.

Merleau-Ponty, Maurice. ([1942] 1963). *The Structure of Behaviour*, trans. Alden Fisher. Boston, MA: Beacon Press.

Mill, J. S. (1882). "Book VI: On the Logic of the Moral Sciences." In *A System of Logic, Ratiocinative and Inductive: Being a Connected View of the Principles of Evidence and the Methods of Scientific Investigation* 8th edn. New York: Harper & Brothers. www.gutenberg.org/ebooks/27942 (accessed 24 March 2017).

Ostrom, Elinor. (1998). "A Behavioral Approach to the Rational Choice Theory of Collective Action: Presidential Address, American Political Science Association, 1997." *American Political Science Review* 92(1): 1–22.

Ostrom, Elinor. (1991). "Review: Rational Choice Theory and Institutional Analysis: Toward Complementarity." *American Political Science Review* 85(1): 237–243.

Ostrom, Elinor, James Walker, and Roy Gardner. (1992). "Covenants With and Without a Sword: Self-Governance Is Possible." *American Political Science Review* 86(2): 404–417.

Pinker, Steven (1997) *How the Mind Works.* New York and London: Norton/Penguin.

Pitts-Taylor, Victoria. (2010). "The Plastic Brain: Neoliberalism and the Neuronal Self." *journals.sagepub.com* 14(6): 635–652.

Polya, G. (1990) *Patterns of Plausible Reasoning.* Princeton, NJ: Princeton University Press.

Rabin, M. (2002). "Inference by Believers in the Law of Small Numbers." *Quarterly Journal of Economics* 117(3): 775–816.

Real, L. A. (1991). "Animal Choice Behavior and the Evolution of Cognitive Architecture." *Science* 253: 980–986.

Real, L. A. and T. Caraco. (1986). "Risk and Foraging in Stochastic Environments." *Annual Review of Ecology and Systematics* 17: 371–390.

Rizzolatti, G. (2006). *Mirrors in the Brian: How Our Minds Share Actions, Emotions, and Experience.* New York: Oxford University Press.

Ross, Don. (2012). "Cognitive Variables And Parameters in Economic Models." In Ron Sun (ed.) *Grounding Social Sciences in Cognitive Sciences*, 287–334. Cambridge, MA: MIT Press.

Shallit, Jeffrey. (2016). "Yes, Your Brain Certainly Is a Computer." *Recursivity*, 19 May. http://recursed.blogspot.com/2016/05/yes-your-brain-certainly-is-computer.html (accessed 23 February 2017).

Slaby, Jan and Suparna Choudary. (2012). "Proposal for a Critical Neuroscience." In S. Choudory and J. Slaby (eds.) *Critical Neuroscience: A Handbook of the Social and Cultural Contexts of Neuroscience*, 27–51. Chichester: Wiley-Blackwell.

Slovic, P. (1995) "The Construction of Preference." *American Psychologist* 50(5): 364–371.

Sun, Ron. (2002). *Duality of the Mind: A Bottom-Up Approach toward Cognition.* Mahwah, NJ: Lawrence Erlbaum Associates.

Sun, Ron (2012). "Prolegomena to Cognitive Social Sciences." In Ron Sun (ed.) *Grounding Social Sciences in Cognitive Sciences*, 3–32. Cambridge, MA: MIT Press.

Suppes, Patrick. ([1960] 1962). *Studies in the Methodology and Foundations of Science: Selected Papers from 1951 to 1969.* Dordrecht: Springer.

Tooby, John and Leda Cosmides. (1995). "Foreword." In Simon Baron-Cohen (ed.) *Mindblindness: An Essay on Autism and Theory of Mind*, xi–xvii. Cambridge, MA: MIT Press.

Turner, John C. (2004). "Introduction." In Bernd Simon (ed.) *Identity in Modern Society: A Social Psychological Perspective*, x–xv. Malden, MA: Blackwell.

Turner, Mark. (2001). *Cognitive Dimensions of Social Science.* Oxford: Oxford University Press.

Turner, Mark (2002). "The Cognitive Study of Art, Language, and Literature." *Poetics Today* 23(1): 9–20.

Turner, Mark (2011). "The Embodied Mind and the Origins of Human Culture." In Ana Margarida Abrantes and Peter Hanenberg (eds.) *Cognition and Culture: An Interdisciplinary Dialogue*, 13–27. Frankfurt and Berlin: Peter Lang.

Von Scheve, Christian. (2011). "Sociology of Neuroscience or Neurosociology?" In Martyn Pickersgill and Ira Van Keulen (eds.) *Sociological Reflections on the Neurosciences*, 255–278. Bingley, UK: Emerald.

Wegner, Daniel. (2002). *The Illusion of Conscious Will.* Cambridge, MA: MIT Press.

Winston, Mark L. (1987). *The Biology of the Honey Bee.* Cambridge, MA: Harvard University Press.

Wrong, D. H. (1961). "The Oversocialized Conception of Man in Modern Sociology." *American Sociological Review* 26: 183–193.

2

STANDARD AND NON-STANDARD APPROACHES TO COGNITIVE SCIENCE

As we saw in the last chapter, the fact that the relationship between the social sciences and the cognitive sciences is underdeveloped and complicated, and that integration faces so many obstacles, is in large part a result of features of the two domains themselves. Social science explanation does not fit the traditional model of scientific explanation in terms of "laws": there simply are none. So "reductionism" in the classical philosophy of science sense, as we have seen, is not an option. But the explanatory structure of cognitive science reasoning and argumentation is also unusual and difficult to fit into the traditional model of scientific explanation. As the example of Gintis (2007) shows, however, some forms of evolutionary psychological explanation do relate, in an odd way, through the attribution of human-like cognitive capacities to animal cognition, making game theory the central explanatory device for integrating cognitive science and the social. And this requires a form of attributing rationality far down the evolutionary scale. This is a topic to which we will return, as it is central to the issue of understanding other minds.

In the preface we noted that the discovery of mechanisms related to this capacity was a remarkable twist: a scientific validation of a form of knowledge important both to social science and social life that was previously regarded as hopelessly subjective and unscientific. But it would be misleading to suggest that this capacity, or even the kind of decision-making discussed by Gintis and made the centerpiece of his effort at integration, was at the core of the standard approach to cognitive science. Just as making decision-making and game theory the core required dismissing or ignoring large chunks of social science and psychology, it also requires ignoring many of the traditional core concerns of cognitive science and cognitive neuroscience themselves, and even ignoring most of the actual attempted applications of cognitive science to social topics.

A general comment about these applications is necessary. They go both ways: from social scientists identifying puzzling topics for which an explanation based on cognitive neuroscience would be useful, and from cognitive scientists working upwards toward the explanation of social phenomenon by reference to cognitive mechanisms they have isolated. There are of course many opportunities here for talking past one another. Cognitive processes are complex and messy, so cognitive science explanations normally depend on a strategy of reducing complexity by beginning with those aspects of mind that can be most readily simplified and treated in isolation, such as perception and body movements. Traditional social science topics, such as social interaction, which cannot be readily simplified, are something of an afterthought. Even the simplest social interaction involves many capacities, from facial recognition and memory to mind-reading and responsiveness to embodied action, signaling, and so forth. Nevertheless, much can be said about these issues and about the challenges of attempts to bring cognitive science to bear on social science topics, and for social scientists attempting to frame topics in forms that cognitive science can be applied to.

The developing field of social neuroscience approaches the relationship from the bottom up: from the identification of cognitive mechanisms grounded in neural processes with observable, measurable correlates, to known social phenomena such as empathy or free-rider punishment. In contrast, social scientists typically are interested in validating and improving social science concepts which have long been assumed to have a basis in psychological mechanisms, such as charisma (Schjoedt et al. 2010) or group biases (Amodio 2014), by showing that they in fact do correlate to observable and measurable neural processes. Sometimes these approaches converge on common concepts such as empathy (Decety and Jackson 2004) or political orientation (Graham et al. 2009); the number of these convergences is gradually increasing. Some of them will be discussed in later chapters.

There is, however, a different aspect to the relationship between the social sciences and the cognitive sciences which is closer to the heart of the philosophy of cognitive science itself: the problem of the general model of the mind and the person, and of their relationship to the environment. One's commitments on this topic have deep connections to the ideas one can have of the social world. What is possible to put into the category of "the social" depends on what one takes to be the properties of the persons who compose it and of the interactions that produce the contents of "the social."

These extensions of standard models of cognition to account for social facts face serious difficulties – so serious that they call the standard model itself into question – and provide support for the radical alternative models that have been proposed (see Hutto 2004; Hutto 2005; Gallagher 2008; De Jaegher 2009; Chemero 2011; Hutto and Myin 2017). In this chapter we will trace the background of these explanatory problems to their roots in the standard model; discuss the kinds of revisions that the social, cultural, and developmental data seem to require; and briefly discuss what is entailed by the alternatives to the standard model.

The Standard Computational Model and Its Logic

The major division within cognitive science is between two broad approaches to the subject; in the rest of the book the contrasting implications of these approaches will be returned to over and over, in one context after another. These approaches have different implications for the possible integration of the social sciences into cognitive science, and go about it in different ways. There is no consensus model of the mind, but there is a family of notions that fit together into something that approximates a single model. Each element is or can be construed to be logically independent, but in the course of constructing and grounding explanations of actual phenomena the elements are difficult to separate. The core of the model is computationalism. It is claimed that "over 80 per cent of articles in theoretical cognitive science journals focus on computational modeling" (Miłkowski 2013: 1, citing Busemeyer and Diederich 2010; see also Gershman et al. 2015). In this tradition, "cognition is information processing in the physical symbol system" (Miłkowski 2013: 3, citing Newell 1980) "or that it is computation over representations" (Miłkowski 2013: 3, citing Fodor 1975). But as Miłkowski notes, all approaches to cognitive science are in some sense computational: they differ in what they think is computed, how it is computed, and what the units being computed with are. So the standard approach is an approach within computationalism.

What I will call, for convenience, the standard approach models the mind on computers and the symbol-processing capacities of computers, and ascribes most of the mind's capacities to an "architectural" feature – fixed computational units, called modules – which perform computations on representations. The standard approach is characterized by an emphasis on "specific components of cognition (e.g., perception, memory, learning, or language)" (Sun 2005: 3) which are taken to be universal.

The grounds for this assumption of universality come from evolutionary psychology. The claim is that:

> our cognitive architecture resembles a confederation of hundreds or thousands of functionally dedicated computers (often called modules) designed to solve adaptive problems endemic to our hunter-gatherer ancestors. Each of these devices has its own agenda and imposes its own exotic organization on different fragments of the world. There are specialized systems for grammar induction, for face recognition, for dead reckoning, for construing objects, and for recognizing emotions from the face. There are mechanisms to detect animacy, eye direction, and cheating. There is a "theory of mind" module, and a multitude of other elegant machines.
>
> (Tooby and Cosmides 1995: xiii–xiv)

These mini-computers operate on information, or representations, and these operations comprise cognition. Moreover, there is a strong reason for thinking that these modules cannot possibly arise in any way than as "the carefully crafted product of thousands or millions of generations of natural selection" – namely that, "the only known explanation for the existence of complex functional design in organic systems is natural selection" (Cosmides and Tooby 1994: 86).

This in turn implies that they are universal: "what they construct is the same for all people, from whatever culture; the representations produced by these universal mechanisms thereby constitute the foundation of our shared reality and our ability to communicate" (Tooby and Cosmides 1995: xiii-xiv). As will become evident in later chapters, accounting for cognitive diversity, and especially cultural diversity, becomes a special problem for the standard approach and for reasons related to the speed of computation: local cultural quirks also seem to be cases of "second nature" or unconscious and opaque cognitive response which would require fast processing.

The core computationalist model – consisting of a pre-given architecture in which complex modules have evolved from more rudimentary ones – sets the contours for how the standard model applies to social phenomena. The strategy generally attempts to shows how complex observable phenomena can be produced by means of computer-like symbol processing in something approximating the rapid response of real subjects. It generally proceeds by providing a "functional" analysis that breaks down a given cognitive process or capacity into computationally simple units, and then provides a computational model for the units' performance of the task. Many of the computational models and related analyses of cognitive processes, such as Gallistel's analysis of ant navigation (1989), involve imputing to the subject a vast array of complex computational capacities such as, in his account, a dead-reckoning module, among many other needed computational "modules," which are bits of cognitive architecture that operate by transforming informational inputs. The key argument for this approach is that even very simple acts, such as catching a thrown ball, once we have broken them down to their functional elements, can be seen to require significant computational power; and this complexity strangely suggests that only a modular account is consistent with the speed with which the brain accomplishes the task.

Computationalism comes in different forms with respect to representations: one view is minimalist and treats information and its processing as a causal process. The strong form of this argument, however, treats representations as complex inferential objects best modeled, even for animal cognition, as parts of syntactic systems. This and similar approaches put their emphasis on the properties of representations or the rules for processing representations. The minimalist view is that "representations" are merely data structures, and virtually every account of mind uses some potentially quite minimal data structure. The analogy cognitive scientists have in mind is to logic, where rules apply strictly but only to "well-formed formulae." If the cognitive processing assumed to be operative is different – as it is, for example, in connectionism – one still needs data structures for processing, but they can be minimal. But there are reasons for thinking that "representations" in a more elaborate sense figure in cognition. The fact that an ant navigates by external points of reference but can continue its direction when these are obscured indicates that it has a mental "representation" of its position that persists in the brain during this period (Gallistel 1989: 56).

The larger motivation for rejecting a limited notion of representation, and its even more limited variants, is that the notion of combination is difficult to construct without something like computational rules to account for the combinatorial properties of the representations. The notion of possessing rules in general seems to be best modeled on syntactic rules. So discussions of these combinatorial properties, as they apply to representations, gradually slides into assuming a model in which rules are shared socially or collectively, as they are supposed to be in the case of language (see Brandom 2009: 197–226). The strong form of this argument is the idea that the brain implements a syntactic and semantic system that is in some sense pre-given rather than learned.

The idea that there needs to be a syntactic system in advance of learning is a consequence of the commitment to the idea that the mind operates on representations: it is difficult to see what sorts of operations these might be unless they were in some sense similar to the logical "operations" of explicit reasoning.

Modules or innate structures are appealed to in order to explain not only the apparently odd way in which language use and theory of mind use appear developmentally, but also their "fast" or automatic character. But the thing being explained requires its own specification, which is typically represented as a flow-chart in which arrows are drawn between boxes representing components of these processes and the arrows representing (usually unspecified) causal and information transforming processes. The boxes are functional units, parts of what is taken to be the minimal set of unitized processes that make up the cognitive conditions for the possibility of some phenomenon (Nichols and Stich 2003: 10).

The choice of the functional units reflects two constraints. First, there is experimental evidence from psychology about the phenomena in question. One might have, for example, evidence of the specific details of the memory capacities of ants returning to a nest as revealed by experiments. Second, there are considerations of economy and simplicity. There should be no more boxes than are needed as "conditions for the possibility" of the total phenomena. The "account" is functional, not physical. The point is to have boxes representing every necessary sub-process that figures in the capacity in question as the experimental evidence has defined it.

What is it that the boxes stand in for? There are of course inputs and outputs that are represented by arrows, and something that happens in the boxes. What happens, however, is a problem. The problem is this: in treating these depictions as explanations, we are in effect explaining brain processes by positing a little human-like operative, a homunculus, in the brain performing the relevant tasks in a manner similar to conscious explicit thought. There certainly are not such things. But the boxes help define the explanatory problem, and enable us to take an additional step: breaking the tasks down into a series of boxes that do not require full-fledged homunculi. Consider, for instance, Daniel Dennett's portrayal (1978: 123–4):

> without saying how it is to be accomplished (one says, in effect: put a little man in there to do the job). If we then look closer at the individual boxes we see that the function of each is accomplished by subdividing it via another flowchart into still smaller, more stupid homunculi. Eventually this nesting of boxes within boxes lands you with homunculi so stupid … that they can be, as one says, "replaced by a machine." One discharges fancy homunculi from one's scheme by organizing armies of such idiots to do the work.

Less colorfully: "They try to explain mindreading (or some other complex cognitive capacity) by positing functionally characterized underlying mechanisms with capacities that are simpler than the capacity they are trying to explain" (Nichols and Stich 2003: 11). In reducing a cognitive capacity to successively simpler underlying processes, the standard model's mechanism-driven perspective implies that combinatorial processes operating on representations play a primary role.

The temptation is to think of the thing that happens in the boxes in computational terms, and specifically in terms of rules. The inputs are conveniently thought of as things that are already in some sense representational, and the processes in the boxes as something that is done with the representations, which involves combining the representations and making them into something different: perhaps a different representation, or a command to a part of the body to act, or, in the case of perception, taking raw inputs and turning them into a representation that can be stored as a memory or matched with a stored memory. Nichols and Stich put it this way:

> the representational account of cognition … maintains that beliefs, desires, and other propositional attitudes are relational states. To have a belief or a desire with a particular content is to have a representation token with that content stored in the functionally appropriate way in the mind. So, for example, to believe that Socrates was an Athenian is to have a representation token whose content is *Socrates was an Athenian* stored in one's "Belief Box," and to desire that it will be sunny tomorrow is to have a representation whose content is *It will be sunny tomorrow* stored in one's "Desire Box."
>
> *(Nichols and Stich 2003: 14–15; italics in the original)*

They note that: "Many advocates of the representational account of cognition also assume that the representation tokens subserving propositional attitudes are linguistic or quasi-linguistic in form" (Nichols and Stich 2003: 15).

Jerry Fodor (2008: 18) makes the reasoning behind this assumption explicit: "compositionality is at the heart of the productivity and systematicity of thought, but also ... determines the relation between thoughts and concepts. The key to the compositionality of thoughts is that they have concepts as theory constituents," and further, "only something language-like can have a logical form." It is difficult to see what the alternative is, given this construction of the problem. The bias toward thinking in terms of representations is overwhelming, in part because it is only representations that can be readily thought of as undergoing combinatorial processes. "Readily thought of," however, implicitly means thought of in terms more or less familiar from folk psychology. The homunculus problem is simply an extreme case of imagining the inner workings of the mind in familiar human terms. The combinations or representations in question are modeled on explicit reasoning, or explicit reasoning as formalized in computer programming.

Some Reservations about the Standard Model

But these claims need to come with a warning. We do not have an argument other than plausibility and the lack of alternatives for believing in the results of boxology, or in modules. There is a sense in which this is simply a sign of our limitations and the limitations of folk psychology: without it, we can't make sense of the actual processes of thought because folk psychology is *how* we make sense of thought, indeed, how we define it. How any of this works in the brain is unknown, and indeed there is a substantial explanatory gap between what we would like to explain (thought, actual speech, consciousness, and the qualities of human experience) and the neuroscience mechanisms we have an understanding of (Horgan 1999: 15–46).

This is not to say that there is no empirical basis for these claims. As noted above, these accounts are constrained by experimental results in psychology: if there is a demonstrated capacity, such as the homing capacity of an ant and its capacity for self-correcting spatial orientation, a functionalist model of this capacity must include the necessary subroutines. There is, however, a physical side to the reasoning. Ideally, the boxes, which represent modularized capacities, should correspond to *something* in the brain. The brain is a variegated organ which has been mapped into different regions, especially as a result of lesion or cognitive deficit studies, which are known to be associated with particular activities or competencies. Ideally, a box should correspond to a cluster of neurons that activate at the appropriate point in the sequence of the boxed processes. Because at least some cognitive processes can be replicated in conditions in which brain activity can be measured, such as functional magnetic resonance imaging (fMRI) machines, it is technically possible to determine where and in what order brain activity occurs – up to a certain resolution. It is a bonus for boxology if these capacities can be localized in the brain; and the fact that many capacities, such as phoneme recognition, can be localized serves as a general warrant for the strategy of boxology.

Boxology arguments depend very heavily on considerations of plausibility. Localizing enhances plausibility. But the two are logically distinct:

> Positing a "box" which represents a functionally characterized processing mechanism or a functionally characterized set of mental states does not commit a theorist to the claim that the mechanism or the states are spatially localized in the brain, any more than drawing a box in a flow chart for a computer program commits one to the claim that the operation that the box represents is spatially localized in the computer.
>
> *(Nichols and Stich 2003: 11)*

This is an important point for what follows. Nevertheless, this bonus, when it can be obtained, for example by localizing certain kinds of thoughts or mental processes, plays an important role.

The standard model's evidential appeal to plausibility, however, is troublesome given other considerations that undermine its plausibility. The modular account depends very heavily on its being universal, on everyone having the same modules to activate, and on the modules being primordial products of evolution, and thus freed from any requirement to make sense of how they are acquired, which would be the case if they varied culturally. The claim is often made that theory of mind is robust at least across several modern cultures. But, although a few basics of theory of mind, such as recognition of goal directedness, do seem universal, theory of mind terms are not universal. Epistemic language varies widely, and even the distinction between true and false belief does not appear in some languages (Needham 1972: 33). Some cultures regard talk about another person's beliefs and mental contents as deeply inappropriate, and treat their minds as opaque (Robbins and Rumsey 2008; Robbins 2008; Schiefflin 2008). And there are a number of other variations in explicit theory of mind talk between cultures.

The problems with the traditional strategy include issues of physical realizability and difficulties with its main concepts, and a problem of underdetermination. As noted earlier, the distinguishing feature of cognitive *neuro*science is that:

> the theoretical posits of a computational explanation are ... tested against neuroscientific evidence: if one can find some stable activation in the brain that corresponds to a category of tasks, the category can be realistically defined in terms of brain functioning.
>
> *(Miłkowski 2013: 98–9).*

This is the problem of implementation, and it is a strong constraint on theory: a difficult test to apply, but one that excludes certain common computational strategies. The concept of levels, as we have seen, is a way to soften this constraint. But it is not a constraint that can be eliminated entirely.

The second problem with the concepts is, ironically, one familiar from Durkheim: the units, such as "representations," are treated as simultaneously causal and semantic (or meaningful), and thus governed by logic. But the concepts of representation used in the computational accounts themselves, such as the purely formal notion of "information," are not semantic or meaningful in the required sense (Miłkowski 2013: 2).[1] So there is an additional "levels" problem: the semantic or meaning level still needs to be connected to its supposed realization at the computational level. The problem of underdetermination is a result of the fact that "one and the same phenomenon could be modeled by a classical symbolic program, a connectionist network, dynamically, or using some hybrid methods" (Miłkowski 2013: 94), and indeed, very different models of each kind can produce the same outputs from the same inputs. Consequently, deciding between them requires considerations other than purely computational ones. The "partial" character of the "autonomy" between levels is relevant here: the deciding considerations come from other levels.

Beyond the Standard Model?

The difficulties with the standard model are many, but there is no comparably developed alternative: critiques are typically partial, and many of the explanatory practices that make up the model are employed by critics of the model as part of their own larger account. The alternative approach is usually associated with the term "embodiment," but is related to a full range of alternative responses to the standard approach (Varela et al. 1991; Noë 2004; Thompson 2007; DiPaolo 2009; De Jaegher et al. 2010; Chemero 2011; Kiverstein forthcoming). The alternative strategy involves "embodiment" in that it takes the unit of cognition to be the whole body; is "enactive" in that it considers the core cognitive processes to involve the sensory-motor system of the active, acting subject; is "extended" in that it emphasizes the role of external surrogates for thought and as a part of action; is "embedded" in the sense that it takes all cognition to be part of a local environment or situation; and is "ecological" and "dynamic" in that it understands cognitive processes as part of a changing total system of relations between the environment and the subject.

The alternative "embodied" approaches turn the standard strategy on its head. They start from the idea of grounding the basic cognitive process not only in the substratum of the brain but also in the body, that is to say in sensorimotor experiences, experiences of acting and adapting, which are intrinsically tied to the body's relation to the world (Garbarini and Adenzato 2004: 101). The argument for this approach rests on a somewhat indirect consideration: the amount of computational work that the system must perform to execute a task. Embodied cognitive scientists typically respond to issues of computational speed by showing how features of the body facilitate abilities, such as the ability of the diving gannet (which fishes by identifying prey from the air and dives deeply into the water) to avoid injury by closing its wings just before hitting the water. Rather than performing complex calculations, it is claimed, gannets rely on optic flow, the changing visual patterns they see when coming close to the water (Chemero 2011: 123). The alternative approach thus replaces much of the processing work assumed to be required by the standard approach by considering the situation of the subject, and stresses the ways in which the body, the activity of the agent in navigating the environment, and the dynamic relation of the environment and the agent serve to solve the puzzle of how cognitive tasks are accomplished in a computationally economical way.

In its more radical forms, this approach explicitly rejects one source of computational complexity: the positing of an intervening body of hidden mental procedures in which representations or "content" that is meaning-bearing are created and processed, which is central to the symbolic processing approach to cognition. For Hutto and Myin (2013: 137) "basic cognition is not contentful; basic minds are fundamentally, constitutively already world-involving." They treat higher computation-like processes, such as thinking about something apart from the more fundamental cognitive process of acting, as outgrowths of these basic capacities. As they put it, "the capacity to engage in decoupled contentful activities is derived, in both a logical and a developmental sense, from activities that involve the manipulation of external vehicles" (2013: 152–3). Similarly, the direction of the explanation of higher cognitive processes is from the external to the internal: "activities involving external symbols undoubtedly transform and augment cognition" (2013: 153).

The attraction of the alternative approaches is that by conceptualizing these tasks differently, in terms of the organism's use of features of the environment rather than elaborate computations, it is possible to reduce computational complexity to levels that are more plausible for the tasks and organisms in question. The general strategy is to avoid positing complex, indirect, and computation-heavy processes and searching for direct, causal, correlational links, for example in accounting for perception (cf. Wilson 2004; Wheeler 2005; Wheeler 2010; Clark 2008; Chemero 2011). The strategy also overcomes some of the issues with attributing elaborate fixed capacities to systems: the relations with the environment are understood dynamically or interactionally (Bickhard 2009; Menary 2010; Gallagher 2013), which fits better with the image of an active, task-setting, and performing embodied system, changing locations and extensively interacting with a changing setting and other changing systems. These approaches are less well developed, however, and raise many other issues, especially in relation to traditionally central concepts such as representation and the traditionally important role assigned to semantic properties of thought.

One ongoing issue is this: the ideas of representation and computation are defined so broadly and ambiguously it is possible to argue that the supposed alternatives are themselves forms of computationalism and representationalism. The differences in approach are nevertheless substantial. The core of the issues is summarized by Anthony Chemero (2011) under two headings: mental gymnastics, and the kind of arguments from explanatory necessity that identify supposed "conditions for the possibility of" capacities. By mental gymnastics Chemero means that most of the models of representational-cum-computational processes require an astonishing amount of computational activity to reproduce, through reverse engineering, the kinds of activities that are being explained. A case in point is the problem of animal navigation. Here the question is, first, do animals such as ants and bees have representational systems? The same considerations underlying the standard model apply: animals have quite astonishing capacities to orient themselves, to communicate position to other animals in some cases, and to recover from errors. To model these capacities representationally and computationally requires a lot of complex mathematics and a lot of computational power to make these capacities operate in real time, though it is vague as to what "a lot" means in this context (Gallistel 1989; Gallistel 2011).

Is it plausible that the ant brain works in this way? And, if not, is it plausible that our brains also might work in some other way? It is also claimed that some mental activities are "representation hungry," which is to say that to construct a model of them requires us to attribute a lot of "representing" to the mind performing those activities. These claims serve to justify attributing "mental gymnastics" to their subjects: to perform representation hungry tasks requires mental gymnastics. As applied to humans, as Chemero summarizes it, this is a "conditions for the possibility" argument that "will be impossible to explain truly cognitive phenomena without mental gymnastics." There is a second, related argument, which is a *tu quoque* argument: that not only are these matters of explanatory necessity, the supposed alternatives, which we will discuss below, also "actually do attribute representations to cognitive systems" (Chemero 2011: 33). And, as we can see even in the case of ants, it is difficult to separate the notion of representation from the notion of combinatorial processes – whatever is combined in mental processes turns out to look like a representation. A data structure which has combinatorial properties, for example, is representing something with special properties mimicked by the mental properties that allow for combination, and is thus, more or less by definition, a representation.

The problem of mental gymnastics is, however, a self-created problem: if we assume that the brain is a computer-like system with programs and rule-following calculations, even the apparently simplest activities, such as an ant returning to its nest, turn out to require a massive amount of computing power and complex mathematics. Modularity is a kind of solution: modularization makes increased speed plausible, but it is a solution with some odd properties. It is designed to satisfy our conscious and reflective ideas of what an inference or combination in the circumstances might be, even if these inferences are being reduced to the simplest elements. But this is an odd criterion for accepting anything: why should fundamental brain processes have properties that mimic our explicit and self-conscious ways of performing tasks or communicating? In the history of physics, there was a point at which the older criteria of "intelligibility" simply had to be abandoned: it became clear that there were phenomena like action at a distance that could be described mathematically but were not "intelligible." A person cannot produce action at a distance – how could a planet? Answering this kind of question required giving up one's anthropomorphic sense of what could cause what, a sense derived from pushing objects around – and not substituting anything for it.

Representations Reconsidered

This is all very abstract. What is at stake here for "the social"? The answer to this is also abstract – but interesting, and important, and also difficult to explain. The term "representation" comes at a long remove from Kant, who famously says:

> There can be no doubt that all our knowledge begins with experience. For how should our faculty of knowledge be awakened into action did not objects affecting our senses partly of themselves produce representations, partly arouse the activity of our understanding to compare these representations, and, by combining or separating them, work up the raw material of the sensible impressions into that knowledge of objects which is entitled experience? In the order of time, therefore, we have no knowledge antecedent to experience, and with experience all our knowledge begins.
>
> *(Kant [1787] 1929: 41)*

What is meant by this is that we do not have direct understanding of the world, but knowledge mediated and organized by categories. The usage itself loads the dice in favor of the idea that representations are the sorts of things that are organized into a system, and, moreover, a system that is supra-individual, or shared. But the key to the problem of representation is what representations are supposed to do in a model of the mental; and this, as we will see, leads us back to the idea of a shared system.

As Fodor noted, the thing that representations (or whatever one chooses to call the basic units of mental processes) need to be able to do is to be transformed through combinations. The case of dead reckoning is a case in point: in actual dead reckoning one takes angles from the point of departure to some fixed points and then draws on charts to fix position; only then does one do the calculations of headings and speed that make up dead reckoning. Dead reckoning is a material practice in which one is trained. The computations combine these data points to produce something new, namely a compass heading which, if it is followed, will get you to the place you have targeted.

The data points need, however, to be in the correct form in order to be transformed according to the rules of navigation – "over that way" is not good enough. And this is a general property that the units in the mental system need to have. One can think of the problem in this way. In biology we have two kinds of variation: normal statistical variation, on some sort of dimension; and variation in code, for example the kind of variation in the units in the DNA molecule. These variations are not distributed statistically around a mean. They come in units that combine according to rules. This was Mendel's great discovery about peas: that their inheritance followed combinatory rules rather than some form of statistical variation that was a product of the variable traits of parents.

The paradigm of coded data points and combinatory rules is the digital computer. And it shows the immense power of calculation and speed of calculation that is possible on the basis of codes and rules. One could imagine analog rather than digital versions of these processes – machines like clocks integrated with other machines like clocks to produce calculative outcomes automatically. But these would be clunky compared to machines based on codes and rules.

Conventionally the coded data points are thought of in terms of "representations," a term with a technical meaning. If one wished to incorporate the reasoning in terms of a slogan, it would be "no computation without representation." And a great deal follows from this, together with the assumption that the brain is a computational machine operating on representations. Gallistel and King discuss a minimalist form of this thesis based on the mathematical notion of information, which they call "the only rigorous definition that we have and the foundation on which the immensely powerful theory of information has been built" (2009: ix). The basic lesson is drawn out by Claude Shannon (1948):

> Shannon's conception of the communication process requires that the receiver, that is, the brain, have a representation of the set of possible messages and a probability distribution over that set. Absent such a representation, it is impossible for the world to communicate information to the brain, at least information as defined by Shannon.
>
> *(Gallistel and King 2009: ix)*

This in turn becomes the controlling fact in neuroscience, which cannot be avoided and must be realized in the physical processes of the brain. To understand how the brain itself works, one must understand the way in which combinatorial processes work. And these processes can, and indeed must, be modeled as symbols, since this is what computation works on, which are, and have to be, simultaneously physical facts: "the physical stuff of computation and representation" are "the physical entities in memory that carry information forward in time." The concept of information, symbol, codes, processing, and so forth are merged with the physical facts of the brain. The physical facts are realizations of the code processing model and are thus "real" and "not just a model" (Gallistel and King 2009: x).

Real and not just a model: this is a crucial claim. It is precisely the one challenged in the controversial quotation from Epstein in Chapter 1. And it requires an extensive excursus to understand. The issues here recur throughout this book, so what follows is not exhaustive. But it is important to understand the core issues and intellectual motivations for this claim, and what kind of argument it is. The argument depends on the "must": this is a claim about what must be in the brain in order for something else to happen, in this case compositionality or combination through codes. But do we need to say that compositionality *of this kind*, namely as a matter of operations on coded objects, is in the brain? Or is this only a feature of our models of cognitive processes? Could the brain work in a different way, a way that our models – which are, after all, constructed to replicate a highly selective set of cognitive processes described in a particular way – do not actually correspond to? The answer to this, from the computationalist, is that the things being modeled are highly general properties of all cognitive processing, so there is no way around the need to model this particular kind of compositionality. Begin with the problem of what is a model and what is real. The core issue is this: as Miłkowski points out, all models of cognitive processes are computational models. The main rival to the standard model, connectionism, is just as much a computational model as the more familiar rule-governed, program-like computational models of the standard approach.

Computational models all face similar problems, which they address in different ways. Each "solution" leaves some aspect of cognition hanging, difficult to assimilate to the model and in need of auxiliary hypotheses to enable the model to be consistent with known facts, such as facts about cognitive development. Nevertheless, there are some very basic considerations that drive the standard model. Two of them have to do with the basic things "cognition" is supposed to do: to take some sort of content and then to transform it by combination into another form of content.[2] The ideas of "representation" and "information" refer to this content, and both are controversial, but difficult to avoid. The key to understanding them is understanding what they are supposed to do: combine into something else. It is easiest to model combination on the model of a computer: bits of information in a specific form that can be transformed according to rules are transformed according to rules to produce more bits of information in the specific form necessary for being transformed according to rules. Rules and well-formed formulae are central to formal logic: this is one of the models of cognition for the standard view. Without information in the right form, formal rules cannot perform transformations.

This is a major constraint. But is it a constraint on formal models of cognitive processes, or a constraint on actual cognitive processes? Is it the only way we can think about modeling the processes, or a hard limit on what the processes could possibly consist of? Before turning to these questions, and some additional puzzles that go along with them, there is one other major constraint that drives us toward the standard model: the fact of memory and its role in effective action. In the first place, this is a constraint on our notion of information or representation. To perform the combinations of representations that need to happen to go from sensory signals to action, representations have to be computable or combinable, preferably in ways that allow for a lot of combination.

Memory becomes important here because the combinations the brain needs to perform include combinations with representations or information "stored" in memory, not just the immediate sensory inputs. And this adds two other requirements: storage and addressability. The representations not only get stored, they also have to be connected to the new inputs, or be accessible to our conscious efforts at remembering, and to whatever else requires memory or the results of learning. Again, the standard model has a computer-like answer to this problem:

> A read/write memory frees the composition of functions from the constraints of real time by making the empirically specified values for the arguments of functions available at any time, regardless of the time at which past experience specified them.
>
> (Gallistel and King 2009: x)

This is a big demand: a kind of memory that allows for and indeed guarantees that novel inputs will be matched up with and combined with historical inputs in an efficient way. And this requires not only "storage" but also what are called "efficient representations," with a lot of power to compose into something new.

Puzzles of Encoding

This is a tremendously compelling story. It seems to follow directly from the simplest and most general premises about computability. But it has implications that are more difficult to swallow, and raises some considerations that are at the least deeply puzzling. The implications are well developed by Fodor and his followers, and they focus on the idea of basic concepts – a particular kind of representation with compositional properties. His thesis is that all basic concepts – non-combined ones that get combined to form non-basic concepts – are innate. The argument involves the problem of learning: how does one learn a concept or, to put it differently, acquire a representation with compositional properties. Merely inputting stimuli is not enough: the world is, as William James put it, a buzzing, blooming confusion. To extract anything from this world requires prior selective mechanisms – some filters, or, if we think of learning as a kind of hypothesis, testing, very strong "a priori constraints on the kinds of hypotheses the learner is going to try out" (Piattelli-Palmarini forthcoming). If we think of learning as testing hypotheses, where do the hypotheses come from? They have to already be in the form of concepts or representations with combinatory properties in order to be the kind of thing that can be tested. You have to have a meaning before you test a meaning, for example, in social interaction.

Then there are oddities of learning words: "The acquisition of even very simple concepts requires things like a theory of mind, the understanding of relevant aspects of a situation, understanding the syntax of the sentences that contain them" and so on, according to the literature on the acquisition of the lexicon (Piattelli-Palmarini forthcoming). Moreover, words don't seem to be learned in the slow trial and error way posited by learning theories. We need a different model, in which the concepts are turned on or activated by the right inputs.

> Evidence, suitably labeled (what Jerry calls Mode of Presentation (MOP)), can "activate" them, but not "engender" them, for all the above reasons. Lila Gleitman and collaborators have carried out, over the years, an impressive series of experiments showing that word meanings are very frequently acquired upon one single exposure, under clear conditions that correspond to MOPs (in Fodor's terminology).
>
> *(Piattelli-Palmarini forthcoming)*

All this fits with the idea that we have a large and diverse set of basic concepts innately, and that they are "activated" by the right situations. The arguments for this come down to two related theses: that there is no learning theory that can account for the acquisition of basic concepts; and that the arguments for "the poverty of stimulus" long made about the acquisition of syntax by Chomsky apply here as well. The term "basic" is critical here: we can learn easily enough through being instructed in or making combinations of concepts, such as "red dog." But getting the things that combine is a different matter. If the basic units of cognition, i.e. the things that compose – representations, concepts, or units of information – are not already well formed or standardized they cannot be learned inductively. One cannot learn a code, a scheme, or a system of compositional properties by trial and error, without having a code already. We "learn" too quickly for this learning to be the result of trial and error, feedback, and so on. And this implies that we don't really learn these things at all: we merely have our innate concepts brought into contact with the words of others. As Piattelli-Palmarini puts it, "The effects on the growth of the child's mind of receiving relevant linguistic data bear a close analogy to the effects of triggers." And even if one could show, as connectionist cognitive scientists have shown, that something like this learning can happen through the brute force of trial and error learning, this form of learning is too slow to account for what is actually learned by children mastering a language. Moreover, even connectionist models require data in a pre-constructed standard form, which is the thing that needs to be explained in the first place: what are the basic units of cognition?

There are, however, plausibility problems with this line of argument, however compelling it seems to be on computational grounds. In the first place, there are many languages, and they are highly diverse – so diverse that even Chomsky's version of the innateness hypotheses is open to a great deal of skepticism (Ibbotson and Tomasello 2016).

Extending this hypothesis to "concepts," itself a problematic term, as will be discussed later, runs into other problems. One must claim that although there are many languages, there is only one innate and therefore universal underlying language. Jerry Fodor (2008) calls this "mentalese." All the other languages would need to be derivative from or consistent with this language – to be alternative realizations of the same underlying concepts – because mentalese is supposed to be the actual language of thought itself, and thought itself is supposed to be linguistic and done with units of thought that have "semantic properties."

This works for some issues, but raises many others. Children learn a lot of language quickly. They don't learn much of it through having concepts explained to them as the compositional products of more basic concepts, as Chomsky himself notes (1975: 161):

> Language is not really taught, for the most part. Rather, it is learned, by mere exposure to the data. No one has been taught the principle of structure dependence of rules ... or language-specific properties of such rules. ... Nor is there any reason to suppose that people are taught the meaning of words. (...) The study of how a system is learned cannot be identified with the study of how it is taught; nor can we assume that what is learned has been taught. To consider an analogy that is perhaps not too remote, consider what happens when I turn on the ignition in my automobile. A change of state takes place. ... A careful study of the interaction between me and the car that led to the attainment of this new state would not be very illuminating. Similarly, certain interactions between me and my child result in his learning (hence knowing) English.

So it is necessary to suppose that mentalese is very extensive, and indeed corresponds with the set of all learnable concepts. As Massimo Piattelli-Palmarini summarizes:

> You tell me what you think is learned when a concept is learned, call it X, and I show you that X (whatever that is) must be assumed to be innately available to the learner. In a nutshell, it seems to me clear and unquestionable that learning word meanings is a process of activation, not of construction by means of progressive guesses and trial-and-error.
>
> *(Piattelli-Palmarini forthcoming)*

This has big implications. If virtually all concept acquisition is through activation, not learning, we have a big puzzle about the apparent diversity between societies with respect to concepts. If they are innate, the innately given set of concepts must be very large.[3]

But if we look at the question of what "basic concepts" are empirically, by looking at the whole range of actual languages and asking what terms are in fact universal, we get a very short list, of forty or so terms. And this list does not include many of the terms that the hypothesis of mentalese would like to explain. The idea that children have a theory of mind that is activated at some particular stage of development is a case in point: it would make sense that if this was a universal feature of human development the "theory" was, so to speak, in the mind ready to be activated. But the actual list of basic terms constructed by linguists includes almost nothing in the way of terms about the mind. And even such apparently basic mental terms as "belief" turn out not to be universal, or not to mean the things that are studied in research on the theory of mind. This is an issue we will take up in the next chapter.

And there are other issues intrinsic to the idea of codes. Much of this argumentation involves "have to" claims: if there is computability in the brain, there must be a code. If there is a code, it must be innate. If it is innate, it must be universal. If it must be physically realized in the brain, it is physically realized in the brain. There are attempts to go beyond these "have to" claims, however, and it is worth thinking some of them through. Gallistel (forthcoming), again, is explicit about them. The way he frames the conflict is between "the hypothesis that memories consist of experientially altered synaptic conductances" and the reality that computational accounts require symbolic processing, and therefore symbols, and therefore encoding.

This difference points to a much larger difference, which recurs in multiple places, such as the issue of epigenetics. We can distinguish two kinds of biological processes: computational processes that involve coding, such as DNA replication and RNA "messaging"; and normal biological variation, which typically is described in terms of a dose–response curve. The two combine to produce outcomes in many cases: one's height, for example, is the result of genetics (which are in code) and post-genetic influences, including such things as nutrition, that alter the outcome in various directions. The phenotype – you – is the result of both, and one can't read the code from the outcome. Many brain processes are dose–response relations; the presence and quantity of particular chemicals and enzymes in the brain, or the degree of synaptic input. These do not translate in any obvious way into units of thought, or anything encoded, except perhaps in a very abstract way as informational signals in simple on-off form. These can be said to be associated in such a way that neurons that fire together wire together, i.e., increase the strength of the synaptic connections. But association is not enough to produce the kind of thought or linguistic capacity – compositional or combinatorial use of symbols – that the strong computationalist, as distinct from the computational minimalist (such as the connectionist), thinks must be explained. As Gallistel (forthcoming) says, "synaptic conductances are ill-suited to symbolic processing."

The issue with encoding is that there has until recently been no plausible physical account of how encoding at a higher level, namely objects of thought with compositional properties, or memory, the preservation of accessible encoded thought, is possible within the brains. The orthodoxy of memory as strengthening of synaptic connections stands in the way of this – but at least we know what these are in physical terms. What the encoder needs is a physical means of encoding. But there is a model for this: DNA and RNA. And recent discoveries point to the idea that "acquired information" in at least one validated case, of conditioned response in a ferret, "resides within individual … cells" (Gallistel forthcoming; Hesslow et al. 2013). The cell is thus a signal transforming device: "synaptic inputs indicate simply and only the onset of a conditioned stimulus" and produce "a complex spike-train output that is informed by acquired temporal information stored within the cell" (Gallistel forthcoming).

Gallistel suggests that "the symbols are in molecules inside the neurons, and the machinery that operates on them is intracellular molecular machinery" and each neuron is a computational machine. Does this get us the basic units of thought, or computation, that are the general basis of cognition and brain processes? Perhaps, but a comment Gallistel adds raises some questions: "Could it be that the process of evolution has found a way to make use of [the machinery of DNA symbols] – or the closely allied RNA machinery – to store acquired information and make computations with it?" RNA and DNA, so to say, speak to each other in the same code, which is just to say that they react to each other chemically in a way that can be modeled computationally as code. This seems different than the "complex spike-train output" that is supposed to be the code for the ferrets' cellular response. And indeed, there is a whole body of naturalized computational mathematics devoted to this and other natural processes. These models don't seem to produce symbolic outputs that speak to the symbolic outputs of other models – they involve different mathematics for different computable biological processes. This raises questions about the interface between encoded processes: if we have multiple codes, how do they talk to each other?

In a trivial sense, there is a basic "informational" level for these processes: chemical processes in the cell that can be modeled computationally. But we are a long way from mentalese in these cases. And one wonders how something like mentalese, which consists of concepts, or any higher-level symbolic unit of cognition could be generated by DNA? We are back to the issue of normal biological variation: why are the structures in my head not subject to the same variation as, for example, the relative size of different parts of my brain? Or other aspects of brain function, which vary on a dose–response basis? It seems that we must hypothesize an essential, universal coding system underlying the phenotypic facts of actual diversity in thought, in language, and so forth, without having any way of explaining how this system is produced, how it is the same for everyone and stays the same for everyone: and why it is unlike even genetic inheritance which is subject to at least some normal variation.

Innateness and Universality

This question points to one of the largely undiscussed bonuses of universalistic "innate" accounts. If we think that there is an underlying code of basic thoughts shared by all persons, we can explain how people are able to communicate, share languages, and so on without having to resort to explanations involving learning. Learning, indeed, is an irritating add-on to innateness. It needs to be integrated with it, which is why replacing much of learning with activation helps reduce the amount of learning that needs to be accommodated. But what is acquired or learned still needs to fit into what is innate: if the code is innate, what is learned also needs to be in a compatible code. And this fits with a certain kind of representationalism in which representations are already there – in the computational brain – in an innately coded form. Representations can then be "learned" and added computationally by combinations of existing representations.

The explanatory bonus comes with a price, which will loom large in the next chapters. We can divide cognitive material into three rough categories: innate and universal, local or socially distributed, and individual. These can be further subdivided: there are universals that are innate because they arrive through a universal mechanism such as DNA directly to the brain and are already encoded, or are instead responses to universal experiences, such as the experience of embodiment. Similarly for local or social, as we will also see: there are levels and types of local commonalities operating through different mechanisms, from contagion to discursive participation. And there are levels of individual contents, from the deeply subconscious to overt actions with full consciousness. The price is that explaining the local and the individual, which is subject to variation, becomes a problem for the innateness theorist. The temptation, as we have seen, is to deny a significant role to learning and to say that things are not learned, but that universal, innate contents are triggered by exposure to data. This allows a neat division between data and innately given structures, and avoids the problems of accounting for learning through trial and error, which seems too inefficient a process to account for what is actually acquired. But to accept this approach is to ascribe a great deal of content to innateness, and therefore to mechanisms of genetic transmission that are unknown and mysterious, and subject to the problems with multiple codes mentioned earlier. And it sits oddly with the actual content of local practices, such as the gift-giving practices described by Merleau-Ponty, which do not seem plausibly to be the sorts of things that are triggered by data.

The alternatives include different basic views of the brain, which happen to fit better with the conventional view of learning as involving synaptic connections and the changing strength of these connections as a result of new data.[4] These alternatives make learning itself the central feature of cognition, and provides a new model of learning. Andy Clark explains the "predictive coding" approach as follows:

The basic idea is simple. It is that to perceive the world is to successfully predict our own sensory states. The brain uses stored knowledge about the structure of the world and the probabilities of one state or event following another to generate a prediction of what the current state is likely to be, given the previous one and this body of knowledge. Mismatches between the prediction and the received signal generate error signals that nuance the prediction or (in more extreme cases) drive learning and plasticity.

(Clark 2011: n.p.)

This is a partial response to the case made by innatists against the possibility of learning the kinds of things that would need to be learned in order to perform in various ways, such as speaking grammatically. The argument was that existing learning theories could not account for the rapidity of acquisition because they depended on slow inductive processes which could never produce concepts, or required conceptualized hypotheses to test, and therefore required the learner to have the relevant concepts in advance.

The predictive coding model rejects this picture of learning as induction, and replaces the idea of pre-existing conceptualized hypotheses. As Clark (2011: n.p.) puts it:

We may contrast this with older models in which perception is a "bottom-up" process, in which incoming information is progressively built (via some kind of evidence accumulation process, starting with simple features and working up) into a high-level model of the world. According to the predictive coding alternative, the reverse is the case. For the most part, we determine the low-level features by applying a cascade of predictions that begin at the very top; with our most general expectations about the nature and state of the world providing constraints on our successively more detailed (fine grain) predictions.

General expectations, not a panoply of pre-existing concepts, do the work of starting the process of learning, which takes the form of reducing signal noise, or irrelevance, in the buzzing, blooming world. This is a model that fits both local and individual variation. Our social experiences are limited to what is local to us: the predictions we develop and improve on, such as the prediction of an appropriate gift, are based on our local experiences. They would fail to predict in other local settings. And our individual experiences of the world differ as well.

A further point can be made about this approach. This learning process occurs at a subconscious level, though it might be aided by overt additions such as instructions. It is part of what John Searle (1983: 154) calls "the background," which he explains:

is not a set of things nor a set of mysterious relations between ourselves and things, rather it is simply a set of skills, stances, preintentional assumptions and presuppositions, practices and habits. And all of these are, as far as we know, realized in human brains and bodies.

As Daniel Hutto (and Michael Schmitz) note, there is a contradiction in the intellectualist language that Searle uses here. As Hutto puts it:

> Schmitz ... highlights the basic tension in Searle's discussions of the Background. He identifies the latter's tendency to invoke the intellectualist language of presupposition, assumption and stance taking, on the one hand, and contrasts it with Searle's explicit claim that the Background is essentially nonrepresentational, on the other. Searle is well aware of the awkwardness of his attempts to characterize the Background. He recognizes that "there is a real difficulty in finding ordinary language terms to describe the Background: one speaks vaguely of 'practices', 'capacities', and 'stances' or one speaks suggestively but misleadingly of 'assumptions' and 'presuppositions'. These latter terms must be literally wrong, because they imply the apparatus of representation with its propositional contents, logical relations, truth values, directions of fit, etc. (Searle 1983, 142)."
>
> *(Hutto 2012: 39)*

The issue is this: is the stuff in the background like overt utterances, with semantic-like properties, including combinatorial ones? Or is it something different entirely, like skills and habits, which we usually don't think have these properties?

This is an issue to which we will return in the next chapter. But it is an issue which looms large in the philosophical literature on cognitive science, and can be understood in terms of the discussion of concepts and representations we have already had. And one's answer to this question leads either in the direction of the standard model of the brain as computer or toward the alternatives: the brain as embodied and primarily concerned with physical actions, with even its higher-level cognitive powers dependent on the same processes that embodied action is dependent on, processes that are evolutionarily prior to higher thought and which higher thought can be best understood of as a form of.

Notes

1　This is a problem for hybrid accounts, which typically mix non-semantic connectionist learning, which works through association, with symbolic processing components, producing a problem of how the kinds of learned associations could have the properties necessary for the kinds of combination and logical transformation characteristic of symbolic processing, and therefore of meaning.

2　A fancier formulation of this is found in Gallistel and King (2009: x): "Computations are the compositions of functions. A truth about functions of far-reaching significance for our understanding of the functional architecture of the brain is that functions of arbitrarily many arguments may be realized by the composition of functions that have only two arguments, but they cannot be realized by the composition of one-argument functions. The symbols that carry the two values that serve as the arguments of a two-argument function cannot occupy physically adjacent locations, generally speaking. Thus, the functional architecture of any powerful computing device, including the brain, must make provision for bringing symbols from their different locations to the machinery that effects the primitive two-argument functions, out of which the functions with many arguments are constructed by composition."

3   From the naïve point of view, and perhaps from a philosophically sophisticated one, this amounts to a *reductio ad absurdum* of the concept of concept, as used here. The question of the status of concepts – or more generally of what in the philosophical literature is called "content –" is an important and vexing question which will be mostly avoided in what follows, which is written from a "social science" perspective. However, a few comments can be made here by way of orientation to what a social science perspective on content might entail. The point of talking about concepts or content is that they are in some sense truth-bearing, or are part of, or conditions of, something that can be said to be true or false. From a social science perspective, the question is somewhat different. First, there is the problem of the psychological reality of concepts. There is abundant, and suggestive, psychological evidence that people do not have, in long-term memory, stable concepts, in the strict sense envisioned by philosophical theories of content. Ask them about their concept of dog and they will give different answers at different times and in different context (cf. Wu 1995; Barsalou et al. 1999). Yet of course there are plenty of external markers from which the internal fact of the concept of dog may be derived – pictures of dogs labeled as "Dog," for example. As to truth, a social science approach might start with Steiner's (1954) classic essay on Chagga truth, which makes the suggestive point that our Western notion of truth derives historically from something external as well, namely witnessing – an act, one may note, that is typically surrounded by complex rituals, such as oath-taking. The sufficiently cynical sociologist of science would note that scientific truth is also surrounded by complex rituals, such as peer-review and publication in sacred journals. In terms of the language that will be used in this book, but only introduced in later chapters, the speech act of asserting a truth is a declaration, and the concept of concept (and content) itself is within what will be called "the *Verstehen* bubble" – which is to say that it is a term we use among ourselves to enable mutual understanding, with no special relation to truth in an absolute or metaphysical sense. Social science itself is an activity within the bubble, with no pretensions to metaphysical truth. Philosophy, however, purports to transcend the bubble and to account for the relation between what is in the bubble and what is not. This is a deep, but questionable, metaphilosophical claim that implicates the whole of Western philosophy since Plato. Needless to say these issues cannot be pursued here, and I do not intend to go beyond these cryptic comments. For an excellent survey of the complexities of these issues in relation to cognitive science, see Hutto and Myin 2017. For an eliminativist approach to content, which is more or less consistent with these cryptic remarks, see Rosenberg 2014.

4   See Kandel et al. (2014).

References

Amodio, David. (2014). "The Neuroscience of Prejudice and Stereotyping." *Nature Reviews Neuroscience* 15: 670–682. www.nature.com/nrn/journal/v15/n10/pdf/nrn3800.pdf.

Barsalou, L. W., K. O. Solomon, and L. L. Wu. (1999). "Perceptual Simulation in Conceptual Tasks." In M. K. Hirage, C. Sinha, and S. Wilcox (eds.) *Cultural, Typological, and Psychological in Cognitive Linguistics: Selected Papers of the Bi-Annual ICLA Meeting in Albuquerque, July 1995*, 209–228. Amsterdam: Benjamins.

Bickhard, M. H. (2009). "The Interactivist Model." *Synthese* 166(3): 547–591.

Brandom, Robert. (2009). *Reason in Philosophy: Animating Ideas*. Cambridge, MA: Harvard University Press.

Busemeyer, Jerome and Adele Diederich. (2010). *Cognitive Modeling*. Thousand Oaks, CA: Sage.

Chemero, Anthony. (2011). *Radical Embodied Cognitive Science*. Cambridge, MA: MIT Press.

Chomsky, Noam. (1975). *Reflections on Language*. New York: Pantheon.

Clark, Andy. (2008). *Supersizing the Mind: Embodiment, Action, and Cognitive Extension*. New York: Oxford University Press.

Clark, Andy (2011). "Predictive Coding: What Scientific Concept Would Improve Everybody's Cognitive Toolkit?" *Edge*. www.edge.org/response-detail/10404 (accessed 17 February 2017).

Cosmides, Leda and John Tooby. (1994). "Origins of Domain-Specificity: The Evolution of Functional Organization." In L. Hirschfeld and S. Gelman (eds.) *Mapping the Mind: Domain-Specificity in Cognition and Culture*, 85–116. New York: Cambridge University Press.

De Jaegher, Hanne, Ezequiel Di Paolo, and Shaun Gallagher. (2010). "Can Social Interaction Constitute Social Cognition?" *Trends in Cognitive Sciences* 14(10): 442–447.

De Jaegher, Hanne. (2009). "Social Understanding through Direct Perception? Yes, By Interacting." *Consciousness and Cognition* 18: 535–542.

Decety, Jean and Philip L. Jackson. (2004). "The Functional Architecture of Human Empathy." *Behavioral and Cognitive Science Reviews* 3(2): 71–100.

Dennett, Daniel. (1978). *Brainstorms: Philosophical Essays on Mind and Psychology*. Cambridge, MA: MIT Press.

DiPaolo, Ezequiel. (2009). "Extended Life." *Topoi* 28: 9–21.

Fodor, Jerry A. (1975). *The Language of Thought*. Cambridge, MA: Harvard University Press.

Fodor, Jerry A. (2008). *LOT 2: The Language of Thought Revisited*. Oxford: Oxford University Press.

Garbarini, F. and M. Adenzato. (2004). "At the Root of Embodied Cognition: Cognitive Science Meets Neurophysiology." *Brain and Cognition* 56: 100–106.

Gallagher, Shaun. (2008). "Inference or Interaction: Social Cognition without Precursors." *Philosophical Explorations* 11(3):163–174.

Gallagher, Shaun (2013). "The Socially Extended Mind." *Cognitive Systems Research* 25–26: 4–12.

Gallistel, C. R. and Adam Philip King. (2009). *Memory and the Computational Brain: Why Cognitive Science Will Transform Neuroscience*. Malden, MA: Wiley-Blackwell.

Gallistel, C. R. (1989). "Animal Cognition: The Representation of Space, Time, and Number." *Annual Review of Psychology* 40(1): 155–189.

Gallistel, C. R. (2011). "Prelinguistic Thought." *Language Learning and Development* 7: 253–262.

Gallistel, C. R. (forthcoming). "The Neurobiological Bases for the Computational Theory of Mind." In Lila Gleitman and Roberto G. De Almeida (eds.) *Festschrift in Honor of Jerry Fodor*.

Garbarini, Francesca and Mauro Adenzato. (2004.) "At the Root of Embodied Cognition: Cognitive Science Meets Neurophysiology." *Brain and Cognition* 56: 100–106.

Gershman, Samuel J., Eric J. Horvitz, and Joshua B. Tenenbaum. (2015). "Computational Rationality: A Converging Paradigm for Intelligence in Brains, Minds, and Machines." *Science* 6245(349): 273–278.

Gintis, Herbert. (2007). "A Framework for the Unification of the Behavioral Sciences." *Behavioral and Brain Sciences* 30(1): 1–61.

Graham, Jesse, Jonathan Haidt, and Brian A. Nosek. (2009). "Liberals and Conservatives Rely on Different Sets of Moral Foundations." *Journal of Personality and Social Psychology* 96(5): 1029–1046.

Hesslow, G., D.-A. Jirenhed, A. Rasmussen, and F. Johansson. (2013). "Classical Conditioning of Motor Responses: What Is the Learning Mechanism?" *Neural Networks* 47: 81–87.

Horgan, John. (1999). *The Undiscovered Mind: How the Human Brain Defies Replication, Medication, and Explanation*. New York: Free Press.

Hutto, Daniel and Erik Myin. (2013). *Radicalizing Enactivism: Radical Minds without Content*. Cambridge, MA: MIT Press.

Hutto, Daniel and Erik Myin. (2017). *Evolving Enactivism: Basic Minds Meet Content*. Cambridge, MA: MIT Press.

Hutto, Daniel D. (2004). "The Limits of Spectatorial Folk Psychology." *Mind & Language* 19(5): 548–573.

Hutto, Daniel D. (2005). "Starting without Theory: Confronting the Paradox of Conceptual Development." In B. Malle and S. Hodges (eds.) *Other Minds*, 56–72. New York: Guilford.

Hutto, Daniel D. (2012). "Exposing the Background: Deep and Local." In Z. Radman (ed.) *Knowing without Thinking: Mind, Action, Cognition and the Phenomenon of the Background*, 37–56. Basingstoke: Palgrave Macmillan.

Ibbotson, Paul and Michael Tomasello. (2016). "Evidence Rebuts Chomsky's Theory of Language Learning." *Scientific American* 315(5): 70–75.

Kandel, Eric, Yadin Dudai, and Mark Mayford. (2014). "The Molecular and Systems Biology of Memory." *Cell* 157(1): 163–186.

Kant, Immanuel. ([1787] 1929). *Critique of Pure Reason* 2nd edn. Trans. Norman Kemp Smith. New York: Macmillan.

Kiverstein, Julian. (forthcoming). "Extended Cognition." In Albert Newen, Shaun Gallagher, and Leon de Bruin (eds.) *Oxford Handbook of 4E Cognition*. Oxford: Oxford University Press.

Menary, Richard. (2010). "Cognitive Integration and the Extended Mind." In Richard Menary (ed.) *The Extended Mind*, 227–243. Cambridge, MA: MIT Press.

Miłkowski, Marcin. (2013). *Explaining the Computational Mind*. Cambridge, MA: MIT Press.

Needham, Robert. (1972). *Belief, Language, and Experience*. Chicago, IL: University of Chicago Press.

Newell, A. (1980). "Physical Symbol Systems." *Cognitive Science* 4(2): 135–183.

Nichols, Shaun and Stephen P. Stich. (2003). *Mindreading: An Integrated Account of Pretense, Self-Awareness, and Understanding Other Minds*. Oxford: Clarendon.

Noë, Alva. (2004). *Action in Perception*. Cambridge, MA: MIT Press.

Piattelli-Palmarini, Massimo. (forthcoming). "Fodor and the Innateness of All (Basic) Concepts." In Lila Gleitman and Roberto G. De Almeida (eds.) *Festschrift in Honor of Jerry Fodor*.

Robbins, Joel and Alan Rumsey. (2008). "Introduction: Cultural and Linguistic Anthropology and the Opacity of Other Minds." *Anthropological Quarterly* 81(2): 407–420.

Robbins, Joel. (2008). "On Not Knowing Other Minds: Confession, Intention, and Linguistic Exchange in a Papua New Guinea Community." *Anthropological Quarterly* 81(2): 421–429.

Rosenberg, Alexander. (2014). "Disenchanted Naturalism." In B. Bashour and H. D. Muller (eds.) *Contemporary Philosophical Naturalism and Its Implications*, 17–36. London: Routledge.

Schiefflin, Bambi B. (2008). "Speaking Only Your Own Mind: Reflections on Talk, Gossip and Intentionality in Bosavi (PNG)." *Anthropological Quarterly* 81(2): 431–441.

Schjoedt, Uffe, Hans Stødkilde-Jørgensen, Armin W. Geertz, Torben E. Lund, and Andreas Roepstorff. (2010). "The Power of Charisma: Perceived Charisma Inhibits the Frontal Executive Network of Believers in Intercessory Prayer." *Social Cognitive and Affective Neuroscience* 6(1): 119–127.

Searle, John. (1983). *Intentionality: An Essay in the Philosophy of Mind*. Cambridge: Cambridge University Press.

Shannon, Claude E. (1948). "A Mathematical Theory of Communication." *Bell Systems Technical Journal* 27: 379–423, 623–656.

Steiner, Franz Baermann. (1954). "Chagga Law and Chagga Truth." *Africa: Journal of the International African Institute* 24(4): 364–369.

Sun, Ron. (2005). "Prolegomena to Integrating Cognitive Modeling and Social Simulation." In Ron Sun (ed.) *Cognition and Multi-Agent Interaction: From Cognitive Modeling to Social Simulation*, 3–26. Cambridge: Cambridge University Press.

Thompson, Evan. (2007). *Mind in Life: Biology, Phenomenology, and the Sciences of Mind*. Cambridge, MA: Harvard University Press.

Tooby, John and Leda Cosmides. (1995). "Foreword." In Simon Baron-Cohen (ed.) *Mindblindness: An Essay on Autism and Theory of Mind*, xi–xvii. Cambridge, MA: MIT Press.

Varela, F., E. Thompson, and E. Rosch. (1991). *The Embodied Mind*. Cambridge, MA: MIT Press.

Wheeler, M. (2005). *Reconstructing the Cognitive World: The Next Step*. Cambridge, MA: MIT Press.

Wheeler, M. (2010). "In Defense of Extended Functionalism." In Richard Menary (ed.), *The Extended Mind*, 245–270. Cambridge, MA: MIT Press.

Wilson, Robert A. (2004). *Boundaries of the Mind: The Individual in the Fragile Sciences: Cognition*. Cambridge: Cambridge University Press.

Wu, L. L. (1995). *Perceptual Representation in Conceptual Combination*. Ph.D. diss., University of Chicago.

3

FOLK PSYCHOLOGY, THE BACKGROUND, AND THE STANDARD MODEL

We closed the last chapter with a puzzle: what is in "the background"? Is it something that is a simulacrum of explicit speech, with semantic properties, which operates by combining representations and is itself best represented as a kind of talking or reasoning in the head? Is the best model for the background the kind of thing Gallistel models for ants as the dead-reckoning system? Or is this transposition of a human practice into a module in the brain just a kind of projection, unwarranted by any physical facts, but instead a "must be so" story to account for experimental facts about behavior for which it might not need to "be so" because there might well be an alternative mechanism. We are, at this stage in the development of instrumentation and modeling, unable to go beyond arguments about the relative plausibility of these claims. But there is a big difference between ants and human practices. In the case of ants we are usually talking about innate mechanisms. The balance of plausibilities changes when we get to the background, which is far more plausibly regarded as the product of mostly implicit or tacit learning processes of some kind, or tacit processes in conjunction with explicit processes, in the form, for example, of interiorization or habituation of forms of action that were originally explicit or public and conscious rather than automatic, such as finding one's way home.

The philosopher and wit Sidney Morgenbesser once had an exchange with B. F. Skinner in which he said "Let me see if I understand your thesis. You think we shouldn't anthropomorphize people?" (Ryerson 2004). This is the problem with the background as well. To put it somewhat differently, the question is whether we should ascribe the same kinds of things – beliefs, intentions, semantic properties of combination, and so forth – to the background. Or should we regard these attributions merely as convenient fictions that are an aid to understanding only if we don't take them seriously as a guide to the real underlying processes?

What Can Be Learned and What Can't Be

Recall a passage from the last chapter: "The acquisition of even very simple concepts requires things like a theory of mind, the understanding of relevant aspects of a situation, understanding the syntax of the sentences that contain them" and so on, according to the literature on the acquisition of the lexicon (Piattelli-Palmarini forthcoming). This gives us a neat chicken and egg problem: if we need a theory of mind and a complex set of social understandings, as well as an understanding of the syntax of sentences, to learn a word, how does one acquire these without being linguistically competent in the first place? The Chomskyan answer to the problem of understanding syntax, as we have seen, is that it cannot be done inductively, but must be an innate capacity which is triggered by exposure to data, not produced by learning. The reason is "the poverty of the stimulus": there is simply not enough data or time for learning to produce knowledge of syntax, if indeed it is possible to learn it from data at all. But does this answer extend to the other conditions listed here? Fodor and his followers, as we have seen, wish to extend it to a vast range of concepts. But does this include the concepts that would make up a theory of mind? And what about "the understanding of relevant aspects of a situation"? Where and how does one acquire this?

Understanding the issues here requires a couple of excursions, which are necessary to get a better sense of what the conflicts here are. The conflicts are characteristic of issues of cognitive science: what looks like a strongly plausible answer to a question from the point of view of one set of issues looks implausible and ad hoc from another. Chomsky's linguistics is a good case of this. His basic idea is what

> we may call the Basic Property of human language: The language faculty provides the means to construct a digitally infinite array of structured expressions, each of which has a semantic interpretation expressing a thought, and each of which can be externalized by means of some sensory modality. The infinite set of semantically interpreted objects constitutes what has sometimes been called a "language of thought": the system of thoughts that receive linguistic expression and that enter into reflection, inference, planning and other mental processes, and when externalized, can be used for communication and other social interactions. By far, the major use of language is internal – thinking in language.
>
> (Chomsky 2016: n.p.)

The fundamental thought about the basic property of language, in short, is this: language is a means of externalizing internal thought, which is then used for communication and social interaction. Thought – meaning reflection, inference, planning, and the like – is already in the form of language, in Fodor's case the language of mentalese. All that is added by learning a specific language is the ability to express these internal linguistic operations externally for the purposes of social interaction and communication.

One major problem with this line of thinking is that animals plan, infer, and do many more cognitive things, and humans also do these things in the course of acting. Do the animals possess mentalese, or whatever we wish to claim is the basic code of human thought, but lack the means to express it? Where does this sharing of code end? With ants, or sea slugs? A standard answer to this puzzling problem is to distinguishing a "narrow language faculty" from a "broad language faculty," with the

> "narrow language faculty" (LFN), encompassing aspects that are specific to language, and a "broad language faculty," which includes more general cognitive functions, not unique to humans but shared differentially with non-human animals, with some possessing some capacities and others lacking them. This distinction served to preserve the idea that language was specifically and uniquely human. And the unique feature was specified: at the core of LFN is "recursion," a specifically human computational mechanism at the basis of language grammar. It was also conceded that this mechanism "might have evolved for functions other than language" (Hauser et al. 2002: 1569).
>
> *(Gallese 2007: 665)*

The last clause about evolving for functions other than language is a revealing concession. Chomsky's key argument, as we have seen, is the fact that children acquire language quickly, and therefore without the slow trial and error process of ordinary learning. As he says, "the intricate knowledge of the means of even the simplest words, let alone others, is acquired virtually without experience. At peak periods of language acquisition, children are acquiring about a word an hour, that is, often on one presentation." And he concludes from this the "must be" we encountered in the last chapter. "It must be, then, that the rich meaning of even the most elementary words is substantially innate." But he admits that "The evolutionary origin of such concepts is a complete mystery, one that may not be resolvable by means available to us" (Chomsky 2016: n.p.).

The concession that the language faculty may be based on a computational mechanism evolved for another purpose is a way of reducing this "complete mystery" to merely a big mystery. But it opens the door to a series of questions about the relation between the elements with which we began in discussing the acquisition of even simple concepts, as Bloom (2001) had listed them: a theory of mind, the understanding of relevant aspects of a situation, and understanding the syntax of the sentences that contain them. The questions are these: isn't it odd to think that the computational mechanisms for these are themselves entirely distinct: with the syntax capacity coming from "evolution"; the theory of mind also coming from evolution but with its distinctive behavioral outcome, mind-reading, apparently shared by other animals (Krupenye et al. 2016); but the third, which is clearly "local," coming from social experience and learned in a non-mysterious manner?

Moreover, given the fact that language is acquired socially, that is to say in interaction with other people, and as Chomsky himself admits, is, in its external aspect, "for" social interaction and communication, is it not also odd that the form of acquisition is only social in one, albeit essential, respect? Two aspects are presumably modularized, and one is not; yet they necessarily and essentially work together to produce the acquisition of concepts. If the separate origins of these aspects was not a "complete mystery," and possibly an insoluble one, as Chomsky admits, wouldn't it be plausible to invert the problem of which came first, and seek the answer to the question of how concepts are acquired in the process of social interaction? After all the experience and setting of acquisition is completely undifferentiated: there is no "mind" moment separate from the syntactic moment and the knowing the social setting moment. So why not attempt to solve the question of what the learning process is on the assumption that it is learning in the course of social interaction? In the next chapter this possibility will be considered more fully.

This kind of question points to another necessary excursion, about the problem of explanatory necessity and the role of inexplicable facts left over from the main explanation. One can begin with the example of Chomsky himself. He was a critic of the behaviorist theorists of language who thought language learning conformed to normal psychological models of learning and drew conclusions about language accordingly. Chomsky pointed out the anomalies left over by this account: the fact of the poverty of stimuli, meaning the fact that there was not enough data being given to the child to explain what was being learned, one-off word learning, and especially the astonishing rapidity of language learning at a certain age. He built his own account by starting with these anomalies, arguing that the only explanation of them was that basic linguistic capacities were extensive and innate and only needed to be triggered. If they were innate, however, they had to be universal; so his project was to show that syntactical structure was universal, or rather that all actual syntactical structures could be understood as variants of a basic innate structure.

His theory ran into its own anomalies, and to the criticism that the defenses against his critics had changed the relevant definitions, so that he had come to define language in such a way as to make the theory true by definition. The anomalies are what interest us here: a linguist discovered a language that does not employ the supposedly defining feature of human language, recursion. What is recursion? Here is an example. Sentence (i) is recursive, while the sentences in (ii) are not:

i John said that Mary thinks that John falsely believes that the moon is made of green cheese.

ii John spoke. Mary thinks. John is wrong. John believes. The moon is green cheese.

The anomaly is this: in Pirahã, the language in question, there is no recursion – all the sentences are like (ii). This has been dismissed as an irrelevant exception, and the evidence has been challenged. But the more interesting result is that the argument for the Chomskyan position has changed. The new Chomskyan view is that people *think* recursively even if this is not manifest in their language.

The discoverer of this language, a Chomsky critic, builds an alternative account of the role of recursion out of the anomaly and the revised Chomskyan claim that recursion can occur in thought, and therefore still be universal and innate, but might not appear in a given language. He argues instead that "recursion facilitates thought and helps language increase the rate at which information can be transmitted." Sentence (i) and the sentences that make up (ii) communicate the same things, but more slowly and cumbersomely. He concludes that "Recursion is not the biological basis for language. It is an enhancement of human thought" (Everett 2017: n.p.).

This is a kind of argument we will find elsewhere, and it is critical to claims about what can and cannot be learned. Many of the arguments about the limitations of learning assume that learning is composed entirely of raw induction and the emergence of associations. The major alternative to the standard model of the brain as computer is connectionism, which models brain processes on a different form of computation – parallel distributing processing with back propagation – which "learns" by finding associations that correctly predict outcomes and is not programmed by rules but by learning algorithms. This kind of learning is relatively slow. But if it is enhanced by other forms of recognition and knowledge acquisition, the rate or speed might increase. And indeed, we can find in social interaction many possible facilitators of this kind, such as empathy and external facts – such as an actual dog.

Starting from the Anomalies

My point here is not to adjudicate these claims, but to show how a particular form of argument works. What the critic of Chomsky has done is to start with the anomaly and turn the argument on its head by making the anomalous fact the explanation of the fact that the standard account purports to explain. Here is another example, from Dan Sperber and Deirdre Wilson, commenting on the difference between their approach and Grice's account of norms of communication:

> A more radical difference between Grice's approach and relevance theory is this. Grice's principle and maxims are norms which communicators and audience must know in order to communicate adequately. Communicators generally keep to the norms, but may also violate them to achieve particular effects; and the audience uses its knowledge of the norms in interpreting communicative behavior.

The principle of relevance, by contrast, is a generalization about ostensive-inferential communication. Communicators and audience need no more know the principle of relevance to communicate than they need to know the principles of genetics to reproduce. Communicators do not "follow" the principle of relevance; and they could not violate it even if they wanted to. The principle of relevance applies without exception: every act of ostensive communication communicates a presumption of relevance. It is not the general principle, but the fact that a particular presumption of relevance has been communicated by and about a particular act of communication, that the audience uses in inferential comprehension.

(Sperber and Wilson 1986: 162)

Relevance, in short, comes first. It is not something that gets established after communication happens governed by a tacitly known principle; it is a condition or presumption of particular speech acts. Another example, which will concern us later, is the phenomenon of enthymemes, or suppressed premises. A standard way of thinking of these is that an inference with a suppressed premise is valid because there is a structure of linguistic norms lurking behind our inferential speech which can be accessed to validate and complete our inference by pulling the suppressed premise out of a hidden common pot, making it explicit (Brandom 1994). This is a pretty implausible account, in one sense: it assumes a big "it" out there with a highly elaborated logical structure lurking behind ordinary inference that can be made explicit. But one can start the other way around, by taking the enthymeme or suppressed premise as the starting point and seeing ordinary inferences as the sorts of things that people understand by inventing interpretations on the fly that make the inference make sense (Lewis 1979: 341). In this case there is no hidden structure: there is only the commonplace human capacity to make sense of a statement by attributing the elements that make it intelligible to us. If a mother says "Carolyn should have taken her umbrella today," for example, we can infer that Carolyn did not take her umbrella, which is a suppressed premise for what was actually said. But this premise is the invention of the hearer, and we are good at inventing them, and routinely and without much thinking invent them in order to understand what we are told, though of course it is prone to error, underdetermination (because more than one attributed premise might fit), and other forms of misunderstanding, such as misunderstanding the social situation in which the words were uttered – for example as part of a joke.

This trick of making the thing that seems to be a leftover nuisance into the basis for the explanation of the phenomenon in question is at the core of the problem of cognitive science and the social. For much of cognitive science, the social *is* the leftover nuisance. Cognitive science, especially in the standard model, is focused on showing how the brain, as a computer-like thing, can come to perform recognized human acts, such as speech. Sociality is just another thing to be explained. Consequently there has been a strong focus on such universal traits as rationality, empathy, and altruism, with the thought that one could build up to an account of morality and normative behavior, or collective identification, from these traits. The task is to find the neural basis of these traits and show how they arise developmentally in the individual, and to then use the individual constructed in this manner to account for observed social facts such as norm-following. But these efforts have the character of add-ons to the standard model of computer-like cognition. It is not too misleading to characterize them as follows: if we need to explain collective activity, we search for, or hypothesize, a neural item that enables the brain to produce collective activity; if we want to explain "society" as distinct for asocial individuals, we hypothesize a "social" added capacity which we then find in the brain, for example as altruism or empathy or as a dedicated system (Sliwa and Freiwald 2017); similarly for explaining religion, for which we can claim, however implausibly, that there is a gene.

But this strategy too can be turned on its head. From the point of view of the universalizing explanations of morality, most of the actual moral practices and beliefs of the past and indeed the present world are anomalies. If we start with actual historical normative behavior and explicit normative beliefs, we find that morality in almost all its forms, except the most modern and abstract kind of universalizing philosophy, is a kind of transaction with nature. The idea of *tabu* is one of automatic punishment by impersonal forces. The fetishes – physical objects – created to assure contractual compliance in Africa were attempts to invoke impersonal natural forces to punish violators. Most of ancient religion involved sacrifice – a physical transaction in a sacralized ritual. Animism, ancestor worship, and the like also involved agency in nature. In these cases, the beliefs in question were not of some unusual "moral" kind, but beliefs about processes in the natural world. This approach does not need to ignore the brain; but it points to different parts of cognition, such as those involving purity and danger (Douglas 1966). It is not inconsistent with cognitive science findings, for example about reciprocity (Fehr et al. 1997) and disgust (Laan et al. 1994; Laan and Everaerd, 1995; Rellini et al. 2005; Both et al. 2011; Laan and Both 2011). Understanding the cognitive basis of reciprocity with spirits, ancestors, and deities or disgust with the ritually impure is a different matter than extrapolating universalistic explanations of human normative behavior from reciprocity or disgust in primates. But making such things as disgust and reciprocity part of the basic structure of cognition changes our picture of basic cognition and challenges the separation of core cognition from variant social manifestations. These are issues to which we will return later in this chapter and throughout the book.

In what follows, we will have occasion to use this strategy of starting with the anomalies repeatedly. It is at the heart of many of the disputes in cognitive science. And we will also have occasion to discuss variations of the issue with Chomsky's and Fodor's forms of universalism. Here the issues are quite complex, but they come down to three major problems.

(A)   The first is one identified by the critics of Chomskyan responses to evidence of the non-universality of recursion in human languages. If actual universality is not the standard, what are the empirical credentials of the universality claim? The answer for Chomsky's syntactic universals and Fodor's mentalese are the same: the universal cognitive mechanisms in question are not manifest on the surface, but underlie and explain what is on the surface, and are inferred from facts on the surface, such as what people actually say in all its diversity. The argument is that the underlying thing must be there to explain some feature of language acquisition or concept possession. There is an analogy with the genetic code: phenotypes may vary, but the code is the same. In the case of genetics, however, DNA was discovered and the physical basis of the "code" was revealed. But is this analogy valid?

(B)   The second problem is related to the first: the fact of non-universality can be accounted for by the difference between thought and speech. One can accept non-recursion in an actual language but claim that recursion nevertheless occurs in thought for the speakers of this language, and is thus universal in a different way. This is more than plausible, and we will see more examples shortly. But admitting the gap between language and thought produces many problems for notions that are central to the standard view of mind. The idea that all thought is linguistic was convenient for the code model: what was in the head had "semantic properties," as codes do. But maybe the issues were these: the doctrine that all thought is linguistic required the idea of mentalese to be persuasive, given the fact that diversity of actual language, which is great, does not match diversity of thought, which does not seem to be as great, and that much "thought" seems to be shared with non-linguistic creatures. To make the code story work for the brain, the code couldn't be the actual spoken code, but a universal code – but still a code, and with the same concepts as appear in actual speech. But if there is non-linguistic thought, or thought without conceptual content, the anomalies kick in and it raises the question of whether the non-conceptual thought is the real thought and language is something that depends on it but is not a good guide to it.

(C)   This points to the third issue: inferences from manifest form to brain form. One of the responses to Epstein's (2016) statement denying that the brain is a computer that was quoted in Chapter 1 was this: people compute, therefore the brain is a computer. This is a common pattern of inference, and it comes in many forms: if language has syntax, the brain has syntax; if there are collectives, the brain has something corresponding to the collectives; if there is morality, there is something in the brain that corresponds to morality. But the inferences are dubious. If we can find our way home, it does not mean that we have in our brain the things that are analogous to navigation devices – compass roses, charts, protractors, and the like. Two things need to be said about this. The first is that since these are "must be so" inferences, they are immediately vulnerable to alternative hypotheses that show that there is no "must be so" here. The second is that there is another direction to these inner–outer inferences. There is a process that is uncontroversial, which we may call interiorization. Something happens in the brain when one does something like learning to calculate with apples and oranges, or learning to navigate with compass roses and the like. What this is and how this works may not be well understood, but some of how it works, such as habituation, is well understood, or at least well attested. So there is a potential alternative explanation for each of these inferences to what "must be so" in the brain that starts with, or includes, these external facts. These issues all arise with the concept of theory of mind, to which we now turn.

Theory of Mind

In the introduction I commented on the startling fact that neuroscience had validated the idea that there is a special human capacity for understanding other people, a capacity that went beyond what could be derived merely from empirical observation of other people's behavior, based in part, it appears, on mirror neurons. We have implicit mind-reading capacities, demonstrated by experiments such as the famous false belief experiments to be discussed shortly. And these capacities seem to be the basis of social interaction: we could not easily imagine a social world without the employment of these capacities, routinely and as part of every relationship between people, and as a large part of what constitutes their experience of the world.

Prior to the discovery of mirror neurons, whose significance remains controversial, there were two theories about these capacities. The dominant one held that humans had an implicit theory of mind (ToM) which enabled them to reason about and infer the beliefs and aims of other people, which in turn enabled them to navigate the social world. This is known as the "theory-theory". The second was simulation theory, which worked differently. It argued that people had and used a basic capacity to simulate the thought of other people, that this normally operated unconsciously and enabled people to predict and thus respond to the behavior of others. If I watch you coming down the stairs and see that you are about to make a misstep and fall, for example, I can anticipate this. Another version of simulation theory involves higher-level understanding. According to it, we understand by introspecting our own mental states and apply this analogically to others. We will return to simulation theory in a later section. Both simulation theory and theory of mind accounts do some of the same work: mind-reading. But both imply different things about the stuff that is in the mind, and both explain different things: the theory-theory explains, by free-riding on the semantic theory of concepts, our ordinary folk psychological terms, as the explicit articulation of a theory we already have tacitly, and share. Simulation theory does not explain this.

We discursively reason about other minds in terms of notions like belief and motivation, what is sometimes called the belief-desire model of action explanation, which we have already encountered as GOFAT. Sitting around gossiping about the motivations and reasons of others, a familiar pastime, involves this language, which we can think of as implying a theory of mind with terms like belief. This raises the question of whether the ToM implied by the usage is true. Are there such things as beliefs and intentions, for example, or is this just a "folk" usage that does not connect in any way to anything in the brain, and is meaningful only in connection with the "folk" understanding of mental processes that we use to explain ourselves and others in non-scientific contexts. One reason for thinking it is true, that is to say whether the mind really works in a way that has elements that more or less correspond to the concepts of folk psychology, and therefore the correct starting point both for accounts of the brain's role in mind-reading and social explanation, is the very fact of the ubiquity of the relevant concepts. They seem to be like the starting points for our understanding of nature – what is sometimes called by analogy "folk physics": concepts that do descriptive work that science can refine but which are roughly correct already. The fact that we constantly mind-read and can verbally attribute beliefs, intentions, and so forth to other people, and that this theory "works" pragmatically in navigating our social world, is evidence that it is a good approximation and starting point for cognitive science. As Nichols and Stich (2003: 2) note:

> So pervasive is the role of mindreading in our lives that Jerry Fodor has remarked that if the ordinary person's understanding of the mind should turn out to be seriously mistaken, it would be "the greatest intellectual catastrophe in the history of our species" (Fodor 1987: xii).

There is a core fact at stake in this discussion. Humans are highly sensitive to the intentions and mental status of others. But making sense of this fact is not straightforward. Moreover, it seems to be a capacity that is developed as a child develops. A significant breakthrough in defining the problem of how this works came with a series of experiments beginning in 1983 (Baron-Cohen et al. 1985; Wimmer and Perner 1983), with young children, that worked in the following way:

> Children are presented with a story, with props, in which they are able to observe that a person hides an object in a basket and leaves; another person comes in and moves the object, hiding it elsewhere. The child would then be asked where the first person would look for the object. Children under age four typically would answer by saying that the person would look where the object had been moved to; at about age four children began to answer that the person would look where they had left the object originally. In short, they reasoned that the person had a false belief and would act on it.

This requires a "theory" about false belief and its relation to action, and thus about mind, or, to put it differently, if they were reasoning explicitly (or slow reasoning), step by step, justifying each usage of every term, it would be like them having a theory. In this form, the results fit the idea that there is a theory of mind module that is activated, that this was not a matter of learning, because the capacity is not associated with intelligence, or any apparent outward stimulus, but merely appears at a certain age, and, moreover, is more or less universal across cultures. (See Perner 1991; Baillergeon et al. 2010; Sabbagh et al. 2013)

This experiment was subject to many interpretations. It was thought to prove that children "represented" because they had to represent the person as having a false belief; that being able to do this showed a developmental stage at which a child could place themselves in the viewpoint of the other, which in turn was an essential condition for high-level social interaction as well as morality. It also raised questions about whether deficiencies in mind-reading capacity might serve to explain autism, which could be regarded as a kind of mind-blindness. It also was taken as evidence that children develop a theory of mind, which is what enables them to reason about other minds by correctly attributing false beliefs to them. This seemed to support the idea that developing an implicit theory of mind which enabled the child to make inferences about other people that could be explicitly articulated in the language of folk psychology was a universal developmental achievement, and the key to understanding human interaction.

What sort of thing exactly was this theory of mind? And how was it acquired? There were three approaches to this question, and a relevant fact. One approach treated the "theory" as a module, which answered the question of how it was acquired – it was innate and only activated at a certain developmental stage. A second regarded it as learned in the normal way, what is sometimes called "the scientist in the crib" approach: the theory of mind was acquired in the same way as other kinds of knowledge, through some sort of implicit induction or hypothesis testing. A third regarded theory of mind as "cultural." There is another approach to this problem that is distinct, but also theoretical, which to the child is an implicit theory of rationality which functions as a default assumption that enables them to attribute mental states to other people, such as belief and desire, or decision, on the basis of knowledge of their behavior and circumstances. The relevant fact is this: children learn, and begin to employ, the language of mental states as it is applied to others and to themselves, as expressions of their mental states, at the same time (Gopnik 1993: 3–4).

Tacitness, the Background, and Speed

The term "implicit" requires some explanation. As we have already seen, there is a problem about "the Background." Is it full of theories, representations, and so forth? Or is it something different, and non-conceptual in character? The difference is nicely captured in an observation by Adrian Cussins (1990: 149–50), who describes being stopped by the police after being seen dodging traffic and being asked: "Do you know how fast you were travelling?" In the conceptual sense, or at least the discursive sense, he did not – he could not state the speed. In the non-conceptual sense, he did – the motorcycle would have crashed if he had mis-judged the speed. But we might say that he had an implicit theory of physics that allowed him to avoid obstacles and judge speed correctly. What is common to the two answers is that this thinking was done tacitly, and also more or less instantaneously or very quickly.

The idea of the Background, of the tacit–explicit distinction, and questions about innateness and modularization are all closely associated with the problem of cognitive speed. Daniel Kahneman (2011) made famous the idea that there are fast and slow kinds of thinking. The idea is that there are two (or more) systems operating in cognition, at least one of which is fast and the other slow. The slow system is the one familiar from conscious reasoning and folk psychology, and involves reasons, beliefs, and ratiocination. The fast system or systems work in a different way, below consciousness and with somewhat different means – heur-istics, for example – and through automatic processes. The fast kinds, operating with heuristics, produce quick judgments that are biased in certain ways if they are contrasted to slow reasoning, i.e., the kind of explicit or near-explicit rea-soning that we might go through step by step in explaining such things as what we thought would justify the theory of mind conclusion that the person who was unaware that the object had been moved would look in the wrong place for it. The fast–slow distinction seems well based, and it is observable in a variety of places.

Thinking of the mind as modular solves certain crucial problems about speed, the speed needed to perform complex cognitive tasks, and also enables us to think about these dedicated components as both complex and simple at the same time: complex in that they perform complex calculations quickly; simple in that, as components of a process, they can be treated as simple mechanical devices. They are fast, and they are highly specialized operations with simple outputs and are "informationally encapsulated," meaning that they operate on their own kind of informational inputs only and their processes are mandatory. This fits well with the idea of an implicit theory – an explicit theory would take complicated steps to come to a conclusion as well as conscious intervention in the reasoning pro-cess. There is nevertheless an important distinction to be made here. Calling it a theory is only to say that the modular processes can be described as if they amounted to a theory – it is an "as if" claim. Nevertheless it is an important feature of these arguments that they work in this way: they describe the "same" processes in both conceptual terms appropriate to explicit theories and in process terms that are closer to some possible physical realization.

Modules allow for speed together with complexity. The reason for supposing that there is a theory of mind module is the way the capacity appears in the course of child development, and the fact that they are "fast." But the idea of modules comes at a price, as we have seen. It implies, or at least suggests, that they are products of evolution and are innate (Cosmides and Tooby 1994: 86). This leaves out acquired skills and competencies, which are individual rather than universal. Connectionism is another answer to the problem of speed. Speed for connectionism is the product of established connections in the brain. This makes this model of mental processes more appropriate for accounting for the content of the Background, at least the non-innate parts. But it has a problem that goes along with its advantage, which is that, while it accounts for learning, it does not account for fast learning. Thus in each case the model requires some sort of supplementation.

The alternatives to the standard model point to some important limitations to the strategy of positing modules that is central to its explanations. There is certainly some ordinary learning that is reasonably well described by connectionism. The problem with the account is this: if we explain fast thinking by the existence of modules, and slow thinking – the kind we can reconstruct or articulate explicitly – by training and linguistic competence, which is language-specific, we are faced with a conundrum about the things that seem also to fall into the category of fast and difficult to articulate thinking but which are *not* the product of evolution.

What might this category include? The list would involve, as suggested above, everything that is tacit and embodied, which would include such things as habitus, practices, and the kinds of skills that chess masters and other experts have – of acting, thinking, or performing at a high level of proficiency without thinking of rules. It would also include what are sometimes called reactive attitudes (Strawson [1962] 2003), the immediate feelings that are generated in response to an offending act, a wrong, and so forth. Such things as our immediate negative response to the appearance of free-riding, for example, a topic much discussed in the neuroeconomics literature, would also fall into this category (Fehr and Gächter 2000).

Normally culture is taken to be tacit and part of the "fast" kind of thought – very often, though problematically, as "presuppositions" which are taken for granted conditions for social interaction and practice. Moreover, culture is thought to be learned, and at a very deep level, so that it is manifested in such things as techniques of the body, emotions, and so forth. Indeed, culture in general is experienced as fast thinking; moreover, we are unable to articulate its contents, or even identify them, without comparing them to cultures in which people fast think differently. It was considerations like this that led some theory of mind thinkers to suggest that theory of mind was itself cultural: this would make it fit into an established category which we know works in this way and also fits with other things that are acquired by learning (Carruthers et al. 1985).

Why is using the term "theory," or "presuppositions," a problem? This is part of a much larger muddle, which we have seen aspects of already. The key to computationalism, representationalism, and the many other elements of the standard model is analogical reasoning. The only way we can think of mental processes that are otherwise inaccessible to us is in terms of our own overt "folk" psychological and logical concepts. The only way we can make sense of mindreading is as a fast version of slow reasoning about the beliefs, motives, and so forth of the other mind we are reading. We think about the thoughts of others as thing-like, and "represent" them to ourselves explicitly by devices such as cartoon thought bubbles. We then reason that something like this representing goes on tacitly in fast mind-reading or in infant mind-reading, and that this therefore implies "possession" of a collection of relevant concepts.

But how is cultural difference even possible on this account? One can argue that the concepts that differ are mere add-ons and enrichments of the inherited symbolic systems in question. As Dan Hutto explains, a key feature of these arguments;

> is that basic conceptual primitives act as atomistic placeholders – they are stable linchpins, mental items that denote, refer, or pick out items about which we can come to weave a wider set of conceptually-grounded inferences. These conceptual primitives can therefore be built upon through a process of on-going enrichment. On this model, when this happens no new concepts are introduced – instead we acquire expanded conceptions, wider understandings and new inferential connections tethered to our old concepts.
>
> *(Hutto 2017: 832; see also Hutto 2005 for a fuller discussion)*

Hence there is – and can only be – one core mind-reading theory that develops from childhood to adulthood; one theory that, as Ian Apperly (2013) puts it, "grows up" through the introduction of new principles and the expansion of inferential linkages. But the way this argument must be constructed raises questions about the whole strategy of attributing symbolic systems, representations, "content," and propositional thought to infants, ants, and bees.

The whole point of "conceptual enrichment" and the acquisition of new inferential capacities depend on the newly added stuff being of the same type as the pre-existing stuff – the stuff being representations or concepts, for example. And this opens a large door. There must be processes other than evolution by which this new stuff gets generated and acquired. The theory of mind of the ancient Greeks which imputed madness to divine intervention (Dodds 1951), for example, is not a product of genetics. But what is it a product of? Whatever story one tells about how these inferential links or this novel "enriched" concept of mind was generated and acquired has to work like this: it identifies a process. In short, by appealing to conceptual "enrichment" the defenders of theory of mind have introduced a novel, parallel process that they admit is necessary to account for certain kinds of development that happen to include fast thinking as well as the acquisition of concepts.

Conceding that there are other sources of concepts, and even of the elements of cultural or interpersonal fast thinking, is an important concession because with it we can ask what other things this process, whatever it turns out to be, explains or might explain. And one answer could be that it explains – by itself and without reference to evolution and modules – the mentalistic concepts that make up the various folk psychologies that appear in different cultures, or even the core folk psychology that we have and attribute, correctly or incorrectly, to the rest of the world. This is a form of the "start from the anomalies" approach. And it has some powerful reasons to take it seriously.

We can think of the issues in terms of the idea of code. All computational models of cognitive processes operate on coded material; but, as we have already noted, there is a big difference in the nature of the codes. Connectionist models operate on what we might think of as very minimal codes, with no innate semantic or combinatorial properties. The only combination here takes the form of association with other items, and is entirely learned through what is fed into the model as data and associated according to an algorithm. This is a highly individualistic model: each connectionist brain has its own learning history because it is given different data, such as the experiences each individual has. This fits with the physical fact that each brain has its own distinctive signature (Finn et al. 2015; Makin 2016) and its own set of synaptic connections that, according to the conventional view of the physical basis of learning (Kandel et al. 2014: 164, 166, 170), have been produced by neurons that wire together because they fire together. The mentalese model is quite different: every brain is supplied innately with a vast array of concepts that have combinatorial or semantic properties, and are activated by exposure to data. These are and have to be the same for everyone.

One can see why there is a problem with "culture" here. Culture is precisely not that which is the same for everyone. But it is also not, as usually understood, different for everyone: there is significant commonality at the local level. People do interact, they understand each other, and within their zone of experience with others can react, predict, and have appropriate emotions. Outside this zone, they do not. This zone, however poorly defined and bounded, is a "culture." We can leave aside for a few chapters the question of whether it could be that through social interaction something that is more or less shared for a group could arise from individual experiences, or in some other way.

But considerations of speed tug in different directions. Another example made prominent in the literature by Hubert Dreyfus (2014) causes special trouble: skilled, expert performance by such people as chess grandmasters or expert skiers. The skilled performer has learned how to do something, but has surpassed anything that can be done with slow thinking. The performances require ultra-fast cognition but cannot be understood as modules: evolution does not give us a skiing or chess module, or a video game playing module, to be activated.

Simulation Theory

The modularity interpretation was understood to fit the initial experimental results of false belief problems perfectly, in part because it was also claimed, based on a small cross-cultural sample, that all humans developed the same theory of mind. Learning and difference was therefore beside the point: nothing was learned; something was activated that was already there, universally. The conclusion was that an infant does not have a theory of mind yet, but an inbuilt capacity to have one that gets activated at a certain age, and which, once activated, allows them to solve particular problems that they could not solve before it was activated. There is, however, no account of how this activation happens. The plausibility of the modular thesis thus depends largely on the consideration that only evolved processes can be sufficiently fast, which in turn depends on another assumption: that the process of mind-reading involves mental gymnastics which depend on something like a relatively complex theory that is embodied in a large set of simple, informationally encapsulated processes. The theory-theory thus links two ideas: the idea of implicit theory and the idea of universality and innateness (though, as noted, there is a variant suggestion that theory of mind is cultural). Simulation theory provides an alternative: a basic mechanism of thought that is used in a wide variety of contexts but which has special application to mind-reading.

This close relation to empirical findings came to an abrupt end, with a second set of experiments based not on the verbal reports of children but on another widely used technique which detected children's increased attention in response to unexpected inputs. These experiments showed that there is a problem with the experimental protocol that produced the initial widely replicated results. The verbal interactions involved in answering the relevant questions – "elicited response tasks" – are complex and require abilities beyond merely recognizing false beliefs. Experiments that do not involve eliciting verbal responses, but measure spontaneous non-verbal responses, turn out to produce different results. Indeed, they show that 15-month-olds had expectations consistent with an understanding of false beliefs. The measurements involved what the children paid attention to in different scenarios depicted for them. Children reliably paid more attention – looked longer – when they were watching cases in which the unaware agent reached for the box containing the toy rather than for the box in which the agent last saw the toy (Baillargeon et al. 2010: 110–11). Using this method, it was shown that children as young as eight months seem to be capable of solving the false belief problem. The special attention paid by the children suggests they were surprised and, in turn, suggests their expectations were consistent with the unaware agent possessing a false rather than a true belief. Moreover, there is evidence that 13-month-olds use their mind-reading skills to take a third-person perspective to others' intentions and to evaluating their harmful actions – the key elements to social cognition generally (Choi and Luo 2015; Lee et al. 2015), and that by 18 months they are sufficiently advanced (though preverbal about it) to use this understanding to help others in tasks that require a grasp of their false beliefs (Buttelmann et al. 2009; Hamlin et al. 2011; Thomsen et al. 2011; Hamlin 2013). These results are revolutionary, but still wildly controversial (see Gagne and Coppola 2017). Nevertheless, the explanation has a more general relevance and applicability.

So it appears that the reason for the failure of three-year-olds to respond correctly is not their inability to detect others false beliefs but their inability to perform the additional mental tasks of articulating answers to queries about the false beliefs of others. This is an important distinction – there is discursive construction of knowledge about false beliefs, but a prior non-discursive basis for these constructions. (Onishi and Baillargeon 2005; Baillargeon et al. 2010; Choi and Luo 2015). This drives a large wedge between two considerations that "code" thinkers who stress conceptual relations and try to ascribe conceptual relations to the contents of the physical brain try to bring together: the folk theory of mind and the theory of mind in the brain.

There were other results that pointed in the same direction: they showed that apes also could mind-read and solve the false belief problem. If we think such things as "only humans have concepts," however, the results are troublesome. If one claims that concepts are part of some sort of innate and distinctively human semantic endowment, and also that the theory of mind was part of this uniquely human endowment, one can no longer give the fact that humans can solve the false belief problem as evidence. The results also undermine the neat distinction between two systems: one corresponding to verbal, elicitable content, something which looks more like a "theory" or a matter of "folk psychology," and a mere capacity shared with apes, and perhaps even with much of the rest of the animal kingdom. Some theorists have accommodated these results by ascribing the relevant concepts, such as the concept of belief, to the infants. As Dan Hutto (2017: 832) says:

> Taken at face value the infant data suggests that very young children must have some command of the concept of belief in place very early on. This is so even though much older children lack the capacity to pass standard, verbally based, false belief tasks – tasks that were previously taken to be the litmus tests for possessing the concept of belief.

But this serves to indicate the extent to which the standard representational model can accommodate any result; that it is immune from empirical refutation.

The idea of concepts can be thought to have a physical or computational side in the brain as well as an overt, explicit side in language itself and conventional semantic relations within language. Concept is a concept that has both sides – possessing a concept is supposed to be a brain state. In the case of these experiments, the discursive construction of a concept in speech, one sense of possessing a concept, is distinct from performing mental acts as if one possessed the concept discursively. But there is a huge muddle here which we will deal with in a later chapter, after a discussion of language and scaffolding. The theory-theory depends on there being such a thing as concepts – which might not seem controversial, but which is an issue like many of the other issues presented so far. It is a case where we have a public object, a word in a language, which we ascribe to the brain as a tacit possession. In the next chapter we will deal with more of these cases, such as those that appear in intentional language and the language of belief.[1]

The main rival to the theory-theory of mind explains mind-reading on a different level than the conceptual. The basic idea of simulation theory is that we are acting beings who not only can act and predict the consequences of our actions; we can also go off-line, that is to say to use the action and input parts of our brain without actually acting, and thus anticipate the consequences of our actions, and also do the same thing by analogy with other persons, to understand their actions by simulating them as though they were our own actions with a predictable course of inputs and action outcomes. Moreover, this is presumably done entirely at a subconscious level.

This might have remained a speculative theory, though an appealing one, without the discovery of mirror neurons. This provided a plausible physical basis for the idea of simulation and the idea of off-line prediction. The initial discovery was of "a new class of visuomotor neuron in the monkey's premotor cortex: mirror neurons." They were called mirror neurons because they:

> respond both when a particular action is performed by the recorded monkey and when the same action, performed by another individual, is observed. Mirror neurons appear to form a cortical system matching observation and execution of goal-related motor actions.
>
> *(Gallese and Goldman 1998: 493)*

This is a condition of simulation, and confirms the idea of off-line prediction. The implications for mind-reading were clear:

> According to "simulation theory", other people's mental states are represented by adopting their perspective: by tracking or matching their states with resonant states of one's own. The activity of mirror neurons, and the fact that observers undergo motor facilitation in the same muscular groups as those utilized by target agents, are findings that accord well with simulation theory but would not be predicted by theory theory.
>
> *(Gallese and Goldman 1998: 493)*

The issue of prediction is important here; but for reasons to be discussed below, it is difficult to construct crucial experiments between these rival accounts. There is also another reason: these theories are often supplemented by more or less ad hoc additions which account for the relevant facts by hypothesizing special capacities that "explain" the experimental outcome. As we will see, this strategy is common in dealing with social topics. Nevertheless, there are findings that strongly support the simulation approach to mind-reading. One involves lesion studies, which show that the anterior insula is involved in reading disgust in the facial expressions of others, and that when it is damaged the patient is unable to read the facial cues indicating disgust. Simulation theory fits this finding; the theory-theory does not. Of course, as suggested, the theory-theory might be revised to account for this.[2] Indeed, such revision in the course of competition between theories is a major source of progress in science, and to be expected.

One of the major questions raised by the discovery of mirror neurons in monkeys was over whether the activities of mirror neurons went beyond mere bodily movements to contribute to the understanding of intentions, that is to say that they were the basis of mentalizing. Eventually the evidence mounted that they did. Iacoboni et al. (2005) did an fMRI experiment that compared clips showing just hand actions and clips showing more context, such as a teacup in a tray for tea with other related objects, and clips combining action and context, which would enable predicting of intentions rather than mere motion. The result was that the clips showing context and motion showed significant activation in the pre-motor cortex, in contrast to the other clips. They then asked the subjects about intention, and found that the subjects associated the motor action of the hand in the context of the tea objects with the intention to drink tea. This is a significant step because it connects the pure neural fact of activation with the verbal expression of beliefs about intention, rather than merely with prediction or imitation; they were actually attributing intentions and using their mirror systems to do so (Shanton and Goldman 2010: 530; see also Goldman 2008).[3]

This study involves another style of argument, which might be called the "part of and essential to" argument. Simulation, as a basic mental process of predicting by operating "off-line," can be said to be part of and essential to such things as mind-reading, but also to such overt exercises in theoretical thinking, such as "as if" reasoning. A famous example of this in another context is Hans Kelsen's argument ([1979] 1991) that one must treat the law as if it is normatively valid. Einstein famously employed "as if" thinking and Vaihinger ([1925] 2009) showed its role in many fields (see also Howard 1990). But we can also take it as a common mode of explicit "slow" reasoning. We would then say that it is based on (or employs, to sound anthropomorphic) our implicit capacity to simulate – to imagine without acting and to draw conclusions by going off-line. If we did not have this cognitive capacity, it is hard to see how we could have the capacity for *explicit* "as if" reasoning; and it is difficult to see how one could theorize at all without entertaining hypotheses that departed from our prior intuitive or common sense ideas by identifying possibilities which we would then test and make sense of by thinking of the thing to be theorized about as if some novel claim – such as "markets consist of utility maximizers exchanging with one another" – were true.

But this same form of argument, like one of those Russian dolls with more dolls within it, can be made about simulation itself. Empirical analysis shows that mirror neurons are *involved in* simulation. But "involved in" is not the same as explain: they need to be there for simulation to occur, but are not enough to explain it. They don't explain, for example, how one goes off-line in the course of simulation. This is explained by something else – inhibitors. But even adding inhibitors to the account leaves us very far from a full understanding of how mirror neuron activations produce or fail to produce such things as a conscious sense of the intentions of others, or the capacity to verbalize claims about intention.

Notes

1 "We argue that theory-of-mind (TOM) approaches, such as 'theory theory' and 'simulation theory', are both problematic and not needed" (Gallagher and Hutto 2008: 17).
2 "The straightforward explanation of NK's and B's selective inability to mind read disgust is that they lacked the ability to *mirror* disgust by virtue of their anterior insula damage. This implies that normal mind reading of disgust – at least through facial and other perceptual cues – is causally based on a mirrored (re)experience of disgust, just as ST predicts" (Shanton and Goldman 2010: 530; emphasis in the original).
3 "These data indicate that, even when they had not been explicitly instructed to do so, subjects associated the hand actions in the intention clips with intentions. For example, subjects associated the whole-hand prehension in the array of objects set for tea with the intention to drink the tea. This seems to confirm Iacoboni et al.'s conclusion that subjects were not merely predicting actions or mimicking" (Shanton and Goldman 2010: 530).

References

Apperly, Ian. (2013). "Can Theory of Mind Grow Up? Mindreading in Adults, and Its Implications for the Development and Neuroscience of Mindreading." In S. Baron-Cohen, H. Tager-Flusberg, and M. V. Lombardo (eds.) *Understanding Other Minds: Perspectives from Developmental Social Neuroscience*, 72–92. Oxford: Oxford University Press.

Baillargeon, Renée, Rose M. Scott, and Zijing He. (2010). "False-Belief Understanding in Infants." *Trends in Cognitive Sciences* 14(3): 110–118.

Baron-Cohen, S., A. M. Leslie, and U. Frith. (1985). "Does the Autistic Child Have a 'Theory of Mind'?" *Cognition* 21: 37–46.

Bloom, Paul. (2001). "Precis of 'How Children Learn the Meanings of Words.'" *Behavioral and Brain Sciences* 24: 1095–1103.

BothS., E. Laan, and W. Everaerd. (2011). "Focusing 'Hot' or Focusing 'Cool': Attentional Mechanisms in Sexual Arousal in Men and Women." *Journal of Sexual Medicine* 8: 167–179.

Brandom, Robert. (1994). *Making It Explicit: Reasoning, Representing and Discursive Commitment*. Cambridge, MA: Harvard University Press.

Buttelmann, David, Malinda Carpenter, and Michael Tomasello. (2009). "Eighteen-Month-Old Infants Show False Belief Understanding in an Active Helping Paradigm." *Cognition* 112: 337–342.

Carruthers, Michael, Steven Collins, and Steven Lukes. (1985). *The Category of the Person.* Cambridge: Cambridge University Press.

Choi, You-jung and Yuyan Luo. (2015). "13-Month-Old's Understanding of Social Interactions." *Psychological Science* 26(3): 274–283.

Chomsky, Noam. (2016). "Noam Chomsky on the Evolution of Language: A Biolinguistic Perspective." Interview by C. J. Polychroniou, *Truthout* 24 September. www.truth-out.org/opinion/item/37725-noam-chomsky-on-the-evolution-of-language-a-biolinguistic-perspective (accessed 20 February 2017).

Cosmides, Leda and John Tooby. (1994). "Origins of Domain-Specificity: The Evolution of Functional Organization." In L. Hirschfeld and S. Gelman (eds.), *Mapping the Mind: Domain-Specificity in Cognition and Culture*, 85–116. New York: Cambridge University Press.

Cussins, Adrian. (1990). "Content, Conceptual Content, and Non-Conceptual Content." In York Gunther (ed.) *Essays on Non-Conceptual Content*, 133–163. Cambridge, MA: MIT Press.

Dodds, E. R. (1951). *The Greeks and the Irrational.* Berkeley: University of California Press.

Douglas, Mary. (1966). *Purity and Danger: An Analysis of Concepts of Pollution and Taboo.* London and New York: Routledge.

Dreyfus, Hubert. (2014). *Skillful Coping: Essays on the Phenomenology of Everyday Perception and Action.* Oxford: Oxford University Press.

Epstein, Robert. (2016). "The Empty Brain." *Aeon*, 20 May. https://aeon.co/essays/your-brain-does-not-process-information-and-it-is-not-a-computer (accessed 24 March 2017).

Everett, Daniel. (2017) "Chomsky, Wolfe and Me." *Aeon.* https://aeon.co/essays/why-language-is-not-everything-that-noam-chomsky-said-it-is (accessed 2 November 2017).

Fehr, Ernst and Simon Gächter. (2000). "Cooperation and Punishment in Public Goods Experiments." *American Economic Review* 90(4): 980–994.

Fehr, Ernst, Simon Gächter, and Georg Kirchsteiger. (1997). "Reciprocity as a Contract Enforcement Device: Experimental Evidence." *Econometrica* 65: 833–860.

Finn, Emily S., Xilin Shen, Dustin Scheinost, Monica D. Rosenberg, Jessica Huang, Marvin M. Chun, Xenophon Papademetris, and R. Todd Constable (2015). "Functional Connectome Fingerprinting: Identifying Individuals Using Patterns of Brain Connectivity." *Nature Neuroscience* 18: 1664–1671.

Fodor, Jerry. (1987). *Psychosemantics.* Cambridge, MA: MIT Press.

Gagne, Deanna and Marie Coppola. (2017). "Visible Social Interactions Do Not Support the Development of False Belief Understanding in the Absence of Linguistic Input: Evidence from Deaf Adult Homesigners." *Frontiers in Psychology* 8: 1–21.

Gallagher, Shaun and Dan Hutto. (2008). "Understanding Others through Primary Interaction and Narrative Practice." In J. Zlatev, T. Racine, C. Sinha, and E. Itkonen (eds). *The Shared Mind: Perspectives on Intersubjectivity*, 17–38. Amsterdam: Benjamins.

Gallese, Vittorio and Alvin Goldman. (1998). "Mirror Neurons and the Simulation Theory of Mind-Reading." *Trends in Cognitive Sciences* 2(12): 493–501.

Gallese, Vittorio. (2007). "Before and Below 'Theory of Mind': Embodied Simulation and the Neural Correlates of Social Cognition." *Philosophical Transactions of the Royal Society B* 362: 659–669.

Goldman, A. I. (2008). "Mirroring, Mindreading, and Simulation." In J. Pineda (ed.) *Mirror Neuron Systems: The Role of Mirroring Processes in Social Cognition*, 311–330. New York: Humana.

Gopnik, Alison. (1993). "How We Know Our Minds: The Illusion of First-Person Knowledge of Intentionality." *Behavioral and Brain Sciences* 16(1): 1–14, 29–113.

Hamlin, J. Kiley, Karen Wynn, Paul Bloom, and Neha Mahajan. (2011). "How Infants and Toddlers React to Antisocial Others." *Proceedings of the National Academy of Sciences of the United States of America* 108(50): 19931–19936.

Hamlin, J. Kiley. (2013). "Failed Attempts to Help and Harm: Intention versus Outcome in Preverbal Infants' Social Evaluations." *Cognition* 128: 451–474.

Hauser, Marc D., Noam Chomsky, and W. Tecumseh Fitch. (2002). "The Faculty of Language: What Is It, Who Has It, and How Did It Evolve?" *Science* 298(22): 1569–1579.

Howard, Don. (1990). "Einstein and Duhem." *Synthese* 83: 363–384.

Hutto, Daniel D. (2005). "Starting without Theory: Confronting the Paradox of Conceptual Development." In B. Malle and S. Hodges (eds.) *Other Minds*, 56–72. New York: Guilford.

Hutto, Daniel D. (2017). "Basic Social Cognition without Mindreading: Minding Minds without Attributing Contents." *Synthese* 194(3): 827–846.

Iacoboni, M., Istvan Molnar-Szakacs, Vittorio Gallese, Giovanni Buccino, John C. Mazziotta, and Giacomo Rizzolatti. (2005). "Grasping the Intentions of Others with One's Own Mirror Neuron System." *PLoS Biology* 3: 529–535.

Kahneman, Daniel. (2011). *Thinking, Fast and Slow*. New York: Farrar, Strauss, Giroux.

Kandel, Eric R., Yadin Dudai, and Mark R. Mayford. (2014). "The Molecular and Systems Biology of Memory." *Cell* 157(1): 163–186.

Kelsen, Hans. ([1979] 1991). *General Theory of Norms*, trans. Michael Hartney. Oxford: Clarendon.

Krupenye, Christopher, Fumihiro Kano, Satoshi Hirata, Josep Call, and Michael Tomasello. (2016). "Great Apes Anticipate that Other Individuals Will Act According to False Beliefs." *Science* 354(6308): 110–114.

Laan. E. and S. Both. (2011). "Sexual Desire and Arousal Disorders in Women." *Advances in Psychosomatic Medicine* 2011(31): 16–34.

Laan E. and W. Everaerd. (1995). "Habituation of Female Sexual Arousal to Slides and Film." *Archives of Sexual Behavior* 24: 517–541.

Laan E., W. Everaerd, G. van Bellen, and G. Hanewald. (1994). "Women's Sexual and Emotional Responses to Male- and Female-Produced Erotica." *Archives of Sexual Behavior* 23: 153–170.

Lee, Young-eun, Jung-eun Ellie Yun, Eun Young Kim, and Hyun-joo Song. (2015). "The Development of Infants' Sensitivity to Behavioral Intentions when Inferring Others' Social Preferences." *PLoS ONE* 10(9): 1–16.

Lewis, David. (1979). "Scorekeeping in a Language Game." *Journal of Philosophical Logic* 8: 339–359.

Makin, Simon. (2016). "New Evidence Points to Personal Brain Signatures." *Scientific American*, 13 April. www.scientificamerican.com/section/news/new-evidence-points-to-personal-brain-signatures1/ (accessed 20 June 2017).

Nichols, Shaun and Stephen Stich. (2003). *Mindreading: An Integrated Account of Pretense, Self-Awareness, and Understanding Other Minds*. Oxford: Clarendon.

Onishi, Kristine H. and Renée Baillargeon. (2005). "Do 15-Month-Old Infants Understand False Beliefs?" *Science* NS 308(5719): 255–258.

Perner, J. (1991). *Understanding the Representational Mind*. Cambridge, MA: MIT Press.

Piattelli-Palmarini, Massimo. (forthcoming)."Fodor and the Innateness of All (Basic) Concepts." In Lila Gleitman and Roberto G. De Almeida (eds.) *Festschrift in Honor of Jerry Fodor*.

4

EXPLAINING AND UNDERSTANDING ACTION

The paradoxical result of the last chapter is this: while empathy and under-standing are real, in the sense that they are grounded in physical features of the brain distinct from and in addition to mere inductive data gathering in the case of mirror neurons, the explanation of how empathy and understanding work may undermine the familiar language of folk psychology and the language of intention itself. Moreover, at the same time that we acknowledge the actuality of empathic understanding, and that it is distinct from the intellectualist picture of under-standing as imposing a hypothesis on behavioral data, we come face to face with another consideration: the limitations of our own self-understanding and the fact that our means of understanding, in the case of the theory-theory of mind, a theory that we tacitly possess, is itself tailored to our cognitive limitations.

The alternatives of the theory-theory of mind and simulation theory are a place to start on the issues. To reiterate, the theory-theory holds that the child, as well as the adult, has a tacit theory of mind that enables them to infer intentions, beliefs, and desires, and perhaps other things. It is a "theory" because the things that are inferred, and serve both to explain behavior and make it understandable or meaningful, are not directly accessible, but can be best thought of as theoretical constructs, like gravity (Gopnik and Wellman 1992: 146). Moreover, thinking of the capacity to understand as based on a tacit theory allows us to treat the changes in capacity in the course of the child's development to adulthood as a kind of theoretical revision or improvement. The simulation alternative holds that the child, and for that matter the adult, "need not really understand the mind, in the sense of having some set of beliefs about it. She bypasses conceptual under-standing by operating a working model," her own mind, which she learns to use by "running simulations ... and applying the results to others," enabling

Rellini, H. A., M. K. McCall, K. P. Randall, and M. C. Meston. (2005). "The Relationship between Women's Subjective and Physiological Sexual Arousal." *Psychophysiology* 42: 116–124.

Ryerson, James. (2004). "Sidney Morgenbesser, b. 1921: Sidewalk Socrates." *New York Times Magazine*, 26 December.www.nytimes.com/2004/12/26/magazine/sidewalk-socrates.html (accessed 20 February 2017).

Sabbagh, Mark A., Jeannette E. Benson, and Valerie A. Kuhlmeier. (2013). "False Belief Understanding in Infants and Preschoolers." In Maria Legerstee, David Haley, and Marc Bornstein (eds.) *The Infant Mind: Origins of the Social Brain*, 301–323. New York: Guilford.

Shanton, Karen and Alvin I. Goldman. (2010). "Simulation Theory." *Wiley Interdisciplinary Reviews (Wires): Cognitive Science* 1(4): 527–538.

Sliwa, J. and W. A. Freiwald. (2017). "A Dedicated Network for Social Interaction Processing in the Primate Brain." *Science* 356: 745–749.

Sperber, Dan and Deirdre Wilson. (1986). *Relevance: Communication and Cognition.* Cambridge, MA: Harvard University Press.

Stich, Stephen and R. Ravenscroft. (1994). "What Is Folk Psychology?" *Cognition* 50: 447–468.

Strawson, P. F. ([1962] 2003). "Freedom and Resentment." In Gary Watson (ed.) *Free Will*, 59–80. Oxford: Oxford University Press.

Thomsen, Lotte, William E. Frankenhuis, McCaila Ingold-Smith, and Susan Carey. (2011). "Big and Mighty: Preverbal Infants Mentally Represent Social Dominance." *Science* 331(28): 477–480.

Vaihinger, Hans. ([1925] 2009). *The Philosophy of 'As If': A System of the Theoretical, Practical and Religious Fictions of Mankind*, trans. C. K. Ogden. New York: Harcourt Brace.

Wimmer, H. and J. Perner. (1983). "Beliefs about Beliefs: Representation and Constraining Function of Wrong Beliefs in Young Children's Understanding of Deception." *Cognition* 13: 103–128.

improvement through learning from the success of predictions from running this model (Gopnik and Wellman 1992: 145).

In both cases we face limitations, but slightly different ones. Simulation is limited by what we can do or intend – it is an extension of our bodily capacities. To the extent that it is supported by mirror neurons, it involves neurons being activated by perceiving what are normally used in performing actions. Our capacities for action and what we perceive are bound together. For example, dancers perceive and respond to ballet moves differently than non-dancers (Cross et al. 2006). And this binding of capacity and understanding extends, perhaps, to understanding in general. We may "share" a core base of bodily capacities, and therefore capacity to simulate, but we also learn. In the case of the theory-theory, we are limited: we are completely dependent on the truth of this theory – if the theory-theory is correct – in understanding, and thus subject to its limitations and the possibility of its fundamental erroneousness that eliminativism argues for. The eliminativist argument is warranted by questions about the physical realization of its "theoretical" terminology: do we need an account of action and understanding with intentions, beliefs, and desires if there is an empirically plausible, physically based alternative? It also follows that we are limited to our own cultural horizons: we can't attribute intentions or beliefs that we can't already, in some sense, understand – an issue we will address shortly.

In what follows, I will separate two issues, familiar from the history of social science itself, to which I will occasionally refer. One is this: what is "really" going on in the brain when people act? The other is "what enables us to understand other people?" The answer we have seen earlier with Fodor is that folk psychology, which answers the second question, must also be more or less the answer to the first one; eliminativists think folk psychology is just wrong. But folk psychology is not the only answer to the question of how we understand – simulation theory is another. It does not tell us what is in the brain, in the sense of giving us a set of theoretical concepts that we can try to locate in brain places or processes. But it does point to mechanisms that might be found to be realized in specific brain processes or neurons.

If we ask the slightly different question of why we have the tacit theory of mind we have (if indeed we have a tacit theory of mind), the usual answer divides into two: one is that it is just correct; the other is that it has evolved. The two answers do not coincide, and much can be said about why they might not. Our capacity to understand, whether it is through a tacit theory or through something like simulation and empathy, evolved not to answer scientific questions but to enable us to quickly respond to social situations. The false belief problem is an example: people (and great apes and other animals) imitate; if we only imitated and did not have the capacity to detect false beliefs, we would be disadvantaged in many situations involving other people and their actions. We would err by imitating or by jointly attending with them toward some object, such as in a game about trying to hide something, rather than using our own knowledge and memory to recognize that the place the other person was looking was the wrong one. But our capacity to detect false beliefs itself rests on our capacity to understand.

If we think of how this capacity came to be, in evolutionary terms, we can think of how it was adaptive, and why it was especially adaptive for humans – emphasis on the "think" – because our knowledge of the relevant mechanisms, such as epigenetic transmission and transformation, and the environment in which it was "adaptive" is limited. But it is reasonable, indeed incontrovertible, that social life, social structure, and these capacities co-evolved, so that these social skills were adapted to the social life as well as making the social life possible. We need to add to this something else. The terms we use when we apply the theory of mind or our understanding of others are the same as, and arrive developmentally along with, the terms we use when we describe our own mental processes. Put simply, the theory of mind that we use to introspect, or perhaps only to express our introspections, is the same theory that evolved for the purposes of navigating social life. And just as this theory, or capacity, is limited, so is our capacity to introspect.

This bears directly on social interaction, and points to a basic issue: much of what we do and get out of social interaction is not part of what is normally considered "folk psychology." The standard picture is something like this: the platitudinous generalizations we might make using folk mental concepts are "the consciously accessible consequences of a substantially richer set of mostly tacit or unconscious psychological rules" and "these tacit rules and generalizations also play a central role in explaining folk psychological capacities" (Stich and Ravenscroft 1994: 459). The explicit part of folk psychology is thus limited, though how limited is an open question. It is clear, however, that basic facts about social interaction are not covered by "folk psychology" or even by understanding. As Gonzalo Munévar puts it:

> We meet a new person and the almost instant non-verbal "processing" of the information depends on a great many clues that themselves depend on unconscious processes based on evolutionary reasons or on a long history of personal experiences. This new person seems trustworthy, interesting, etc., but we often have no idea why the actual conscious experience is connected to these reactions, and we might not even be aware of the reactions themselves.
>
> *(Munévar 2014: 198)*

Some range of reactions, in short (how big we cannot say) are not accessible to introspection; and to the extent that we can even talk about the reactions – which shape our responses in ways we are also unaware of – we do so on the basis of practices or theories. These may be therapeutic or religious theories of the self. Our reasoning is based on data that is behavioral data about other people together with simulative testing of our own emotional responses. This is itself a procedure that is limited by our own limitations in introspection, and in our limitations in talking about the results of our introspection.

There is another large problem here, which is important to sociology and anthropology. Folk psychology is limited in the kinds of inferences it can make about "beliefs." The limitations are crucial for social science because they become apparent at one of the crucial points at which social science explanations begin: the point where our normal ways of understanding other people break down. If our core model of understanding and explaining action is the belief-desire model of intentional action, we run into difficulties when we cannot understand the beliefs and desires. We cannot understand them when we can't empathize with them in a way that enables us to understand them – nor can we identify their beliefs and desires. We simply don't understand them. We cannot infer a belief in *mana* in ordinary social interaction if we don't have a concept of *mana* ourselves. We would simply be mystified by what the "believer" told us. To be sure, we may construct a translation based on concepts we do possess, such as "ghost," or social scientific usages like "charisma." But these involve inferences and considerations far beyond the ordinary inferential workings of our theory of mind in doing something like solving the false belief problem. And they are reconstructions from our own point of view and for the purposes of enabling us to understand. The reconstructions are not indicative of the contents of the Background for the *mana* user. They are indicative of what we need to attribute to the user of *mana*-talk in order to make sense of them.

The Background, the tacit cognitive stuff, is not accessible to us or to the *mana*-speaker. Introspection alone cannot tell us much about what our own culture is, for example. What is "cultural" and what is merely normal about our own practices is invisible to us. It is only when we encounter a culture that does things differently that we recognize our way of doing things as a practice. When we encounter another culture, our normal capacity to understand and the inferences and predictions we are used to making break down: for a culture based on *mana*, *mana* is simply a fact; for us it requires elaborate analogical thinking to grasp. The mana-speaker has acquired mana-talk and its application directly and as primary descriptive language about the world, and has in the Background the cognitive mechanisms for using it. What makes *mana* a fact for them is tacit Background we do not share. The same holds for the reasons we make certain natural inferences, or how we manage to walk or ride a bicycle: we cannot pull this Background up to consciousness by introspection. Nor could we introspect and reveal our implicit folk psychological theory or the syntactical theory that we supposedly rely on to understand the speech of others and to generate our own speech. They are both buried in the tacit. We might reflect on what we normally say, and ask what it would be like if there was a theory that justified it, but that is different than saying what is actually in one's head.

This raises questions about just what we are talking about when we use the term "folk psychology," and what relation the explicit language of belief, desire, intention, and so forth has to the implicit theory that the theory-theory, if there is such a thing, tells us we are operating with. It is no picnic to make sense of the various alternatives here, but a rough guide would distinguish at least the following options:

a   a pure simulation and mirror neuron account in which understanding is pre-theoretical and partly learned, but learned by improving on base capacities to "mirror" the actions of others;
b   universal theory-theory, typically with a universal semantic model;
c   cultural, with a local tacit semantic model and a local tacit theory of mind;
d   narrative, i.e., based on the publicly articulated forms of expression about the mind.

The "cultural" answer is that the sorts of content that make up the tacit theory of mind are acquired locally by the same mechanisms by which culture is acquired. This helps with the fact that overt theories of mind, at what I am calling here the narrative level, vary considerably between cultures. The explicit theory just reflects the implicit one in each culture. The non-cultural answer just treats the folk theory of mind as more or less the common property of humankind. This of course requires a different mechanism, but it can be innate or a result of universal human experience and universal human mechanisms of acquisition. "Narrative," as used here, refers to the overt theory of mind, the platitudes, and the accepted forms of public reasoning – the forms that are intelligible to others in a group – as they relate to traditional mental concepts, such as belief, which of course also vary between societies.

There is a close relation between the idea of an implicit theory of mind and another idea: rationality. The point of posting a tacit theory of mind is to explain inferences, such as the inferences involved in the false belief problem. But where there is inference there is rationality, the rationality that figures in the most basic relations in the belief-desire model of action, which connects the beliefs and desires to the act that they explain. The act needs to be a rational response to the belief and desire. It is for this reason that many philosophers want to see the relation involved in action explanation as "normative" rather than causal. There is another attraction to this view. If we regard this relation as rule-governed, it fits nicely with the standard view of the brain: the brain can be thought of as an operating system which is programmed in various ways – the tacit theory of mind is one of these programs. Indeed, both the innate theory of mind account and the cultural account can be thought of in this way.

But rationality, especially in the sense of decision-making rationality, can be read back (as we have seen with Gintis) into the "actions" of evolving animals, to the point of explaining their relations in terms of game theory. And we can also treat the developing child as a "scientist in the crib" revising their primitive theory of mind rationally, in response to new data, or even constructing a tacit theory of mind out of the data inputs themselves – an achievement that would require a high level of rationality. Thus one could construct a parallel list: starting with primitive animal rationality; treating the implicit theory of mind as merely a by-product of developing human rationality; and explaining actual action as itself rational. And this has "social" implications for humans as well. Human society can be interpreted as the product of rational choices in a game-theoretic structure.[1]

There are some affinities and generic issues that need to be noticed here. The a) and d) accounts potentially mesh. As Stich and Ravenscroft noted years ago, the status of folk psychology has been a matter of intense dispute, with some authors arguing that:

> commonsense psychology cannot be regarded as a causal or explanatory theory because its principles are partly normative or largely analytic. Others maintain that the basic function of folk psychology is not to predict and explain, but to warn, promise, congratulate and to do a thousand and one other jobs that are fundamental to the smooth workings of our interpersonal lives.
>
> *(Stich and Ravenscroft 1994: 449)*

If we take this seriously, there is no reason to expect that commonsense or folk psychological concepts match up with anything in the brain or explain anything, at least in the sense of matching up to the actual cognitive processes which do explain action.

But we *can* regard them as having other roles than prediction. They can be largely empty, as an explanatory theory, but central and useful for a wide variety of other purposes (Morton 1996; Mercier and Sperber 2011; Mercier and Sperber 2017). As

> Churchland points out, "we use the resources of folk psychology to promise, to entreat, to congratulate, to tease, to joke, to intimate, to threaten, and so on" (Churchland 1989, 231; see also Wilkes 1981; Wilkes 1984). Others have emphasized different roles for folk psychology including coordinating behavior (Morton 2003), making judgements of moral responsibility (Knobe 2003; Morton 2003), identifying intentional action (Knobe 2003), perceiving intentions (Gallagher 2004), understanding others (Hutto 2004; Gallagher 2001), justifying behavior (Davidson 1963; Andrews 2004), regulating behavior (Hobson 2007; Mameli 2001; McGeer 2007; Zawidzki 2008), and providing reasons (Davidson 1963; Hutto 2008). Each of these views stems from an insight about one or more of the myriad ways in which we interact with others.
>
> *(Andrews 2012: 186)*

We can lump these purposes under the heading of "narrative" for two related reasons. One is that the purposes listed above all involve the public use of folk psychology to do such things as assign blame, which is itself a social practice. The second is that these concepts do play a role in sense-making, and this role is also social in the sense that the sense is being made of the behavior of others, or is directed toward others in the form of such things as justifications. This is consistent with the actual diversity of uses in different cultures and the "eliminativist" idea that folk psychology is a false theory. But it can also be consistent with a view of social science as itself narrative based, in a broad sense that needs to be explained – and will be later in this chapter.

The issues and affinities related to b) and c) have been partly described above. If we have a computer programming model of the mind, we can claim that the theory of mind is programmed in, innately, as part of the innately given semantic structure, or programmed "culturally," for example with a cultural semantic structure that is tacitly acquired and tacitly behind the actual inferences and platitudes that make up the local folk psychology. There are plenty of issues with this picture, some of which have been discussed above. How does this programming happen? How does some sort of extremely complex system get transported into people's heads "culturally" given that people have enough trouble understanding overt, public speech and more trouble learning such simple systems as basic arithmetic? And since we have no idea what the actual rules of a tacit semantics, or a tacit theory of mind, or indeed a tacit syntactical system are or might be, or a way of figuring out what they are, what grounds do we have for regarding the idea as plausible, especially if there is a remotely plausible alternative explanation?

Dan Hutto points to another issue, with the identification of the Background as a whole as "intentional," a claim of Searle's which actually points to a much larger muddle about intentions. Hutto comments on a "deeply entrenched assumption" which he calls "the semantic thesis of intentionality":

> To adopt this thesis is to subscribe to an explanation of intentionality that is modeled directly on the kind of semantic, truth conditional or referential content associated with sophisticated speech acts and mature folk psychological states of mind. This fuels standard assumptions about what is, in general, definitive of directedness; even forms of directedness associated with the most basic forms of activity. Accordingly, anything that qualifies as any kind of directed activity must be ultimately explained by appeal to states of mind with non-derived, fully representational, psychosemantic content.
> *(Hutto 2012: 42–2)*

This is rather a mouthful. But the issue is an important one, and it figures in many other thinkers, such as Gallistel (2011), who wishes to model all thought (even of insects) in this way, as mimicking speech. The point of these arguments is to identify intentionality or directedness with something that can be understood in familiar terms. The term "understood" as distinct from "explained" is relevant here: it springs from the idea that the eliminativists reject, namely that mental content is like verbal content and public speech, and the desire to make mental content, the stuff in the Background, into something that can be "understood."

Searle (1983: 4) makes this claim explicitly: "Intentional states represent objects and states of affairs in the same sense of 'represent' that speech acts represent objects and states of affairs." The reason to be tempted by this assumption is this: the "mental" that is involved with action goes beyond what is conscious, accessible to introspection, or part of the conventional action explanation. The considerations involved in meeting a person mentioned earlier are exemplary: "the almost instant non-verbal 'processing' of the information [that] depends on a great many clues that themselves depend on unconscious processes based on evolutionary reasons or on a long history of personal experiences" (Munévar 2014: 198). The success of actions, learning from trial and error about actions, all involve this additional stuff. It is not passive or entirely fixed: at least some of it changes with action and with learning, or "activation." So it seems natural to extend the notion of intentionality to this unconscious stuff, and then to think of intentional states as mimicking public speech.

One finds a similar form of analogous reasoning in connection with rationality. Animals figure things out about the world. Over the long run they manage to find some sort of equilibrium with the other animals in their species, which they reproduce with and sometimes cooperate and also compete with. We can "understand" this as rational. But this means only that we can build models of their behavior that more or less fit that are rational decision-making or game-theoretic models. If one looks carefully at the studies that confirm this, one sees that there is a lot of randomness. But there is a lot of randomness in the case of humans, who we do understand, though we don't need models to do so. This distinction between fitting a model and really understanding seems to hang on the consideration of whether the actions are really intentional – a muddled concept to which we now turn.

The Trouble with Intention

Begin with a finding from cognitive science. It is well known that children over-attribute intentionality, for example to physical objects. This bias does not disappear entirely with development. The evidence is clear that even "adults have a bias to interpret all behavior as intentional until proven otherwise … when evaluating an agent and an action, an intentional inference is automatically activated as the cause of the action" (Rosset 2008: 778). This bias leads us to treat accidents as intentional, and for people to impute conspiracies to coincidental conjunctures of events. Yet there is another relevant finding: infants are able very early on to distinguish intentional and unintentional actions by persons in relation to them (Woodard 2009; Sakkalou and Gattis 2012; Ammaniti and Gallese 2014: 146–7; Choi and Luo 2015; Lee et al. 2015).

This gives us a kind of starting point: there is something like intention that is recognized by infants. Whether this should be understood as pre-conceptual, pre-linguistic, or pre-cultural – or alternatively as the activation of innate capacities – is one of the open questions remaining from the last section. The standard innatist account depends very heavily on its being universal, on everyone having the same module to activate, and on modules being primordial products of evolution, and thus freed from any requirement to make sense of how they are acquired – which would be the case if they varied culturally. As I have noted, the claim is that theory of mind is robust at least across several modern cultures. It would seem to follow that infant capacities rely on this innate theory. But there is an issue with the claim of universality. Although the basics of theory of mind, such as recognition of goal directedness, do seem universal, theory of mind terms are not universal. Epistemic language varies widely, and, as mentioned earlier, even the distinction between truth and belief does not appear in some languages: the same declaration implies both that the speaker affirms it and that it is true. But the problem goes beyond this. In some languages believe is the same as "to use"; in others it is the same as trust (Needham 1972: 32–4). Some cultures regard talk about another person's beliefs and mental contents as deeply inappropriate, and treat their minds as opaque (Robbins and Rumsey 2008; Robbins 2008; Schiefflin 2008). And there are a number of other variations in explicit theory of mind talk between cultures, including cultures within the Western tradition.[2]

So it is an open question as to what is universal and what is not – a question about what is actually happening when an infant understands an act as an intentional act. Here we seem to have two things going on: first, a primordial core of responsiveness, perhaps involving mirror neurons, which amounts to a basic kind of empathy that consists in the recognition of what someone is doing. This is all the infant needs to distinguish "intentional" actions from accidental ones. Then we have something quite different, namely an understanding that conforms to and allows the utilization of the whole range of language of the theory of mind, including "intentional" but also terms like belief and desire. We might think of this as full understanding or empathy in the full sense (Gallagher 2012: 169). We might also think of empathy of this more comprehensive kind as incorporating and depending on the more basic capacity shared with infants, apes, and so on, in a "part of and essential to" way.

The relevant distinctions here map directly onto some familiar distinctions in social science, particularly in Max Weber. Weber defined sociology restrictively as the study of meaningful social action, which he described as *verstehende Soziologie*, or understanding sociology. He avoided philosophical language, including terms like intention. His account of *Verstehen*, or understanding, was not hermeneutic in any traditional sense. It focused instead on the capacity for employing empathy and achieving *Evidenz* with it that distinguished sociology, and by extension other sciences of action, from natural science. His thought was that for some kinds of action we have empathic understanding that is evident, that is to say requires no further grounding and is perhaps – this is one contemporary meaning of *Evidenz*, found in Brentano ([1930] 1966: xv–xvii) – also evident to anyone observing the same action.

The example he gives is a man chopping wood. This is a physical act that fits into the most basic of the categories of mind-reading listed earlier: it is not linguistic; it does not involve inferences requiring a theory of mind; and there is no narrative structure required in addition to the physical act in order to "understand" it. He called this a case of "direct observational understanding" (Weber [1968] 1978: 7). If the directly understood facts together with circumstantial facts formed a pattern which allowed for inferences about something more, such as the woodcutter's aim of selling the wood, the larger pattern would be what he calls "explanatory understanding" and characterizes in terms of "motive," which we see will be qualified in a very specific way. This kind of understanding "consists in placing the act in a more intelligible context of meaning." Thus, in the case of the woodcutter:

> we understand the chopping of wood … in terms of motive in addition to direct observation if we know that the wood chopper is doing it for a wage, or is chopping a supply for his own use, or is possibly doing it for recreation.
> *(Weber [1968] 1978: 8, 12)*

The use of "meaning" and "intelligible" here has a specific meaning. It is what we might call cultural: "The interpretation of a coherent course of conduct is subjectively adequate [i.e., adequate as an interpretation by the observer] insofar as, according to our habitual modes of thought and feeling," and "taken in their mutual relation are recognized to constitute a 'typical' complex of meaning" (Weber [1968] 1978: 11). This is Weber's minimalist notion of culture, which we will contrast to the "tacit theory" notion of culture.

This pattern formed by a typical complex of meaning is not itself a product of a pure act of empathy, but of something that can be recounted in an intelligible narrative. So this account combines a) and d) without appealing to an innate tacit theory of mind, as b) does, or a cultural tacit theory, as c) does. Moreover, there is a sharp division between empathy and narrative: empathy is a universal capacity that can produce evident results, and similarly universal is interpretation through typical complexes of meaning; the contents of interpretation, the concepts used to interpret and describe, and to construct the narrative, are located firmly on the side of culture, and depend on our habitual modes of feeling and thinking – these habitual modes are what makes the interpretation intelligible to us, as interpreters or audience.

The combination of a) and d) stands clarifying. In the first place, Weber is not using a tacit theory conception of the production of meaning – meaning for him is a matter of patterns found in coherent courses of conduct, such as chopping wood for the market. In the second place, by taking content to be relative to local habitual modes of thinking and feeling, he makes interpretation "relativistic," in the sense that it is for us and our audience and must be intelligible to us. Making a course of conduct intelligible is to place it in what I am calling here a narrative form. These forms are relative to the particular audiences that respond to them in local habitual ways. From this point of view, folk psychology – understood as a narrative form that hooks into local habitual ways of thought – is a perfectly legitimate source for narrative structures: one can talk about beliefs and desires, emotions, and so forth as they are part of the habitual modes of thinking of one's audience. But these will differ from audience to audience: the explanation of a given course of conduct by a modern historian will employ different mentalistic concepts than an explanation given by someone from an alien culture, and also different descriptive concepts, because such concepts are "local."

So for Weber, folk psychology is indispensable, but only because it is the language of the culture in which we formulate our questions and answers. And he has arguments as to why this is how social science is compelled to formulate its problems. For him, folk psychology need not be a true theory of mind, or even an approximation. It is simply a way of talking about the world disclosed by understanding or *Verstehen*. Yet it does have something to do with empathy and the finding of patterns. How this works is not entirely clear from Weber's discussion, but a reconstruction might be given to answer some questions that are raised by his account. The first question concerns "meaning." Where does that come from? A standard account is that meaning involves a system of meanings – that is to say a tacit theory, like the semantic structure posited by Fodor – or a "cultural" tacit theory shared by a community. That is not how Weber proceeds. He starts with core empathic facts that themselves have meaning, such as the man chopping wood. The "meaning" that we gain from our empathic response, that gives us evident knowledge, is knowledge of what he is doing – an action rather than a mechanical set of movements.

This is "meaningful" in a very basic sense: we know what he is doing. When we string together a set of these kinds of "knowing what he is doing" facts and other circumstances we get patterns. The patterns are meaningful because their content is meaningful: they are cases of second order pattern recognition in which the elements of the pattern are meaningful. The relation between the elements is something we recognize, a pattern, which is not meaningful in the primary sense that our empathic response to the woodchopper and our recognition of what he is doing is meaningful. The "meaning" character of the elements of the pattern makes this a pattern of something that is already meaningful. These elements in turn can become the subject of joint attention, and be narrated according to the habitual modes of thought and feeling of the audience, for example when we piece together that the woodchopper is chopping for the market.

Weber makes two other points that bear on the issue of folk psychology, one of which bears especially on the subject of patterns and intelligibility. The first relates to the intentionalizing bias. He commented on the necessity, for understanding, of our attributing human mental traits to animals, but also on the problematic character of these attributions. The problem lay in distinguishing the effects of mechanical and biological causes from the kinds of things we "understand" by analogy with humans. But he extended this problematic to human action as well. He noted that several of the phenomena he was providing a "meaningful" analysis of also had concurrent physical or biological causes, and that it was an error to think that the purely sociological meaningful action approach was a complete explanation of the phenomena. He says that the sociologist must take account of the "continual interaction" of biological non-meaningful causes with meaningful action. Biological causes, he says, are "often of decisive importance." He adds that this is "particularly true of all 'traditional' action [because it is the result of habituation and thus barely counts as 'action'] and of many aspects of charisma." His comment on charisma is telling: these aspects "contain the seeds of psychic contagion" (Weber [1968] 1978: 17).

This results in an odd, and non-reductive, division of labor between social science and biology: "These types of action are very closely related to phenomenon which are understandable only in biological terms or can be interpreted in terms of subjective motives only in fragments." Nevertheless, "all these facts do not discharge sociology from the obligation, in full awareness of the narrow limits to which it is confined, to accomplish what it alone can do" (Weber [1968] 1978: 17). The narrow limits are defined by the capacity to empathize, particularly to identify actions. Weber also recognized that we as human beings have a capacity to understand ideational systems, such as law and mathematics, as well as individual actions, at least in certain cases, by "direct understanding" rather than by inference.[3] We can think of his sociology as social science within the limits of understanding, but with a full recognition that many relevant processes lie beyond these limits.[4]

Weber's solution to the problem of the status of folk psychology may seem somewhat awkward, but it gets him the best of several worlds. He gets the full conceptual advantages of being able to use the rich language of his own local speech community, including the language of folk psychology, without any need to commit himself to its "reality," or correspondence with the brain, or ultimate causality, for example, in the form of the theory of free will. He can acknowledge the role of biological causes, contagion, and so forth in human action. The awkwardness comes in the admission that this set of concepts does not integrate with the local conceptual language. It acknowledges that we intentionalize or give meaning to acts that have large unintentional or meaningless components or are not intentional or meaningful at all. But this division of labor between sociology and biology allows him to accommodate the relativistic character of folk psychology: the fact that there are multiple "folk" conceptions of action and the mental.

Finally, though I will not discuss these issues here, Weber is able to give an account of the relation of models, such as rational choice, to actual understanding through empathy: models, which he calls "ideal-types," are tools that abstract from the richer world of actual action but are constructed to be more intelligible than actual action, at least sometimes and in some respects, and additionally can be made accessible by constructing narratives around patterns including meaningful, or empathically accessible, elements. He also finds a way to give these narratives a particular kind of "causal" significance that does not involve scientific laws stated in terms of general rather than local concepts.

There is, however, an extension of the mode of understanding that does not involve direct understanding that raises important problems. As will be discussed in more detail later in this chapter, we are good, as humans, at filling in blanks in patterns – an example of which is supplying missing premises for statements. We do this in the normal course of understanding other people. An extension of this ordinary part of social interaction to other cultures, or alien viewpoints, is to say that they have different (and perhaps identifiable) presuppositions or assumptions, and that their culture consists of such assumptions. This is a quite different claim: it amounts to saying that they have a tacit theory and – as with the cultural version of the theory of mind thesis – that this is the resource on which they draw when making overt public statements or in general in making inferences. It is, so to speak, an inside-out approach to meaning: the basis of meaning is what is inside the speaker's head, in the form of a culture or shared semantic system. In later sections of this chapter, and more extensively in Chapter 8, we will consider some outside-in alternatives to this conception.

The Alternatives

From a neuroscience perspective, Weber's distinction between the subject matter of the "understanding" sciences and other sciences rests on a solid basis. As a consequence of the discovery of mirror neurons, empathy, in Weber's sense, is the subject of a large neuroscience literature (Decety and Ickes 2009). The rehabilitation of empathy, as I suggested in the preface, is a striking departure from the standard model of the brain as computer, and has not been assimilated to it. But the alternatives that have been proposed by the opponents of the standard model are more congenial to empathy. More importantly, the alternatives point to, though they do not directly provide, an alternative to what appears to be the strong suit of the standard model: its ability to account for rational action and decision-making. In what follows I will briefly describe these alternatives, and then go on to provide, based on other sources in the cognitive science literature, an alternative account of action itself, consistent with some central findings in neuroscience that are also difficult to assimilate to the standard model. I don't mean to treat this alternative as a full-fledged theory. It is simply my attempt to fill in some gaps using available ideas to sketch out what alternatives might be constructed.

Cognitive science's dominant computationalist paradigm has always been contested, and always plagued by fundamental problems. The alternatives, however, have not added up to a similarly comprehensive approach. Nevertheless, there are strong affinities between some of them. Richard Menary (2010) has referred to a central grouping of four distinct movements we have already encountered, known as the 4Es of cognition: embedded, embodied, extended, and enactive. Alternatively, they are listed as "embodied, ecologically situated, extended, and enculturated" (Hutto 2017a: 1). Sometimes "emotion" and other "E's" are added to the list. More recently, attempts have been made, by Andy Clark, to link enactivism with predictive processing (PP). These various movements require some further explanation, as does predictive processing.

Clark (2016: 3) presents predictive processing as a radical alternative to traditional computational models. The basic idea of predictive processing is that the brain is "an ever-active prediction machine: an inner engine continuously striving to anticipate the incoming sensory barrage." But there are different ways to take this. As Clark (2015c: 3) puts it:

One way (Conservative Predictive Processing) depicts the predictive mind as an insulated inner arena populated by representations so rich and reconstructive as to enable the organism to "throw away the world." The other (Radical Predictive Processing) stresses the use of fast and frugal, action-involving solutions of the kind highlighted by much work in robotics and embodied cognition. But it goes further, by showing how predictive schemes can combine frugal and more knowledge-intensive strategies, switching between them fluently and continuously as task and context dictate.

Radical predictive processing fits with an action-oriented conception of the brain. As Dan Hutto (2017b: 2) explains the argument, "brains, tirelessly and proactively, are forever trying to look ahead in order to ensure that we have an adequate practical grip on the world in the here and now. Focused primarily on action and intervention, their basic work is to make the best possible predictions about what the world is throwing at us." They are, as Clark says, "action oriented engagement machines" (2016: 300).

What makes it radical is that it replaces "the passive input-dominated view of neural processing" with a picture of cognition having a "restless, pro-active, hyperactive and loopy character" (Clark 2015a: 1–2). What it provides is something that the 4E approaches have lacked, namely a neuro-computational partner. Predictive processing potentially does this by "combining elements from work in connectionism and artificial neural networks, contemporary cognitive and computational neuroscience, Bayesian approaches to dealing with evidence and uncertainty, robotics, [and] self-organization" (Clark 2016: 10).

This fits, roughly, with something the 4E movements share: a focus on what is called embeddedness or situatedness. In its radical form, it also fits with the rejection, common to the 4E movements, of component-dominant systems in which the function of components can be identified in isolation from each other. For interaction-dominant systems, behavior is an emergent outcome that is "the result of interactions between system components, agents, and situational factors, with these intercomponent or interagent interactions altering the dynamics of the component elements, situational factors, and agents themselves" (Richardson et al. 2014: 256). Where the 4E movements differ is in their approaches to embodiment and to the environment. One approach, discussed in the next chapter, derives from Gibsonian psychology and focuses on the notion of affordances – that is to say the parts of the environment that are ready to hand, and that we experience as though they were designed for our use. Others stress the effects of embodied action on cognition.

There is a "torrent of experiments" in support of these ideas. The relatedness of elements of mind, body and environment can be "established by showing that a particular movement of the body or interaction with the social or physical environment makes a measureable difference in cognition." A simple example is this: "holding a cup of warm versus cold liquid in one hand changes how experimental subjects evaluate other unrelated stimuli" (Rosch [1993] 2017: xlvii). A more complex example goes to the heart of the idea of an isolated, modularized, semantic system. As Vittorio Gallese notes:

> Recent behavioral studies, though, show that the syntactic system is penetrable. Syntactic ambiguities are evaluated using non-linguistic constraints like real-world properties of referential context. Empirical research shows that humans continuously define linguistically relevant referential domains by evaluating sentence information against the situation-specific affordances. These affordances are not encoded as part of the linguistic representation of a word or phrase. Listeners use predicate-based information, like action goals, to anticipate upcoming referents. For example, a recent study … shows that syntactic decisions about ambiguous sentences are affected by the number of referential candidates that can afford the action evoked by the verb in the unfolding sentence. These results suggest that even a key component of the supposed NLF [narrow language faculty, which we discussed in the last chapter] is intimately intertwined with action and its embodied simulation.
>
> *(Gallese 2008: 326)*

More simply, people do not deal with language as though they were implementing a rigid code, but interpret what is said in terms of the real world, consisting of the things they have ready perceptual and embodied access to, and in terms of what is being done by them in that world. This is where embodiment, embeddedness, and affordances come together to produce something that can be described as an ecological system.

This interpenetration has implications for our basic picture of what the mind does. As Evan Thompson, discussing enactivism "as a particular version of the embodied cognition paradigm," notes, for enactivists the nervous system is an "autonomous adaptively dynamic system" that "actively generates and maintains its own coherent and meaningful patterns of activity, according to its operation as a self-organizing network of interacting neurons." This is in contrast to the standard view of the brain as processing pre-existing information, organized in code. Rather, the brain "creates information in concert with the rest of the body and the environment." Cognition can then be understood as "sense-making" and as the "exercise of skillful and situated know-how in situated and embodied action" (Thompson [1993] 2017: xxvi).

This is attractive as a general picture of an alternative to the standard model. It fits with such basic facts as the multimodal character of perception (Gallese 2008), the "recruitment" or use of sensorimotor parts of the brain in action and perception, and is a more plausible approach to the problem of evolutionary development than the acceptance of the mystery of the complete development *ex nihilo* of an elaborate innate syntactic or semantic system. And there are ways of connecting embodied action to higher thought processes, even to philosophical positions (Lakoff and Johnson 1980 [2003]). But Clark is right to think that there is a problem here with computationalism, or with what I have been calling here the problem of coding. The strength of the standard model is in building computational models of decisions and inferences, and getting empirical support by showing how well these models do in predicting actual behavior, usually in controlled settings. The alternative approaches have less to say, and typically prefer such concepts as "dynamic systems" or use direct mathematical relations (Chemero 2011), neither of which involve coding and transformations according to rules.[5]

The standard models of rational decision-making and inference required a high level of coded input, so much of the discussion of the issues between the standard model and its possible rivals has concerned "representations" or coded mental units and "representationalism," the doctrine that mental processing requires such units. There are many positions which attempt to combine some sort of representational approach with 4E alternatives. Clark (2015b: 4), for example, admits that while predictive processing "openly trades in talk of inner models and representations, [it only] involves representations that are action-oriented through and through." We need not resolve these issues here. But we can usefully consider the relevance of one of the oldest issues in this literature, from robotics, called "the frame problem" (McCarthy and Hayes 1969; Shanahan 1969; Pylyshyn 1987; McCarthy 2017). The frame problem arises in artificial intelligence (AI) contexts: how can one make a robot identify the relevant inputs for a decision, inference, and subsequent action when it is faced with a plethora of environmental stimuli? How can it frame a situation so that the machinery of inference and decision can operate? Treating robot behavior as a serious model of human cognition requires an answer to this: humans do this effortlessly and continuously, though not always without error. The question is how?

Predictive processing helps, potentially, with this problem: our cognitive relations with the world amount, for predictive processing, to a guessing game. We tacitly absorb the results of correct and false guessing, and consequently we select as relevant that which we have learned at a tacit level as predictive of future perceptions, which in turn are the result of our actions – so this gets us a model of cognitive interaction with the world that allows for the ecological, embedded, and enactive character of cognitive processes to be incorporated. The attempt to ally predictive processing has been critiqued by Dan Hutto, who has suggested ways to radicalize it. For him, predictive processing is still too cognitive, too attached to the standard model, and for reasons that are a variant of the frame problem: "the question of how the brain is able to get into the great guessing game in the first place" (Hutto 2017b: 2). This, as we have seen, was one of the issues with the hypothesis testing model of learning: it only works if one has hypotheses to test, but one cannot get them from the data. So where do they come from?

As Hutto points out, the model of the brain here is that of the scientist learning about the world. He quotes Hohwy (2013: 13), who says that:

> the problem of perception is the problem of using the effects – that is, the sensory data, that is all the brain has access to – to figure out the causes. It is then a problem of causal inference for the brain analogous in many respects to our everyday reasoning about cause and effect, and to the scientific methods of causal inference.
>
> *(Hutto 2017b: 7)*

He notes that Gerrans is even more forceful and direct on this issue: "a scientist explaining some discrepant evidence is *doing the same thing* as the oculomotor system controlling the trajectory of a limb" (Gerrans 2014: 46–7; quoted by Hutto 2017b: 7, adding emphasis).

Hutto's question is this: "Where does the brain get its conceptual resources and background knowledge so that it can represent information and making inferences?"

This points to the core problem of circularity in representationalism, and more generally in coding: where do the representations that are matched to the world come from in the first place? Clark's response is that this is done by an algorithm which operates in the rich and ever-changing world in the following way:

> the world can be relied upon to provide a training signal allowing us to compare current predictions with actual sensed patterns of energetic inputs. This allows well-understood learning algorithms to unearth rich information

about the interacting external causes that are actually structuring the incoming signal.

(Clark 2016: 19)

Hutto rejects this as an evasion of what he and Myin call the HPC – the hard problem of content – which "all explanatory naturalists competing to understand basic cognition must ultimately face up to." He notes that "a straight solution to the HPC requires explaining how it is possible to get from non-semantic, non-contentful informational foundations to a theory of content using only the resources of a respectable explanatory naturalism" (Hutto 2017b: 10). This is precisely what does not happen with algorithms processing "information" unless it has the semantic, combinatorial content in the first place. Looking at the brain does not help. As Rosenberg (2014: 26) says, "networks of human brain cells are no more capable of [intrinsically] representing facts about the world ... than are the neural ganglia of sea slugs!" But sea slug ganglia are good at some things: sea slugs were the animal models of choice for Eric Kandel because of their large ganglia, and he showed not only that they could learn, but also that they have long-term memory (Kandel and Spencer 1968; Hawkins and Kandel 1984; Kandel 1984; Hawkins et al. 1986; Manier 1986: 192). But learning is not representing. So the question becomes: do we need representation, or "content," to explain what needs to be explained? Hutto's response (2017b: 12) is to argue that "contentless embodied expectations of persons ... enabled in major part by brains" do the necessary work of prediction for actual organisms satisfying their specific needs, which do not need to construct a picture of the world in the manner of scientists. He thus, in the name of pure enactivism, rejects the need for the "inner models and internal representations" which are at the heart of the standard picture (Clark 2015b: 4; quoted in Hutto 2017b: 6). In the next section we will discuss the origins of the needs in question.

Despite the emphasis on organisms and ecology, social interaction and the social environment fit this approach – one is tempted to call it a paradigm – very well. The social environment is exactly that place in which massive amounts of input need to be processed, in which people need to find their way around in diverse settings with different groups of people, with their own complex expectations, patterns of behavior, and so on. It is this setting that requires mind-reading to navigate, as well as joint attention and much, much more. But there are issues with extending the paradigm to the human realm, to decision-making, to inferential thinking, and so forth.

It is perhaps useful to step back a bit and use the strategy of starting with the anomaly and solving the problems of the standard view on the basis of our solution to the anomalies. We have already noted the example of relevance given by Sperber: that relevance needs to be presumed by communication, and provides an alternative starting point for understanding communication. Similar considerations about relevance apply to such characteristically psychological phenomena as cognitive dissonance. As classically pointed out by Truzzi (1973), one cannot have dissonance without relevance – and this applies across the board. One cannot apply decision theory without having the frame – cognitive content, preferences, and so forth – that determines relevance. But where does the frame come from? This has been claimed to be a problem with simulation as well: we can choose to think in an as if way about the actions of others by analogizing to what we would do in the same situation; but the idea that this is done automatically in an unconscious way seems to require conditions to be met that can only be met on the conscious level, such as identifying the target of the analogy – a variant of the frame problem. Framing is a problem that is systematically obscured in experimental studies, which create situations in which additional information is unavailable or suppressed in order to create a purified environment which enables the experimenter to exclude alternative explanations. Cognition in the wild is very different.

The Action Model Reconsidered and Replaced

Explaining action using the reason-desire model or decision theory raises intractable problems that are both solved in part and made worse in other ways by modeling brain processes on conscious things, like choices, or things that can be semantically reconstructed, like inferences, which are familiar to us from intelligible sentences. The idea of intention is at the core of these issues – the reason-desire combination is taken to form an intention, which then explains the action. The quest becomes one of finding some neural correlate of this process of formation of intentions. There is, however, a big problem with the "intention" story, which undermines the implied sequence of events leading to action. Experiments done by Benjamin Libet, and repeated many times, show that the neural correlates of intentional acts precede consciousness of intention to act (Libet et al. 1983; Libet 1985). And this suggests a radical revision of the intention story. This requires some digressions.

The first digression involves the notion of intention itself. The intentional action model is odd because it does many jobs: it explains, or pseudo-explains; it relates the action in a logical or normative way to belief, as in a justification; it attributes a mental state; it justifies the use of these attributions for the purpose of making moral judgments and judgments about responsibility. But as an explanation of action is it problematic. The standard way of inferring an intention is to infer it from the actions taken by the "intending" person. But this is circular: the evidence for the intention is the same thing as the thing being explained. There are other ways to justify inferences about someone's intentions, but they are all dependent on this core circularity. One can, for example, cite the profession of an intention as evidence of intention, or the partial fulfillment of an intentional act as evidence for the intention of completing the act; but each of these forms of reasoning depends on there being a normal relationship between the intention and the act, and one can only establish this normal relationship circularly. This is what the 1950s' authors in the long-running reasons and causes debate had in mind when they said the relation was conceptual rather than causal, and what philosophers have in mind today when they characterize the relation between intention and act as "normative." It just doesn't work as a normal causal explanation, because we cannot identify the cause independently of the effect. There is, as the older literature had it, a conceptual connection between intention and act.

There is also an oddity about the nature of intention itself. There are at least two or three levels that need to be separated. The paradigm is some sort of conscious intentionality in the form of an action directed toward a goal with rationally selected means. This is also Weber's paradigmatic form of instrumental action. But there are lower levels as well, such as a kind of directionality, with some additional element that makes it more than the directionality of a falling rock, such as feedback. This is more or less the sense in which one also speaks of the intentional bias, and is presumably the basis of animism and similar beliefs, but is pre-verbal. We can think of this as a heuristic, prone to error as other heuristics are, but useful and "true" in the evolutionary sense. Then there is the empathic sense relevant to Weber's woodchopper, which amounts to knowing what someone is doing, which is also pre-verbal. These distinctions will turn out to be important.

A second digression is also needed. There is another aspect to intentions that is overtly "social." Although we think of intentions as intensely private, in the head, and accessible only to the agent, there is a public form of intention, and also of belief and desire. They can all take the form of declarations. This is especially evident in Needham's account of the linguistic variations with the terms for belief. They include, for example a Navajo language in which "to believe" is the same as "to obey" (Needham 1972: 32–3). This social and declarative aspect of belief is usually treated as incidental; but, in accordance with the strategy of starting with the anomalies, let us treat it as central. Intention talk needs to be learned. It can only be learned socially. There is no way, as we know from Wittgenstein's private language argument, for us to learn how to locate and identify private mental objects apart from learning to use expressions and signs. And it is language with effects on others.

One can then ask: what do we do when we attribute intentions, beliefs, or desires? There is a standard story, coming from Davidson (1963), which assumes the folk psychological account. We infer beliefs, desires, and error by triangulation, an inference which works by using our knowledge or assumptions about two of the three elements – that is the beliefs, the desires, or the actual state of the world to which they refer – to infer the third element or to infer error if the action does not match the belief. The inferences of course assume the validity of the model of action itself. And we can ask the question of whether this model, and our folk psychology on which it depends, is true or a cultural artifact. This is not, it should be noted, a question of whether the model can be used in social science. It can be used in a Weberian sense, which is to say as an indispensable part of our means of making action understandable to a particular cultural and historical community which employs these concepts.

If we start from the outside rather than the inaccessible inside of the mind, we can say the following, which fits with Needham's interesting list of terms that combine with "belief": declarations of intentions, beliefs, and desires are speech acts. The speech act can be understood to be the primary sense of the use of these concepts; that is, that other uses, such as the attribution of beliefs to others, depend on this primary sense: they are learned on the basis of learning this primary use. We can derive attributions of undeclared intentions, beliefs, and so on from the primary sense as declaration. To say "I believe x" is not to consult one's inner mental state and pull out a belief from a filing case in long-term memory, but to make a promise-like statement with public consequences; nor is attributing an intention an act of going into the mind of the other and identifying its contents. An undeclared intention or belief can be understood as follows: to say someone has a belief or intention is to say that they would, if prompted, sincerely declare the intention or belief. To say that one had an undeclared belief or intention of one's own is to say that one would sincerely declare it. This is a secondary or derived usage: declaration is primary.

Understanding intention talk in this way allows us to separate two things: the cultural practice and the problem of explaining experimental facts about intention and belief. The primitive form of empathy and intention ascription is pre-verbal, but attuned to such things as "false belief" detection. One must take care not to read into these capacities a "concept" of intention or of "belief." All that ascription of intention means in such contexts as infant intention detection is determining what a person is doing, as in Weber's woodchopper example. Solving the "false belief" problem, similarly, does not require a concept of "belief" at all, since what is being detected is what the person appears to be doing and the mismatch between what the person appears to be doing and the facts about the setting known to the detector. This may require some minimal sense of directionality – the sense necessary to distinguish an action from the motion of an object, such as a falling rock. Directionality, which is part of the list of universal semantic items, needs to be something more than motion in a direction – perhaps motion with apparent feedback, or motion with accompanying signs that it is more than pure motion. But this sense is the kind of thing we can associate with evolutionary truth: it is important for people and animals to make this distinction. It does not validate a theory of intentions and beliefs as mental objects.

By making this separation between intentions as mental objects and intentions as part of a cultural practice we can assign intentional language to other sources: we can take it to be the product of innate semantics; as a part of an implicit cultural theory of the mental; or as a narrative form used to communicate about the results of our primitive empathy, in identifying what someone is doing. We can abandon, or bracket, the mentalistic concepts of intention and belief themselves, and look for a replacement that better fits with such things as the Libet results. This may seem like a very tall order: the standard belief-desire model of action explanation is deeply entrenched, both in our own culture and in the discourse that social science and philosophy have constructed based on it. Nevertheless, it is worth seeing what a replacement might look like, if only to open a discussion of what it would look like to have an approach that could bridge the gap between the understanding of action through empathy and the known facts about cognitive processes. This will need to be a radical exercise, simply because the known facts have been described in terms of the concepts of belief and intention.

An Alternative Account of Action

If we start with the classic Weberian discussion of action, we get this: the paradigm of action is a rational, conscious selection of appropriate means to ends, followed by the action itself. We understand actions that fall short of this standard as though they were intentional, and we have an intentionalizing bias which leads us to attribute intentionality to acts that are marginally intentional, such as habitual actions. At the extreme limits of the concept of action are involuntary acts, acts which seem to have some directionality but lack the rest of what makes an action intentional, such as conscious choice. These are the anomalies of the conventional account of action. If we then apply the strategy of starting with the anomalies, we would take involuntary action as the paradigm of action, and explain fully conscious, rational action in terms of this paradigm.

Is there involuntary action? Weber and the neuroscience literature (Ioannou et al. 2016) provide us with the example of contagion, which is both involuntary and a primitive form of empathy. And we can provide many more, especially from animals: the mammal running for cover when the shadow of a hawk passes over, our reactions to snakes, and so forth. There is even evidence of a syndrome in adults in which actions are involuntarily imitated, which fits with mirror neurons and the idea, which we will pursue below, that a major component of action is inhibition – something marginal to the standard account of action. We can, of course, construct, Gallistel-style, accounts of all of these things which make them appear to be rational choices and involve complex boxological sequences. But this would also attribute mental gymnastics where the processes may be much simpler and more direct.

We can construct a model of action in these cases based on some core ideas in the literature. One comes from Herbert Simon, who is often excoriated for his suggestion that the study of cognition could and should be pursued separately from other cognitive neuroscience topics until it is well enough understood to be integrated into a larger picture. But Simon's attempts to apply artificial intelligence methods to the task of mimicking cognitive processes, which included some successes, were more interesting for their failures, or for what they revealed about the differences between what could be neatly modeled and what could not – leading to such notions as bounded rationality and ill-structured problems. One of the topics that especially engaged him was intuition, which he came to understand as subconscious pattern recognition (see Frantz 2003). The key to this concept is that pattern recognition is involuntary. We can, of course, seek patterns. But recognizing them is itself neither voluntary nor something we can reduce to calculation or decision-making. Indeed, it precedes decision-making, choosing, and so forth, as well as anything that might correspond to the forming of intentions. And recognizing a pattern causes actions on its own.

Simon and his collaborators worked on chess. And they immediately recognized that grandmasters do not think in the way that an ordinary computer program would: by projecting moves far into the future and deciding between them on the basis of projected consequences, a strategy that required massive computational power. Instead, they developed a "chunking" theory, which:

> suggests that chess skill depends on memory of specific patterns of pieces on the board. Essentially, grandmasters are stronger because they know more patterns ... and ... makes the assumption that chess mastery stems from knowing thousands of chess patterns. Recognition of one of these patterns during play is said to trigger the memory of an associated plausible move, which may then be selected or investigated by the player. Hence chess skill depends on memory.
>
> (Gobet and Simon 1998: 204, citing Holding 1992: 10)

In Chase and Simon's classic 1973 paper on this, they argued that:

> When the master is staring at a chessboard trying to choose his next move, he is engaged in a forward search through some kind of problem space and that when the move is made in the mind's eye – that is, when the internal representation of the position is updated – the result is then passed back through the pattern perception system and new patterns are perceived. These patterns in turn will suggest new moves, and the search continues.
>
> (Gobet and Simon 1998: 205)

This is a rough and partial model, but useful for human action as well.

Lawrence Barsalou has applied a notion of pattern recognition to social settings and what he calls "situations." He argues that "mirroring is a special case of a basic cognitive process common across species, namely, Pattern Completion Inferences within Situated Conceptualizations (PCIwSC)." This would be a cognitive process similar to predictive processing, but operating on situations rather than perceptual states. According to PCIwSC, the brain is a situation-processing architecture (see Barsalou 2003; Barsalou 2009; Barsalou et al. 2003;

Wilson-Mendenhall et al. 2011; Yeh and Barsalou 2006; Leonard et al. 2016). It works as follows:

> In a given situation, multiple networks implement parallel processing streams that perceive and conceptualize various elements of the situation, including the setting, self, other agents, objects, actions, events, interoceptive states, and mental states. For example, the para-hippocampal gyrus and parietal lobes process the spatial setting; regions of the cortical midline process self and others; the ventral stream processes objects; the motor system processes actions; and so forth. As individual elements of the current situation are perceived and conceptualized, higher-order configural conceptualizations in turn integrate these elemental conceptualizations into a coherent account of what is occurring more globally across the situation. Together, all conceptualizations of the situation across the elemental and configural levels are assembled into a situated conceptualization (SC) that represents and interprets the situation.
>
> *(Barsalou 2013: 2951)*

This formulation explicitly avoids boxology and mental gymnastics: the processing is parallel and simultaneous rather than a sequential set of combinatorial information-transforming processes.

We can bracket and ignore the terminology of concepts, interpretation, and so forth, which tends to anthropomorphize the process and point toward a model of a background semantic system, which is not implied by the argument. All that is really needed in this account is a notion of pattern recognition and the idea that it is a given pattern as a whole that is recognized when the different kinds of stimulation are found together. This gives an account of what happens in meaningful social interaction:

> when some friends wave at you from across the street, an SC of this event conceptualizes the setting as a street, the other people as your friends, their action as waving, and their mental state as friendly. At the configural level, these local conceptualizations are integrated into a coherent meaningful event, with your friends recognizing you, experiencing pleasure on seeing you, and greeting you. The pattern is then "stored in memory" ... and "can be cued later when a similar situation is encountered again, or when just part of the original situation is perceived." Once it is in memory – which need not take repetitive learning – it produces pattern completion inferences (PCIs). On seeing your friends across the street again, for example, the SC stored on the previous occasion might become active and simulate them waving to you as a prediction, further preparing you to wave back and feel positive affect.
>
> *(Barsalou 2013: 2951, quoting (Barsalou 1999; Barsalou 2008))*

This kind of pattern completion inference has implications far beyond such overtly "social" situations. Recall that one of the problems solved by the semantic part of the standard model was that it accounted for human inferential capacities. It did so by modeling them on logic, with premises and conclusions. The idea that there was a structure of implicit inferential rules underlying ordinary speech and reasoning – even an innate one, but possibly only a cultural one – was motivated in part by the phenomenon of enthymemes, and of the fact that we take speech acts to have logical or semantic implications beyond their explicit content. We can think of the idea of a hidden structure of this sort as a wholesale solution to the problem of explaining implications of these kinds. Pattern completion inferences, however, do the same work – but, so to speak, on a retail level. It is necessary only for us to have the capacity to recognize patterns and fill in the missing parts. In the case of the kinds of inferences and enthymemes that motivate the semantic account, the filling in happens when we recognize a pattern that is not complete and fill in the missing parts – the suppressed premise or implication, in these cases. Rather than posit a vast implicit semantic system, we need only think that people recognize and remember many patterns. The patterns need not fit together in a vast whole: they can be and are overlapping, redundant, chunking, and conflicting in the neural responses they invoke (Nelson et al. 2017).

There is another important implication of the idea of pattern recognition and pattern completion. Patterns are not simply semantic: they are learned and recognized in ways that involve multiple parts of the brain at the same time, including such things as affect and the sensorimotor system. And this solves another problem. It is common for enactivists to criticize the standard model and its accounts as overly cognitive, meaning that they reduce cognitive processes to computer-like processes. Barsalou stresses that the components of situated conceptualization (SC) are spread across the brain, and utilize the motor system. In this respect it fits with the stress of enactivism on the basis of activity being in the sensorimotor system. But Barsalou adds an important component: the social.

The patterns include not just perceptions of objects, but "social" elements. Almost all learning, for example, involves a social context, with affectual relations between the participants. Even the learning of simple arithmetic involves the child mind-reading the teacher, feeling authority, and following the patterns provided in the setting for doing math problems: the habitualized methods of responding, of physical elements such as chalk and blackboards, the writing of formulae on them, and the production of inferences. These elements are part of a pattern that students will recognize over and over, and "enact" in response to. The difference is this: pattern-completion inferences do not require reconstruction in terms of premises and conclusions. Premises, conclusions, suppressed premises, implications, and the like are subsumed in patterns, which can be recognized even when they are partially filled in, and can be filled in on the basis of the larger pattern. This may be relevant to some of the mysteries of learning that motivate innateness theorizing: if we consider that it is remarkable that someone learns a word on one try, it may be instead that learning that word is just one piece of a larger pattern of a learning situation with multiple elements – including expectations, emotions, and so forth – that is already well established in experience and which adding a new word merely fills in, as a slightly different variant of the pattern of word learning.

This approach fits with what is known about the enormous human capacity to fill in blanks in this way, and to find patterns even in random assemblages. The process is not error free, and is in a sense overloaded on the side of finding patterns: we are routinely misled by our pattern-recognition capacity (Shermer 2008).

Nevertheless, it is open to improvement. A simple example of this involves experiments in the mirror neuron literature on the identification of motion mentioned earlier. Subjects were shown videos of persons walking in the dark with reflective pads so that only three data points were visible. They were nevertheless able to identify the motions without difficulty, unconsciously filling in the data points. As noted before, when experiments were done on ballet dancers, it was found that they responded more successfully in identifying particular moves than non-ballet dancers, and that women and men ballet dancers were better at doing this for the moves associated with male and female performances (Calvo-Merino et al. 2006; Cross et al. 2006). This showed the link between pattern recognition and sensorimotor capacities. But the lesson is much broader: pattern recognition and filling in are basic cognitive capacities; they are part of skilled performance and improve with embodied experience.

One of the problems with the semantic model of mind, as the earlier extract in Chapter 3 from Sperber and Wilson (1986: 162) indicated, was relevance. Relevance occurs, so to speak, offstage, in the context in which the inferences or utterances are made, which provides the conditions under which the utterances make sense. Applying semantic machinery requires a determination of relevance and context that cannot be done within the semantic machinery itself. More generally, codes need to be specified first and then fed into the combinatorial process. They are not self-specifying. Pattern recognition avoids this issue entirely: the pattern is the determinant of context and relevance; or, to put it differently, the relevant context is part of the pattern. It needs only to be recognized as a pattern: stage and offstage are part of the pattern. This can obviously misfire – we can think we have recognized our friend across the square and wave to them, only to discover it was someone else.

Conscious Effort

We can now combine this picture of cognition as pattern recognition and completion inference with our preliminary account of action. All the elements described here are involuntary or "mandatory" in the usual cognitive science terminology. When Barsalou discusses "interpretation" as something going on in the brain, for example, he is not describing an analogue to self-conscious hermeneutical interpretation of a text, but is thinking about it in the way that Wittgenstein is when he argues that rule-following is not a matter of "interpreting" a rule: it is a direct, unwarrantable, regress-stopping step (Wittgenstein [1953] 1958: 86–8). But action itself cannot be mandatory. Or can it? Contagion is an example of this; empathic responses of the kind measured in fMRI studies would be another – they might lead at least to involuntary flinching. Mirror neuron research shows activity in the action part of the sensorimotor system in response to perception. But alongside the mirror neuron system and the perceptual system are inhibitors: neuron connections that serve to suppress action (Quast et al. 2017). So a plausible take on the problem of explaining action might be this: patterns are recognized; the relevant brain systems are activated by this, including the action system; and action follows if it is a strong enough stimulation, or the right kind – the snake or the hawk's shadow – to produce the action involuntarily and unconsciously. These are the "normal" cases; consciousness is something that arrives when things go wrong. As one blog puts it:

> The brain is essentially a pattern recognition machine, constantly making predictions. Our perception is a combination of our prior expectations – expressed in the form of these automatic predictions – and actual sensory perception. As long as the sensory information matches the predictions, the brain hums along. When there is dissonance, the brain steps into make a correction.
>
> *(Piore 2017: n.p.)*

We have some good models for the ways in which consciousness goes together with things going wrong. There is the famous and much discussed case of the second baseman, Chuck Knoblauch, who was unable to make simple throws to first base (Dreyfus 2007a: esp. 354; also Dreyfus 2007b). In this case, these throws were something that he trained for, were "automatic," and did not require other than minimal "consciousness" and no process of decision, especially in the routine cases. Nevertheless, when Knoblauch thought about what he was doing, he made errors. And this is a common experience: if one is going unthinkingly through a routine, such as driving a car to a familiar destination, and one is prompted or challenged, one experiences a moment of confusion. It is plausible to say that in these cases two patterns come into conflict in the sense that they activate conflicting responses. The habitual driving pattern says "you are on the right path," while the prompt or challenge indicates that you should check your actions, or pull back.[6] Research on the trolley problem points in a similar direction: the problem involves a choice that needs to be made quickly, either to save people by pushing a man onto the track and blocking an errant trolley, or doing nothing and allowing the people to be killed. These represent two different but also familiar patterns that turn out to invoke different responses in different parts of the brain. This is a common pattern. In the case of the trolley problem, Greene et al. (2004: 395–6) found that the selection of a more utilitarian choice revealed a conflict between the "rational" and "emotional" systems. Additionally, they found activation in the anterior cingulate cortex, an area in which activation is thought to reflect conflict between competing brain processes (see also Mulert et al. 2005).The anterior cingulate cortex is associated with "conscious effort" and elements of consciousness itself, such as self-consciousness, as well as such things as embarrassment. "Self-conscious emotions such as embarrassment arise when one's actions fail to meet salient social expectations and are accompanied by marked physiological and behavioral activation" (Sturm et al. 2013: 468).

Lesion studies support this picture of conflict in the case of the trolley problem:

> brain damaged patients more often chose to push the man off the bridge to save the five people on the tracks. This is presumably because they didn't experience an emotional signal (which would normally have been reflected via activity in the mPFC) that would prevent them from endorsing such an action, thereby allowing deliberative mental processes to reign supreme. Simply put, these patients' lack of emotional response led them to the more rational choice.
>
> *(Damasio 1994; quoted in Johnson 2010: n.p.)*

But this same kind of brain damage:

> leads to a much larger set of deficits, including difficulties making economic decisions as well as a tendency to exhibit exaggerated anger, irritability, emotional outbursts and tantrums, particularly in social situations involving frustration or provocation. People with this kind of brain damage also often have difficulty making sound economic decisions.
>
> *(Damasio 1994; in Johnson 2010: n.p.)*

This suggests a complex picture of cognitive conflict which works both through higher-level pattern recognition, such as recognizing the trolley problem as a conflict between emotion and reason, and the suppression of one side of the conflict. Some researchers on charisma claim this occurs in response to emotional speakers by religious believers:

> emotional speakers engage with a neural pathway called the default mode network (DMN). This pathway, also known as the task-negative network, spans multiple areas of the brain (including the amygdala) and is associated with daydreaming, thoughts about others, and remembering things in the past. Interestingly, its activation is often found to be *negatively* correlated with the very circuits we rely upon for analytic thinking – those involved in

executive functions, planning, reasoning, attention, and problem-solving. Interpretations of these conflicts are controversial. "The problem is these two networks have almost no overlap," Boyatzis said. "They suppress each other."

(Piore 2017; emphasis in original. See also Boyatzis et al. 2014)

But others claim the emotional and rational "networks" are closely interdependent.

For our purposes we have no need to settle this question. With this pattern-recognition account we have an alternative to the standard account. The take-away is that most of what the brain does in relation to action is "mandatory" and inaccessible: it is part of the "Background." Rational control of action is something that follows these "mandatory" operations in the background, such as pattern recognition, and works on the conflicts that arise from these operations. "Decision," because of the frame problem, requires prior pattern recognition, which defines the space of decision. Consciousness of these processes, as one would expect from the Libet results, is limited or non-existent; and consciousness of choice is a late outcome, dependent on pattern recognition and perhaps no more than an instance of pattern completion inference rather than a simple determinant of action, as the standard intentional account of action would have it. This approach avoids some major problems with the standard approach to action: it does not depend on positing spooky and problematic mental entities such as intentions. In this case, posits beget posits, such as the posited tacit theory that is the supposed basis of mind-reading. Each of these posits brings its own problems, of the sort admitted by Chomsky: it is a mystery as to how these tacit theories got there. Moreover, the pattern recognition approach allows us to come closer to the physical reality of the brain itself.

Barsalou adds something important to enactivism, which claims that the standard brain as computer approach is too cognitivist. He adds the body and the physical context, the social context, which is incorporated into pattern recognition of situations. In the next chapter we will deal with context, and especially the social context, in more detail, but in terms of the cognitive science concepts that allow us to add to the accounts we have been discussing. We are, nevertheless, still very far from traditional social science issues. In the next chapter we can begin to address some of them.

Notes

1 Even social institutions can be accounted for in this way. See Guala (2016).
2 A vast number of highly diverse examples of mind talk are given here: http://metaphors. iath.virginia.edu/.
3 This is suggested as well in the neuroscience literature (Nickerson et al. 2009: 50). We can think of this "empathically" in terms of joint attention. In cases of joint attention, which has been shown to involve mirror neurons in primates, we "attend" not only to the object but also to the responses of the others attending to the object.

4 There are good reasons, which I will not elaborate here, for thinking that these are the limits of social science generally, because all social science rests, ultimately, on explanations that depend on some form of "understanding" rather than something like natural laws.

5 As Hutto puts it, radicalizing enactivism "only appeals to the scientifically well-grounded notion of information-as covariance. Understood in terms of covariance, a state of affairs carries information about another state of affairs just in case it lawfully co-varies with that other state of affairs, to some specified extent" (Hutto and Myin 2012: xvi). He gives as an example of this the relation of rings on a tree to the age of the tree. Chemero (2011) supplies multiple examples.

6 Mindfulness as a kind of therapy is one concern of the enactivist literature, and one might think of this as a method of disrupting habitual patterns to bring about change.

References

Ammaniti, Massimo and Vittorio Gallese. (2014). *The Birth of Intersubjectivity: Psychodynamics, Neurobiology, and the Self.* New York: Norton.

Andrews, Kristin. (2004). "How to Learn from Our Mistakes: Explanation and Moral Justification." *Philosophical Explorations* 7(3): 247–263.

Andrews, Kristin. (2012). *Do Apes Read Minds? Toward a New Folk Psychology.* Cambridge, MA: MIT Press.

Barsalou, Lawrence W., P. M. Niedenthal, A. Barbey, and J. Ruppert. (2003). "Social Embodiment." In B. Ross (ed.) *The Psychology of Learning and Motivation,* 43–92. San Diego, CA: Academic Press.

Barsalou, L. W. (1999). "Perceptual Symbol Systems." *Behavioral and Brain Sciences* 22: 577–660.

Barsalou, L. W. (2003). "Situated Simulation in the Human Conceptual System." *Language and Cognitive Processes* 18: 513–562.

Barsalou, L. W. (2008). "Grounded Cognition." *Annual Review of Psychology* 59: 617–645.

Barsalou, L. W. (2009). "Simulation, Situated Conceptualization, and Prediction." *Philosophical Transactions of the Royal Society of London: Biological Sciences,* 364: 1281–1289.

Barsalou, L. W. (2013). "Mirroring as Pattern Completion Inferences within Situated Conceptualizations." *Cortex* 49: 2951–2953.

Boyatzis, R. E., K. Rochford, and A. I. Jack. (2014). "Antagonistic Neural Networks Underlying Differentiated Leadership Roles." *Frontiers in Human Neuroscience* 8: 114–129.

Brentano, Franz. ([1930] 1966). *The True and the Evident,* ed. O. Kraus; trans. R. M. Chisholm, I. Politzer, and K. R. Fischer. London: Routledge & Kegan Paul.

Calvo-Merino, Beatriz, Julia Grèzes, Daniel E. Glaser, Richard E. Passingham, and Patrick Haggard. (2006). "Seeing or Doing? Influence of Visual and Motor Familiarity in Action Observation." *Current Biology* 16: 1905–1910.

Chase, W. O. and H. A. Simon (1973). "The Mind's Eye in Chess" In W. G. Chase (ed.) *Visual Information Processing,* 215–282. New York: Academic Press.

Chemero, Anthony. (2011). *Radical Embodied Cognitive Science.* Cambridge, MA: MIT Press.

Choi, You-jung and Yuyan Luo. 2015. "13-Month-Old's Understanding of Social Interactions." *Psychological Science* 26(3): 274–283.

Churchland, Patricia. (1989). *Neurophilosophy: Toward a Unified Science of the Mind-Brain.* Cambridge, MA: MIT Press.

Clark, Andy. (2015a). "Embodied Prediction." In T. Metzinger and J. M. Windt (eds.) *Open MIND*: 7(T), n.p. Frankfurt am Main: MIND Group. doi: 10.15502/9783958570115http://open-mind.net/DOI?isbn=9783958570115.

Clark, Andy. (2015b). "Predicting Peace: An End to the Representation Wars. A Reply to Michael Madary." In T. Metzinger and J. M. Windt (eds.) *Open MIND*: 7(R), n.p. Frankfurt am Main: MIND Group. http://open-mind.net/DOI?isbn=9783958570115.

Clark, Andy. (2015c). "Radical Predictive Processing." *Southern Journal of Philosophy* 53: 3–27.

Clark, Andy. (2016). *Surfing Uncertainty: Prediction, Action, and the Embodied Mind*. Oxford: Oxford University Press.

Cross, Emily S., Antonia F. de C. Hamilton, and Scott Grafton. (2006). "Building a Motor Simulation de Novo: Observation of Dance by Dancers." *NeuroImage* 31: 1257–1267.

Damasio, A.R. (1994). *Descartes' Error: Emotion, Reason and the Human Brain*. New York: Putnam.

Davidson, Donald. (1963). "Actions, Reasons and Causes." *Journal of Philosophy* 60: 685–700.

Decety, Jean and William Ickes, eds. (2009). *The Social Neuroscience of Empathy*. Cambridge, MA: MIT Press.

Dreyfus, Hubert L. (2007a). "The Return of the Myth of the Mental." *Inquiry: An Interdisciplinary Journal of Philosophy* 50(4): 352–365.

Dreyfus, Hubert L. (2007b). "Response to McDowell." *Inquiry: An Interdisciplinary Journal of Philosophy* 50(4): 371–377.

Frantz, Roger. (2003). "Herbert Simon: Artificial Intelligence as a Framework for Understanding Intuition." *Journal of Economic Psychology* 24: 265–277.

Gallagher, Shaun. (2001). "The Practice of Mind: Theory, Simulation or Primary Interaction?" *Journal of Consciousness Studies* 8(5–7): 83–108.

Gallagher, Shaun. (2004). "Understanding Interpersonal Problems in Autism: Interaction Theory as an Alternative to Theory of Mind." *Philosophy, Psychiatry, and Psychology* 11(3): 199–217.

Gallagher, Shaun. (2012). "Neurons, Neonates and Narrative: From Embodied Resonance to Empathic Understanding." In A. Foolen, U. Lüdtke, J. Zlatev, and T. Racine (eds.) *Moving Ourselves, Moving Others: Motion and Emotion in Intersubjectivity, Consciousness and Language*, 167–196. Amsterdam: Benjamins.

Gallese, Vittorio. (2008). "Mirror Neurons and the Social Nature of Language: The Neural Exploitation Hypothesis." *Social Neuroscience* 3(3): 317–333.

Gallistel, C. R. (2011). "Prelinguistic Thought" *Language Learning and Development* 7: 253–262.

Gerrans, P. (2014). *The Measure of Madness*. Cambridge, MA: MIT Press.

Gobet, Fernand and Herbert A. Simon. (1998). "Pattern Recognition Makes Search Possible: Comments on Holding (1992)." *Psychological Research* 61: 204–208.

Gopnik, Alison and Henry M. Wellman. (1992). "Why the Child's Theory of Mind Really Is a Theory." *Mind & Language* 7(1–2): 145–171.

Greene, Josh, L. Nystrom, A. Engell, J. Darley, and J. Cohen. (2004). "The Neural Bases of Cognitive Conflict and Control in Moral Judgment." *Neuron* 44(2): 389–400.

Guala, Francesco. (2016). *Understanding Institutions: The Science and Philosophy of Living Together*. Princeton, NJ: Princeton University Press.

Hawkins, R. D. and Eric R. Kandel. (1984). "Is There a Cell Biological Alphabet for Simple Forms of Learning?" *Psychological Review* 91: 375–391.

Hawkins, R. D., Gregory Clark, and E. R. Kandel. (1986). "Cell Biological Studies of Learning in Simple Vertebrate and Invertebrate Systems." In *Handbook of Physiology*. Bethesda, MD: American Physiological Society.

Hobson, R.Peter. (2007). "We Share, Therefore We Think." In Daniel D. Hutto and Matthew Ratcliffe (eds.) *Folk Psychology Re-Assessed*, 41–61. Dordrecht: Springer.

Hohwy, Jakob. (2013). *The Predictive Mind*. Oxford: Oxford University Press.

Holding, D. H. (1992). "Theories of Chess Skill." *Psychological Research* 54: 10–16.

Hutto, Daniel D. (2004). "The Limits of Spectatorial Folk Psychology." *Mind & Language* 19(5): 548–573.

Hutto, Daniel D. (2008). *Folk Psychological Narratives: The Sociocultural Basis of Understanding Reasons.* Cambridge, MA: MIT Press.

Hutto, Daniel D. (2012). "Exposing the Background: Deep and Local." In Z. Radman (ed.) *Knowing without Thinking: Mind, Action, Cognition and the Phenomenon of the Background*, 37–56. Basingstoke: Palgrave Macmillan.

Hutto, Daniel D. (2017a). "Book Review. Andy Clark *Surfing Uncertainty: Prediction, Action and the Embodied Mind.*" *Australasian Journal of Philosophy*: 1–4. http://dx.doi.org/10.1080/00048402.2016.1274769.

Hutto, Daniel D. (2017b) "Getting into Predictive Processing's Great Guessing Game: Bootstrap Heaven or Hell?" *Synthese*, 1–14. http://dx.doi.org/10.1007/s11229-017-1385-0 (accessed 20 June 2017).

Hutto, Daniel D. and Erik Myin. (2012) *Radicalizing Enactivism: Basic Minds without Content.* Cambridge, MA: MIT Press.

Ioannou, Stephanos, Paul Morris, Samantha Terry, Marc Baker, Vittorio Gallese, and Vasudevi Reddy. (2016). "Sympathy Crying: Insights from Infrared Thermal Imaging on a Female Sample." *PLoS ONE* 11(10): e0162749. www.ncbi.nlm.nih.gov/pmc/articles/PMC5055358/ (accessed 27 April 2017).

Johnson, David Charles. (2010). "The Rational Vulcan." *Neuropoly*, 23 May. https://neuropoly.com/tag/trolley-problem/ (accessed 16 March 2017).

Kandel, E. R. and W. A. Spencer. (1968). "Cellular Neurophysiological Approaches to the Study of Learning." *Physiological Review* 48: 65–134.

Kandel, Eric R. (1984). "Steps toward a Molecular Grammar for Learning: Explorations into the Nature of Memory." In K. J. Isselbacher (ed.) *Medicine, Science, and Society*, 555–604. New York: Wiley.

Knobe, J. (2003). "Intentional Action in Folk Psychology: An Experimental Investigation." *Philosophical Psychology* 16: 309–324.

Lakoff, George and Mark Johnson. ([1980] 2003). *Metaphors We Live By.* Chicago, IL: University of Chicago Press.

Lee, Young-eun, Jung-eun Ellie Yun, Eun Young Kim, and Hyun-joo Song. (2015). "The Development of Infants' Sensitivity to Behavioral Intentions when Inferring Others' Social Preferences." *PLoS ONE* 10(9): 1–16. doi:10.1371/journal.pone.01355.

Leonard, Matthew K., Maxime O. Baud, Matthias J. Sjerps, and Edward F. Chang. (2016). "Perceptual Restoration of Masked Speech in Human Cortex." *Nature Communications* 7. www.nature.com/articles/ncomms13619.

Libet, B., C. A. Gleason, E. W. Wright, and E. K. Pearl. (1983). "Time of Conscious Intention to Act in Relation to Onset of Cerebral Activity (Readiness-Potential): The Unconscious Initiation of a Freely Voluntary Act." *Brain* 106(3): 623–642.

Libet, Benjamin. (1985). "Unconscious Cerebral Initiative and the Role of Conscious Will in Voluntary Action." *Behavioral and Brain Sciences* 8(4): 529–539.

Mameli, M. (2001). "Mindreading, Mindshaping, and Evolution." *Biology and Philosophy* 16: 597–628.

Manier, Ed. (1986). "Problems in the Development of Cognitive Neuroscience, Effective Communication between Scientific Domains." *Proceedings of the Biennial Meeting of the Philosophy of Science Association* 1986(1): 183–197.

McCarthy, J. and P. J. Hayes. (1969). "Some Philosophical Problems from the Standpoint of Artificial Intelligence." *Machine Intelligence* 4: 463–502.

McCarthy, John. (2017). "The Frame Problem." Wikipedia. https://en.wikipedia.org/wiki/Frame_problem.

McGeer, V. (2007). "The Regulative Dimension of Folk Psychology." In D. Hutto and M. Ratliff (eds.) *Folk Psychology Re-Assessed*, 138–156. Dordrecht: Springer.

Menary, Richard. (2010). "Cognitive Integration and the Extended Mind." in Richard Menary (ed.) *The Extended Mind*, 227–243. Cambridge, MA: MIT Press.

Mercier, Hugo and Dan Sperber. (2011). "Why Do Humans Reason? Arguments for an Argumentative Theory." *Behavioral and Brain Sciences* 34: 57–111.

Mercier, Hugo and Dan Sperber. (2017). *The Enigma of Reason*. Cambridge, MA: Harvard University Press.

Morton, Adam. (1996). "Folk Psychology is Not a Predictive Device." *Mind* 105: 119–137.

Mulert, Christoph, Elisabeth Menzinger, Gregor Leicht, Oliver Pogarell, and Ulrich Hegerl. (2005). "Evidence for a Close Relationship between Conscious Effort and Anterior Cingulate Cortex Activity." *International Journal of Psychophysiology* 56: 65–80.

Munévar, Gonzalo (2014). "Damasio, Self and Consciousness." *Philosophia Scientiæ* 3: 191–201. www.cairn.info/revue-philosophia-scientiae-2014-3-page-191.htm.

Needham, Robert. (1972). *Belief, Language, and Experience*. Chicago, IL: University of Chicago Press.

Nelson, Matthew J., Imen El Karoui, Kristof Giber, Xiaofang Yang, Laurent Cohen, Hilda Koopman, Sydney S. Cash, Lionel Naccache, John T. Hale, Christophe Pallier, and Stanislas Dehaene. (2017). "Neurophysiological Dynamics of Phrase-Structure Building during Sentence Processing." *Proceedings of the National Academy of Sciences* (*PNAS*) 114(18). www.pnas.org/content/early/2017/04/11/1701590114.full.pdf (accessed 27 April 2017).

Nickerson, R. S., Butler, S. F., and Carlin, M. (2009). "Empathy and Knowledge Projection." In J. Decety and W. Ickes (eds.) *The Social Neuroscience of Empathy*, 43–56. Cambridge, MA: MIT Press.

Piore, Adam. (2017). "The Anatomy of Charisma: What Makes a Person Magnetic and Why We Should Be Wary." *Nautilus*, 16 February. http://nautil.us/issue/45/power/the-anatomy-of-charisma?utm_source=frontpage&utm_medium=mview&utm_campaign=the-anatomy-of-charisma.

Pylyshyn, Zenon. (1987). *The Robots Dilemma: The Frame Problem in Artificial Intelligence*. Westport, CT: Praeger.

Quast, Kathleen B., Kevin Ung, Emmanouil Froudarakis, Longwen Huang, Isabella Herman, Angela P. Addison, Joshua Ortiz-Guzman, Keith Cordiner, Peter Saggau, Andreas S. Tolias, and Benjamin R. Arenkiel. (2017). "Developmental Broadening of Inhibitory Sensory Maps." *Nature Neuroscience* 20: 189–199.

Richardson, Michael J., Rick Dale, and Kerry Marsh. (2014). "Complex Dynamical Systems in Social and Personality Psychology: Theory, Modeling, and Analysis." In Harry T. Reis and Charles M. Judd (eds.) *Handbook of Research Methods in Social and Personality Psychology* 2nd edn, 253–282. Cambridge: Cambridge University Press.

Robbins, Joel. (2008). "On Not Knowing Other Minds: Confession, Intention, and Linguistic Exchange in a Papua New Guinea Community." *Anthropological Quarterly* 81(2): 421–429.

Robbins, Joel and Alan Rumsey. (2008). "Introduction: Cultural and Linguistic Anthropology and the Opacity of Other Minds." *Anthropological Quarterly* 81(2): 407–420.

Rosch, Eleanor. ([1993] 2017). "Introduction to the Revised Edition." In Francisco J. Varela, Evan Thompson and Eleanor Rosch, *The Embodied Mind: Cognitive Science and Human Experience*, xxxv–lvi. Cambridge, MA: MIT Press.

Rosenberg, Alexander. (2014). "Disenchanted Naturalism." In B. Bashour and H. D. Muller (eds.) *Contemporary Philosophical Naturalism and Its Implications*, 17–36. London: Routledge.

Rosset, Evelyn (2008) "It's No Accident: Our Bias for Intentional Explanations." *Cognition* 108: 771–780.

Sakkalou, Elena and Merideth Gattis (2012). "Infants Infer Intentions from Prosody." *Cognitive Development* 27: 1–16.

Schieffin, Bambi B. 2008. "Speaking Only Your Own Mind: Reflections on Talk, Gossip and Intentionality in Bosavi (PNG)." *Anthropological Quarterly* 81(2): 431–441.

Searle, John. (1983). *Intentionality: An Essay in the Philosophy of Mind*. Cambridge: Cambridge University Press.

Shanahan, Murray. (1969). *Solving the Frame Problem: A Mathematical Investigation of the Common Sense Law of Inertia*. Cambridge, MA: MIT Press.

Shermer, Michael. (2008). "Patternicity: Finding Meaningful Patterns in Meaningless Noise: Why the Brain Believes Something Is Real When It Is Not." *Scientific American*, 1 December. www.scientificamerican.com/article/patternicity-finding-meaningful-patterns/ (accessed 21 June 2017).

Sperber, Dan and Deirdre Wilson (1986). *Relevance: Communication and Cognition*. Cambridge, MA: Harvard University Press.

Stich, Stephen and R. Ravenscroft. 1994. "What Is Folk Psychology?" *Cognition* 50:447–468.

Sturm, V. E., M. Sollberger, W. W. Seeley, K. P. Rankin, E. A. Ascher, H. J. Rosen, and R. W. Levenson. (2013). "Role of Right Pregenual Anterior Cingulate Cortex in Self-Conscious Emotional Reactivity." *Social Cognitive and Affective Neuroscience* 8(4): 468–474.

Thompson, Evan. ([1993] 2017). "Introduction to the Revised Edition." In Francisco J. Varela, Evan Thompson and Eleanor Rosch, *The Embodied Mind: Cognitive Science and Human Experience*, xvii–xxxiv. Cambridge, MA: MIT Press.

Truzzi, M. (1973). "The Problem of Relevance between Orientations for Cognitive Dissonance Theory." *Journal for the Theory of Social Behaviour* 3: 239–247.

Weber, Max. [1968] 1978. *Economy and Society: An Outline of Interpretive Sociology* 3 vols, ed. Guenther Roth and Claus Wittich. Berkeley: University of California Press.

Wilkes, K. V. (1984) "Pragmatics in Science and Theory in Common Sense." *Inquiry* 27: 339–361.

Wilkes, W. (1981). "Functionalism, Psychology, and the Philosophy of Mind." *Philosophical Topics* 12(1): 147–167.

Wilson-Mendenhall, Christine D., Lisa Feldman Barrett, W. Kyle Simmons, and Lawrence W. Barsalou. (2011). "Grounding Emotion in Situated Conceptualization." *Neuropsychologia* 49: 1105–1127.

Wittgenstein, Ludwig. ([1953] 1958). *Philosophical Investigations* 3rd edn., trans. G. E. M. Anscombe. Englewood Cliffs, NJ: Prentice Hall.

Woodard, Amanda L. (2009). "Infants' Grasp of Others' Intentions." *Current Directions in Psychological Science* 18(1): 53–57.

Yeh, Wenchi and Lawrence W. Barsalou. (2006). "The Situated Nature of Concepts." *American Journal of Psychology* 119(3): 349–384.

Zawidzki, T. W. (2008). "The Function of Folk Psychology: Mind Reading or Mind Shaping?" *Philosophical Explorations* 11(3): 193–210.

5

INCORPORATING THE SOCIAL INTO COGNITIVE SCIENCE

Affordances, Scaffolding, and Computational Complexity

It's all about speed. The major difference between the standard approach and its alternatives is how they approach two facts: first, that people make very fast unconscious responses, or act in ways that require very fast unconscious and introspectively inaccessible mental operations; second, that once in place, these operations are, at least sometimes, difficult to change or replace. The standard approach handles these problems with such concepts as modules, and attributes massive computational power to the brain, allowing it to perform complex tasks almost instantaneously, and long before they could be performed by the conscious step-by-step operations that are the basis of boxology models. A whole field of computational psychology is devoted to constructing computational models that show how these processes can even be possible (Sun 2008).

Computational considerations are, arguably, central to cognitive science generally (Gallistel and King 2009) and inevitably central to integrative brain science (Gershman et al. 2015). This field is concerned with combining the knowledge of multiple fields related to the brain, especially those concerned with integrating clinical research with fundamental research, and including such fields as developmental psychology, cognitive science, brain imaging and lesion studies, genetics, the physics and biochemistry of brain processes, and much more. In making sense of "the social" in relation to the brain and cognition none of these topics can be excluded: there are potential connections, and social variations or social implications, of each of these topics. Moreover, paying attention to these social aspects is likely to bear on the project of integration itself, if only because the "social" part of human life is pervasive in its presence and in its causal relations with almost all that is human.

The fields that bear on the brain include linguistics, which provides a useful model. On the one hand, language is a real phenomenon that engages the brain, is related to lesions, and is partly acquired. Speed is central to this story: children acquire language quickly and apparently effortlessly, or without conscious effort or training. Trying to do the same thing without training as an adult is impossible: mimicking this kind of learning through rule-following and memorization, even with the best training methods, is excruciatingly difficult. More importantly, fluency is the ability to speak quickly and without conscious effort. The brain thus needs to be "language ready" for there to be language, and this is a fact that integrative brain science must take into account. But readiness cuts both ways: one needs a conception of the brain that accounts for these features of linguistic competence; but one also needs a conception of language that is consistent with the realization of linguistic phenomena in the brain.

With language, one can have different opinions as to whether this problem was solved, and at what cost. We inherited from the Medievals, who were faced with the problem of teaching Latin to children who already spoke a language, a kind of theory of language in which grammar rather than actual speech was constitutive of language; and it was then claimed that syntactical rules were rooted in more basic, and universal, syntactical rules, such that all brains had to have them. The problem became one of discovering, though in practice this amounted to designing, a brain that was language ready. As we have seen, this led to difficulties, though perhaps not insurmountable ones. But from this example we can see where the standard approach would look for a solution: in universal innate computational capacities. This is, so to speak, an "internalizing" solution. It tries to explain by showing how the computational brain could produce grammatical speech or, in the case of a famous connectionist paper, how they could learn it without it being programmed in (Smolensky et al. 1993: 382). As Lakoff puts it,

> From the perspective of neural computation, a human brain consists of a very large number of neurons connected up in specific ways with certain computational properties. How is it possible to get the details of human concepts, the forms of human reason, and the range of human languages out of a lot of neurons connected up as they are in our brains? How do you get thought and language out of neurons?
>
> *(Lakoff 1999: 5)*

Structured connectionism, his approach, "allows us to construct detailed computational neural models of conceptual and linguistic structures and the learning of such structures" (Lakoff 1999: 5).

Problems of fit go both ways. One can ask whether our conventional concepts of the social, the cultural, and so forth are brain-ready. Many of them clearly are not: they posit forces and collective entities that don't have any plausible realization in the brain. To be sure, these are not clear-cut distinctions, and judicious reinterpretation of common ideas may allow some accommodation with what is known, and what will be known, about the brain. But for many of the relevant concepts, their origins in the nineteenth-century model of disciplinary autonomy are obvious: they were designed to be independent of biology (Meloni 2012). Sociology before Durkheim, in the hands of people like René Worms, was intensely biological. Their intellectual problem was this: how can socialism be made consistent with Darwinism? This was the tradition that was rejected when sociology sought to define its own special domain. The baby that went out with the bathwater with the achievement of autonomy was the problem of fit itself.

In this chapter we will consider a series of "externalizing" solutions to the problem of speed that reflect the aims of integrative brain science rather than autonomy, but which also are "social." They involve causal relationships of the kind that sociological concepts are constructed to address, but with a difference. The language of computational load, affordances, and scaffolding, which we will discuss here is brain-ready. The causal processes described here are similar to, and extensions of, processes that have been studied in connection with perception, cognition, and action in the brain sciences. It would be of course an error to treat any of these topics as settled, and there are many issues, none of which have been examined here, with the scientific understanding of core cognitive processes. But these are empirical and theoretical issues which can be made into answerable questions, and not simply a matter of another perspective on the social.

Computational Load and the Tacit

We have already seen repeatedly that the standard approach models cognition on explicit reasoning. Modules perform the same tasks that can be done explicitly, like dead reckoning, but in a fast, mechanical way, which is possible because the task has been broken down into simple components. Something like modularity is needed because explicit thinking is slow. But modularity implies universality and the long process of natural selection. Yet as active participants in social life, we effortlessly, and without thinking about it consciously and explicitly, navigate not only our physical environment and technology but also a complex set of social interactions. Moreover, much of this navigation involves local skills. When we are out of the social surroundings we are familiar with, such as when we are dealing with a radically different culture or technological setting, or even a different bus system, we can proceed only with difficulty and by explicit thinking – about such things as people's motives, meanings, beliefs, understanding of the situation, and so forth – that we normally process automatically and unconsciously. Thus we think *as though* we have modules, but without modules. Instead we can perform this way because we have acquired skill-like capacities. If it is the case that the kind of effortless responses characteristic of modularity can only be acquired through evolutionary processes, we are left with a puzzle about how we acquire these skills, and how this acquisition can be accounted for within the standard approach. The alternative approach seems, on the surface, better suited to this task. Social interaction described in this way resembles the situation described in the embodied, dynamic approach in which acquired embodied automatized skills enable us to handle complex situations.

The problems here are not well demarcated, and there are numerous perspectives involving different sorts of empirical claims about what we can generally call the tacit. The distinction between tacit and articulated or explicit maps onto a more general distinction, for which the terminology varies. Much of our mental processing, even when we are attempting to solve problems such as making a rational choice, explicitly depends on tacit inferential steps that are the product of learning, or perhaps part of the preconditions for learning, as when we speak of the language-ready brain (Arbib 2012). For convenience I will distinguish in what follows between fast and slow thinking, following Daniel Kahneman (2011). Kahneman was concerned with rationality and the use of fast heuristics in place of slow, fully rational, explicit thinking. But this distinction, between the slow and explicit and the fast and tacit, applies much more broadly than the original context for Kahneman's work, and beyond his concern for rationality. When John Searle discusses the "Background," meaning the inaccessible computational operations underlying inferences, perception, and other cognitive processes (Searle 1991; Searle 1995), and Damasio (1994) discusses the "somatic," they are also referring to fast-thinking processes.

The distinction also maps onto a concept from psychology: cognitive load. The term refers specifically to a distinction between long-term and working memory. Memory is relevant here because the relevant cognitive processes must be implemented through memory: there must be something in memory that is being used when, for example, we make a fast, unconscious inference. The idea is that working memory is sharply limited: we can only pay attention to seven plus or minus two pieces of information at the same time for problem solving or learning. Long-term memory is not limited in this way: we can acquire an indefinite amount of information or develop an indefinite number of habits. Cognitive load refers to the total amount of mental effort being used in the working memory. We can reduce this effort by relying on things stored in long-term memory – such as tacit schemas which allow us to process information without conscious effort (Sweller 1988).

We face a familiar problem with these skills, schemas, and so forth. Ron Sun et al (2001: 208) make the following distinction, taken from Reber (1989): "Declarative knowledge is represented explicitly and thus consciously accessible whereas procedural knowledge is represented implicitly and thus inaccessible [Anderson 1983; Ackerman 1988; Reber 1989; LeDoux 1992]" (Sun et al. 2001: 208). The skills we use to navigate are not consciously accessible to us, at least not in any direct way. Indeed, what goes on at the tacit level may even conflict with what we think consciously: the phenomenon of implicit bias is only one example of this. The term "alief" has been coined to describe belief-like mental states which are belief-like in the sense that they can conflict with beliefs, but are more primitive than belief and desire, which are directly activated by the environment and directly activate behavioral responses (Gendler 2008). Implicit bias works in the same way, at the perceptual level: biased responses may be detected, for example through immediate physical reactions that the subject is not only unaware of but consciously denies (Amodio and Mendoza 2010).

The problem presented by skills, schemas, and so forth is clear but complex. To account for what Reber calls "procedural knowledge," including the kind of knowledge or skills that underlie our social performances and interactions, we need a cognitive science model that allows for consistency between the various levels of neuroscience – including the physical neuronal and embodied level, the level of computational psychology, and the "functional" level of actual performance – and that can be integrated with the concerns, if not the concepts, of traditional social science. The main desiderata is that the cognitive processes in question are computationally plausible: it may be acceptable to produce, to paraphrase Gintis, a predictive model of some human activity for some purpose in which it is assumed that the people involved perform Lagrangian transformations. Producing a realistic understanding of what people actually do, however, requires an understanding of what is actually realized in the brain, embodied, and the external processes related to them.

We can set aside the many issues with the conceptualization of the tacit, however, and concentrate on the issue common to all of them: namely, the problem of how tacit *acquired* capacities can operate in the effortless and fast way that modules are supposed to. This in turn can be formulated in terms of a concept that grew out of the narrow notion of cognitive load: *computational* load, meaning computational effort or cost generally, whether conscious or not (Clark 1997: 47, 133, 150, 244n2). What modules are supposed to do is to reduce this effort: to take an apparently complex computational task and break it down in ways that speed up processing by reducing computational effort by making the elements simple, automatic, and fast. The problem with modularity is accounting for how it is produced in the first place. As we have seen, modules were traditionally associated with evolution, not something that could be learned. But could there be other, acquired, ways of reducing computational load?

What might these be? The internal and external approaches are two non-exclusive solutions in the literature, and they correspond to the two approaches to cognitive science outlined above, but do not conflict, and indeed could be complementary. Sun's innovation was to show how, in a computational model based on connectionism, something module-like could be produced internally, from the learning process itself, in which "rules" were generated, rules that reduced computational effort. Because of the way it is acquired, namely through experience and practice (as skills are), it can be more readily modeled (as Sun does) by uninterpretable or "subsymbolic" representational units in a connectionist network capable of accomplishing learning and accomplishing tasks (see Sun 1994: 43, 45). This approach is not without drawbacks: as a model of the brain it is more realistic than the symbolic processing approach, but still at a high level of abstraction. But this kind of learning is generally accepted and, in the case of skills, does not require implausible amounts of computational power, and fits with the physical features of the brain better than the standard approach. Nevertheless, these models have some important limitations. They are relatively slow to learn and require massive data and response inputs.

An alternative to this kind of learning is to assume that the gains in computational speed are the result of the employment of "schemas," a term which recurs in the psychological literature as well as sociology, as Sun (2012: 12) points out, especially in relation to the idea "that culture may manifest in individual minds as schemas (Fiske and Linville 1980; DiMaggio 1997; etc.)." As the term is typically used, schemas are different from patterns. They are mental forms that can be repeated and shared, for example, to make up a culture. But, as Sun notes, there is a problem with the concept of schemas: they also need to have some reality at other levels. They "can exist and be accessed (and thus affect behavior) only through innate cognitive capacities such as memory, reasoning, and decision-making," So whatever the "notion means in practice, it should be, and can be, more specifically pinned down in a mechanistic, process-based way, as computational cognitive modeling (computational psychology) would provide" (Sun 2012: 12). And these models are themselves constrained by the question of whether they can be implemented in actual brains.[1] This is what Sun's version of "rules" supplies: something that does the work of schemas but responds to the problem of implementation.

Sun also adds another argument that is relevant to the problem of the slowness of connectionist learning by association. He points out, following Reber, that most tacit processes of learning, and most tacit phenomena, are not purely tacit.[2] There is usually, in the cases that concern them, some verbal or slow thinking aspect to the skills or capacities which is intertwined with them in actual practice and in the development of the capacities. Sun distinguishes "top-down" and "bottom-up" learning. In top-down learning, a verbal instruction is followed and the pattern is habitualized; in bottom-up learning, of the kind his rule-constructing computational model simulates, the verbal or explicit content of the skill, such as evaluative language about doing something correctly, can add to the process of learning, and thus speed it up.[3] This is an important point that looms large in what follows because the "social," however it is understood, is causally intertwined with explicit, narrativized, public expressions: the use of them is part of what forms habits and stabilizes patterns in ways that enable situations to be jointly attended to. But the social cannot be reduced to these public forms of expression, to its "discursive" character. This relationship will inevitably dominate much of the discussion in the rest of this book.

Sun's approach is largely "internal" in the sense that he wants to solve the problem of computational load by computational processes, though he acknowledges external elements, such as verbal instructions. The complementary approach is "external" in the sense that it involves external surrogates for internal mental processes. But external approaches also allow for internalization through tacit learning, so the relations between these claims is muddled, and muddled on an important point: what is the status of such things as schemas, scripts, and so forth? And how do they relate to more traditional concepts such as roles? The muddle has to do with sharing. The tacit theory approach assumes that somehow, either through innate mechanisms or "culture," the same tacit theory gets into the heads of the relevant people, either all people in the case of innate mechanisms, or some sort of learning or acquisition in the case of culture. The alternative, which we might dub the "habitualization of narrative" model, denies that there is anything script- or schema-like that is "shared" that didn't get there by people responding to external inputs, particularly from exposure to the actual declarations of others; and, most importantly, there is nothing in common in people's heads, such as a tacit theory, that is anything more than the habitualization of responses to these external inputs.

This may seem like an arcane difference, but it is an important one. The shared tacit theory account and its variants depend on the idea that there is what is sometimes called "high-fidelity social learning" (Tomasello 1999), in which "true imitation resulted in a trans-generational copying mechanism" (Carruthers 2013: 329). The concept is a solution to the problem of acquisition or transmission of culture: it purports to explain how such things as schemas, scripts, and so forth are reproduced with great clarity in the heads of the people in groups. The existence of the mechanism is then taken to explain cultural stability: the reason culture is stable is that people have learned the culture, consisting of this tacit stuff, through this high-fidelity mechanism. One needs such a mechanism because the alternative modes of transmission have two limitations: they are explicit, so we still need to know how something like a tacit (and presumably more extensive) theory is produced by them; they also only produce individual outcomes, such as the particular habits I acquire as a result of my social interactions, rather than some sort of duplicate of the tacit stuff in the head of my neighbor.

The issue is sometimes framed in terms of two alternative kinds of "propagation": reconstructive and replicative. They produce stability in different ways. The reconstructive approach argues that cultural stability is not a result of the power of high-fidelity social learning, an internal explanation, but of the properties of the things being shared, an external explanation (Scott-Phillips 2017). This distinction points to a more basic issue, already raised by Sun: how do schemas, scripts, and other things usually thought of as part of culture, such as roles, actually operate in the mind, and in what sense can they be said to be shared? The replication answer is that they are copied from others through a special high-fidelity copying process, and this explains the fact that they are in common among the members of a group. They then operate in the mind as a tacit theory. But we can explain the same surface facts about stability and "sharing" without reference to such a process.

How might this work? If we start with pattern recognition, and pattern recognition of social situations, we have the basic cognitive mechanism we need: the external facts are the social situations we construct, individually, by recognizing the situation as patterned. We navigate the social world with these patterns – make inferences, act, react emotionally, and so forth. We "share" them to the extent that other people recognize the same social situations as patterned, although they may see them in terms of somewhat different patterns, for example, by connecting them to different emotions. The only sameness between minds and "sharing" we need to account for social interaction is sufficient similarity for understanding to occur. Of course we are also in a world of social interaction in which joint attention is a kind of fundamental social glue. So if we see a policeman and our companion sees the policeman, we are aware of the other and attuned to some extent to their responses, which may be different in detail with respect to the pattern recognition that the policemen evokes in them, but will have something that overlaps with our reaction. This is, from this perspective, all that scripts, schemas, and roles amount to. There is no need for high-fidelity learning because pattern recognition and joint attention – together with, where relevant, narratives that get habitualized – explain both stability and the cognitive side of the process. Patterns in memory, or whatever produced responses to familiar things, are already doing the work of speeding up cognition. And the features of the situations themselves that make them easily recognizable do part of the work of explaining why they are so readily shared.

This approach takes us to one level of externalization. We shift the cognitive load from internal processes to internalized features such as patterns in memory that result from external facts, such as social situations. But we can go one step further and substitute external things for cognitive things, such as memory itself. This step is known as the extended mind thesis (Sutton 2012; Gallagher 2013). The basic thought behind this approach is that for some common mental processes or capacities an external process or thing can substitute for the mental process. This allows for an important innovation, namely the recognition of the role of artifacts, objects, and technology as means of "reducing individual computational load and expanding our behavioral horizons" (Clark 1997: 244n2); the classic example is scissors. In one sense these are simply useful objects. In another they are extensions of our powers to act that transform us by enabling us to do something novel and, once we master them, without thinking about it – thus reducing the cognitive load of a task (cf. Gregory 1981).

The extended mind thesis (Clark and Chalmers 1998) is a way of understanding these substitutes as part of cognition itself. The core thought is that when a prosthesis, such as a memo pad, is substituted for something the brain does, such as remembering, it is part of the mental process, so that "mental" is no longer limited to the brain or even the body. Tacit processes can, similarly, substitute for explicit ones, and sometimes explicit thinking can substitute for tacit processes. Objects and routines, in short, can do the work of the mind. And they can also often reduce computational load by doing so, especially when the routines are invented to perform tasks we would otherwise find cognitively difficult or impossible. As Shaun Gallagher (2013) points out, the externalization argument can be extended in a social direction, to include our reliance on other people. We can memorize the way to walk home and take the route by thinking about every step or turn, that is to say perform the acts consciously as a fully intentional act. But we can get home in other ways: the route can be habituated "in the body"; we can hail a cab and not think about how it gets us there; we can solve the problem socially by asking people for directions; or we can take a bus that follows a predetermined physical route.

Clark (2008: 79) subsequently attempted to exclude such things as other people's opinions by restricting the extended "mind" to those substitutes that were used automatically, were always available, and were endorsed uncritically. Gallagher (2013: 6) argues that these restrictions are arbitrary and introduces the idea of a "mental institution," giving the legal system as an example, which includes local practices that extend our cognitive processes when we engage with or interact with them. This points to an important implication for sociological thinking about institutions: they are an interacting combination of physical artifacts, explicit rules, orders, instructions, and so forth, together with tacitly learned automatic responses both to training and to the patterned experiences of performing actions in the institution.

Affordances

The psychological literature on cognitive load, on the demands placed on working memory, has shown that the poor, the elderly, people in a confusing novel situation, and many other circumstances are forced to think, in the sense of slow thinking, harder and with more difficulty. These are the same kinds of difficulty as those that are produced by conflicting action producing patterns, as discussed in the last chapter. One might associate this insight with historical pragmatism as well: it was a central precept of Dewey's social psychological work, *Human Nature and Conduct* (1922), that experimental, analytical hypothesis generating and testing thought only arose when it needed to as a result of the failure of habitual responses.

The concept of computational load allows us to conceptualize the relation of mind to world in a novel way. Consider the difference between Chemero's diving gannet and Gallistel's ant. The ant, as Gallistel constructs it, lives in the same objective world as we do, and navigates in it with something akin to the advanced mathematical tools of slow thinking, but modularized through evolution into fast operation. The gannet reacts directly to a different world from ours, in which the visual field becomes the feature of the environment that can be the immediate object of low cognitive load, "fast thinking," which does not require complex modular processing. We can generalize the point: we ourselves live in what are in effect two different worlds: the slow thinking world that produces, for example, the physicists' table, consisting of atoms in motion; and the fast thinking world defined by the feature of its accessibility to us, that is accessibility with low computational load. One might suggest that the second of these worlds corresponds to the phenomenological notion of the *Lebenswelt* or life world, or Heidegger's *Dasein*.[4]

Much could be said about the differences between these two "worlds" of different computational accessibility. A few introductory comments are relevant. The ordinary world of experience is prone to error. The habits we acquire are based on a sample of experience with feedback, and are accordingly subject to error: they fail to generalize in new situations. Cognitive shortcuts, such as patterns saved in memory and habits, facilitate fast thinking and reduce cognitive load and demands on working memory. Moreover, they are individualized. My habits are not yours, though they may become in a practical sense more uniform through discipline and the demands of social interaction, particularly joint attention. In consequence, from the point of view of computational load, we each live in different worlds with respect to accessibility and convenience.

One way to conceptualize these differences, and the phenomenon of accessibility, is affordances. The term was originally applied by James Gibson (1977) to natural "properties," and was intended to provide an approach to issues about perception. Thus Gibson worked with a notion of the environment as objective and the same for all. In cognitive science this is still its main role (Chemero 2011), but there it has been entangled with issues over direct perception, or perception unmediated by representations, and therefore entangled with a broader dispute over representationalism as a theory of cognition. We can ignore these disputes for the moment. The subsequent uses of the term extended it radically, and it is these extensions that will concern us here. The importance of the concept, for our purposes, relates to the internal–external distinction. To appeal to affordances serves to off-load the problems that an internal analysis would need to solve by, in effect, locating the cognitive agent in a simpler and more easily navigated world.

The core idea behind the concept of affordances is simple. An affordance is an actionable property that exists in the world. A door knob affords turning; stairs afford climbing. Affordances are the handles by which we act on the world. But they are relative to the user – different animals have different capacities and therefore different affordances. If we consider the different capacities that individuals have by virtue of their tacit acquisitions, we get the same result for humans: people vary in what is an affordance for them. And they also vary in terms of the environment of affordances available to them. Affordances are related to capacities, and both capacities and affordances vary significantly between individuals. The relationship between capacities and affordances is also dynamic: one can get better at using tools, and also improve one's capacities for using them in ways that allow for the use of tools that could not have been used initially. In this way the world of affordances in which a person lives changes.

An issue with affordances is the question of how far the concept can be extended. Are routines, other people, systems, and so forth also affordances? The term is perhaps a bit too useful – it seems to include everything that makes actions easier.[5] Moreover, as we might expect from the pervasive fact of the tacit and causal intertwining with the explicit, it is difficult to separate out the causal elements: this was Weber's point. Thinking and action in any complex case is composed of many elements, including emotion, inferences, and so forth. The idea of convenience is crucial here, and may be understood in terms of the fast–slow distinction and the problem of computational load. We can think of the problem of the relationship in terms of the extent to which performing an action is cognitively convenient. An action that requires a great deal of explicit conscious reasoning or slow thinking is less convenient, and unsurprisingly, as Weber said, rare. But different acts are more or less convenient in this sense: they require more slow thinking. In this case, the white person need not think about presentation of self when making a credit card purchase, while the minority group member might. We can call these "convenience discrepancies," and ask what their role is in determining behavior.

An example from social science can bring the discussion back to earth. Peggy McIntosh's famous list of elements of "white" and male privilege can be readily restated in affordance terms. The list she provides is not intended as a fully specified description of mechanisms. Most of the items on the list state advantages, or opportunities, available to white males that are not available to others, such as the ability to use checks, credit cards, or cash without being concerned that one's skin color will count against "the appearance of financial reliability" (McIntosh 1988). Checks, cash, and credit cards are all, in some sense, affordances. They are designed surrogates for more cumbersome forms of exchange, and are more convenient to employ. But as surrogates they may have properties that differ from the thing that they substitute for, and thus are different as affordances, for example by requiring more trust. This serves as a differentiator: for some people it is more convenient to use these affordances than others; and, as a consequence, they live in a different world of affordances.

The role of fast or tacit thinking is pervasive in accounting for convenience discrepancies. What is convenient for a person to think and act on depends on how much is already built into their fast thinking processes. The conclusions we can easily come to, the ideas we can entertain, and the perceptions we can integrate depend on how much, and what, is already there and does not need to be slow thought. One unthinkingly reaches for a credit card at a check-out counter, for example. But one might also reach for it thinking about how to handle an encounter that threatens to turn into an embarrassing incident in which identification is checked and the manager called. This would be an unthinking response to a pattern recognition, which is turned into a slow-thinking consideration of choices about how to act by the need to further assess the situation. Is the cashier friendly? Is the store unwelcoming and devoid of minority customers? These are all patterns which lead to different action responses. And there are identifiable neural differences between such responses (Aubin et al. 2016).

While there is no reason in principle that someone might not be able to easily step into a group of people brought up with different experiences, especially social experiences with different groups of people, and understand what is going on and respond appropriately, the reality is different: it is characteristic of diverse social settings that the tacit background that enables one to make the right inferences and have the appropriate feelings does not work in other social settings. A traditionally sociological response to the discovery of a setting in which the actions and beliefs are puzzling is to make them understandable by explaining the context in a way that makes them understandable to us. But to do this is to give a slow-thinking account of what is, for the participants, a fast-thinking experience.

What is going on in the encultured brain for those for whom the right responses are "natural," intuitive, and so forth, as distinct from those who are slow thinking their way to understanding? W. E. B Dubois and Erving Goffman provide some useful indications. In a setting in which one's fast-thinking responses lead to failed interactions, in which one's expectations are wrong, in order to present oneself in a way that gets successful responses one must put on, as Dubois puts it, a mask. The mask, in our terms, is a slow-thinking mask, one which one constructs more or less through slow thinking or reasoning, on the basis of advice or observation, with the aim of making interactions seem natural – that is, like the interactions of those who are relying largely on fast thinking. If one is in these settings over time, the mask becomes habituated or automatized, a form of fast thinking itself. But because these novel settings are exceptional, one retains one's alternative habitual responses, emotional connections, and so forth, and must manage an inner life which is divided. If there are different emotional connections or valuations placed on responses with the mask on from those without the mask, one might expect a need for these responses to be regulated on a higher cognitive level, in a different part of the brain, with different connections to emotion-activating parts of the brain, and to generate slow thinking in response – for example in the construction or acceptance of an ideology separating the two. And one would expect these differences to be reflected in identifiably distinct brain processes: interacting with one's own familiar group would involve automatized responses; acting with a mask on would involve slow thinking about what responses are appropriate, strategic, or intelligible to others.

Having to slow think where others can rely on automatized responses is a disadvantage in most situations, especially those in which fast thinking leads to the correct results. People trying to use the affordances presented by other people are limited by the fact that they must overcome such things as the unconscious or conscious biases of others, or even the fear of the unconscious or conscious biases of others: the need to establish trust, for example, can be costly in cognitive effort, or impossible. The differences in affordances available to people, if one takes into account subtle and not so subtle differences in degree, can become very substantial, and account for a great deal of variation in actual behavior. In this sense affordances are a major "external" rival to "internal" accounts of cognition.

Yet one must be cautious here: slow thinking, for example making conscious decisions about such things as how to present oneself, is a large part of social interaction; and, as with Sun's example of the role of explicit instructions in learning, is causally intertwined with fast thinking. One learns, for example, what presentation of self works, and habituates it so that it becomes a fast-thinking response to a situation. But it is also the case that social interactions involve many small choices that require thought: thinking of the right word or the right attitude to take to a situation where one has subconsciously recognized conflicting patterns. So the notion of masks and perhaps the notion in Goffman of front-stage and back stage in the presentation of self both need to be modified: these are cases where the distinction between fast and slow thinking about social interaction is accentuated and obvious. But it is an accentuation of an ongoing process of interaction between fast and slow thinking. Even the act of checking out in a grocery store involves small decisions: assessing the intentions of others in line and deciding how to adjust to them by placing one's purchases in a more convenient position, for example. And these are the sorts of slow-thinking things that also can become, through learning, with or without verbal instruction, fast thinking.

A second wave of thinking about affordances emerged in the design community, with the idea of designing affordances. And here we face another difficulty with the extension of the term to the social realm. As we have seen, the term was originally applied by Gibson to natural "properties," was intended to provide an approach to issues about perception, and worked with a notion of the environment as objective and the same for all. When the concept was later applied to design theory it became practically important to distinguish the affordances that were *perceived* by standard users and those that were actually there: a design whose affordances were not immediately visible and actionable did not achieve its purpose. As Donald A. Norman (1999: 39 put it, the question was:

> When you first see something you have never seen before, how do you know what to do? The answer, I decided, was that the required information was in the world: the appearance of the device could provide the critical clues required for its proper operation.

This reasoning opened the door to a conception of affordances that included such "social" things as conventions: it is immediately evident, for example, that driving on the "correct" side of the road takes advantage of a convention and is an affordance.

Norman, however, argued, on the basis of a kind of rudimentary social theory, that conventions and social things were not affordances:

Conventions are not arbitrary: they evolve, they require a community of practice. They are slow to be adopted, and once adopted, slow to go away. So although the word implies voluntary choice, the reality is that they are real constraints upon our behavior. Use them with respect. Violate them only with great risk.

(Norman 1999: 41)

The contrast with affordances is this: the actionable qualities of affordances are immediate and do not require training or effort: the appearance of a device provides the clues to its proper operation. Conventions, for Norman, are constraints; affordances, though they may be negative in the sense that their use may have negative consequences, are not. For him, constraints reside in a community of practice, while affordances (or perceived affordances) are immediately accessible.

These are obviously problematic distinctions, for reasons that need not be discussed at length here: "conventions" and practices are not simply external in this manner, but are also habituated and automatized, so that something not immediately accessible can become automatically accessible through experience. The distinction between conventions and affordances "that carry the clues to their use on their face" thus turns into a matter of degree. In the design literature this has become an empirical problem: when faced with a new arrangement of designed affordances, to what extent does past experience determine which affordance is most accessible? The evidence indicates that past experience, what I have been calling tacit learning, has significant effects (Still and Dark 2008). Moreover, "conventional" constraints, like affordances generally, expand and restrict behavioral possibilities by expanding and restricting the behavioral possibilities of others: they allow for new ones when they allow predictable outcomes of actions, for example. They are very much a part of the convenient and accessible "world" as distinct from the slow-thinking world, both of which the cognitive agent occupies and moves between.

The distinction between perceived affordances and potential affordances can be more readily understood not as a distinction between properties of affordances but as a distinction between capacities: if one has the relevant capacities, one will perceive the affordance. This is in some ways a quibble, but it points to an important issue. From a design perspective, one must operate with a more or less standardized model of the capacities of the user, simply because one must anticipate what will be taken to be an affordance. In this context the distinction makes sense and is obvious. But from a cognitive neuroscience point of view, the distinction is entirely on the side of capacities: what is taken as an affordance is a matter of cognitive and embodied capacities. These capacities are not fixed, and any standardized model is a simplification and idealization of capacities that are heterogeneous and malleable.[6] This implies also that the "world" of accessibility that each of us inhabits is our own world, the world disclosed as accessible by our own individual capacities.

But what is it that is heterogeneous and malleable? Where do these capacities reside? In bodies to some extent, but, more importantly, in the tacit background as a whole. What appears to a mathematician as an obvious step in a proof will appear to a novice as unintelligible squiggles on a page. What the mathematician has and the novice does not, if we leave aside innate capacities, is a vast fast-thinking capacity developed through practice of solving problems and doing proofs. These are, in short, skilled performances resting on a tacit background that is a product of the performers' training and individual experience, and experience of feedback which modifies the brain and changes capacity – perhaps even negatively, as with Thorstein Veblen's concept of trained incapacity (1914: 347). The more that is automatized, the more readily even the slow-thinking tasks of higher mathematical thinking can be performed: this is why so much of mathematics education consists of repetition, which reduces cognitive load (see Warwick 2003). This brings us closer to the idea of the *Lebenswelt* or *Dasein*: the world for us is the world that is accessible to us given the cognitive shortcuts that enable our own fast thinking.

Scaffolding

Although the term is used in various ways, scaffolding can be best understood as a process made up of steps in which affordances are taken and lead to changes of capacity, which allow other affordances, which in turn change capacities, and so forth. Vygotsky's original example of schooling is a case in point – each step enables future steps, but each step also requires the next affordance (1978). With considerations like these we come to the prospect of multiple successive dynamic interactions in which capacities are altered in ways that create new affordances, which in turn transform capacities. This kind of transformation is characteristic of social change.

Schooling is a case of designed affordances, and is a useful example. Designed affordances are fraught with unintended consequences. They are created and offered in a larger world of other affordances, and heterogeneous capacities of various kinds, and may or may not work to bring about the goals they were designed for. The capacities of individuals to use the affordances depend on the background, the tacit acquisition of fast-thinking routines. This occurs, so to speak, in the wild or bottom-up as well. And we can understand the most famous of sociological theses about massive social change, Weber's Protestant ethic thesis, in precisely these terms, and in terms of Sun's point about the mutual causal interaction of the tacit and the explicit.

Without going into the details and interpretive disputes over this thesis, we can restate the basic outlines of Weber's argument, which appears in a variety of places that expand on the original articles that make up the *Protestant Ethic* (1958), in terms of affordances and capacities. The end point of the argument, as he explained in his lectures on *General Economic History*, was a new type of person:

the worker who was suited to the rational organization of labor (Weber [1927] 1961). The rational organization of labor is itself an affordance: rational organizations are sets of routines in which people are parts, or cogs, as Weber liked to say. But people did not have, in traditional society, the capacity to work in this way. It required a transformation. Incentives were not enough, at least initially – traditionals worked for what they needed, and no more, and felt no guilt about it.

Scaffolding begins with a new affordance: the printed vernacular Bible, which enabled its readers to distinguish and argue about the differences between what the Bible contained and implied, on the one hand, and the magical powers of the Eucharist claimed by the priests, on the other. In the north of Europe, this ignited a vast controversy in which ordinary people participated and were able to come to their own conclusions, based on the text of the Bible itself and the affordances given by the open discussion of the text, something that had never occurred before. These were explicit, or discursive, parts of the process, and served also, as they stabilized, as conventions. The formalization of doctrinal ideas, by Calvin in particular, provided an affordance within this discussion – a tool to be used for various purposes. The passions unleashed in this period were a consequence of the centrality of the problem of salvation within Christianity, and its personal significance to believers (Weber [1968] 1978: 401, 404, 523). These are all results of external facts that changed – they were effects of a new environment of affordances.

The key to the argument, however, is not that doctrine produced action, but that external changes produced internal changes. Weber argued that, despite its overt character, the key Calvinist doctrine of predestination, which followed from the idea of God's omniscience, was rationally compelling, that is to say in our terms well suited to the tacit background of believers and to their slow thinking about consistency. But it was emotionally devastating because it took salvation completely out of the hands of the believer and disconnected it from ordinary ideas of goodness and justice. This negative message, together with Luther's doctrine of justification by faith alone, implied that only those destined to be faithful would be saved, but through God's grace rather than their own efforts. But, Weber argued, this terrifying doctrine was modified, in pastoral practice and indeed in later forms of Protestantism. So what was habituated as a mode of thought, a stabilized pattern that allowed for the recognition of situations in terms of it, was not the doctrine in its original form, but a kind of asceticism which then allowed for new institutions and practices: this is the power of scaffolding.

Much of this story occurs at the level of slow thinking, the thinking involved in making theological doctrine consistent with behavior and understanding the doctrines themselves. The immediate modification involved signs – signs that the believer could take to mean that they were among the elect. These included such things as conformity to God's plan and adherence to God's will as revealed in the individual's conscience. God's plan included a life-task for each person in the form of work in a vocation. Thus a life of scrupulous work in a vocation became evidence to the believer of their place in heaven, and failure to fulfill God's will became evidence of impending damnation. This psychological sanction, Weber argued, was powerful, and produced individuals of a novel, modern, type – people who sought careers, thought of their life as a whole (to be judged by God), and, most importantly, were ascetic. Asceticism, the forgoing of worldly pleasures, was implied by traditional morality, but was one competing value among many stronger ones. The theology of Calvin provided the link between salvation and ascetic purity. But asceticism produced an unintended effect: a transformation of capacities to act and plan. This was the inadvertent internal change that was scaffolded on the external changes.

In terms of affordances, the sequence was this: the theology was an affordance, an accessible and cognitively convenient solution to contradictory experiences and beliefs, and it was psychologically transformative, but in a painful way. Weber stressed the novelty of the psychological sanction represented by the threat of damnation unmediated by the former affordance of an intervening church. Pastoral counseling was another affordance, which mitigated the pain of the prospect of salvation by depicting a godly life of the sort that the Elect, those to be saved, would live. This was the ascetic life. So the ascetic life became the sole option for those seeking salvation, and the specific ascetic life afforded by one's sect became the default form of life. And this life produced a transformation in capacities, which was habituated and embodied. Those who were transformed were reliable, honest, and hard-working, and above all diligent in their work, which is what made them skillful and thus in demand for their products.

The next step was to design affordances in the world of work for this new type of diligent worker. And this is what was done by creating factories with production routines that required skilled diligent workers within a vocational division of labor who would regard work as its own reward, as a sign of salvation, rather than seek meaning or satisfaction in work. The new form of specialized work made possible new kinds of products that were competitively successful; Swiss watches is the example given by Weber, who notes that the factories resembled monasteries with their bells calling to prayer at specific times. Eventually this heightened order and rationalization became standard: work meant working according to routines. The next step involved the withdrawal of the former affordance of "traditional" labor. Market competition – a new affordance created by entrepreneurs who, motivated by the ascetic and planning transformation, expanded the range of people they sold to by cutting prices and squeezing out traditional competitors. Weber's phrase "they wished to work in a calling, we are forced to do so" captures this change in the world of affordances (1958: 181).

This is a highly schematic reconstruction, but the point can be generalized. Scaffolding is a way of understanding the mutual and transformative consequences of different affordances and capacities. And it applies to a wide range of traditional sociological controversies. William Julius Wilson (2009), for example, in *More than Just Race*, tries to find a middle ground or reconciliation between two accounts: in terms of culture and in terms of opportunity. In scaffolding terms, these are not contradictory. The culture of poverty is a response or adaptation to a particular limited set of affordances in which certain short-term outcomes, which may produce negative long-term outcomes, are more accessible and less uncertain. The effects of living under this regime of affordances are transformative, and thus not merely external. This is a point made recently by Orlando Patterson, who discusses effects of the atmosphere of pervasive violence and threat in the inner city in addition to the traditional focus on the causes of violent action. As he observes, "studies on the developing child clearly demonstrate … the neurological mechanism whereby the culture of violence is reproduced. Growing up in the presence of violence tends to make one violent" (Patterson 2015: 11; see also Hackman and Farah 2009). The response is adaptive, and is a case of tacit learning of responses that are only adaptive in the setting of the inner city itself, including such things as the development of a street presentation that wards off the threat of violence by itself threatening violence (Krupnik and Winship 2015). But the automatic responses are built up from experience in a world of joint attention on events, empathy, and so on, rather than on some sort of explicit doctrine about how to behave. Outside the inner city, and in the face of such things as normal employment opportunities, these responses are maladaptive because they are menacing to other people, with predictable negative effects on employment opportunities. The finding that networking does not help inner-city residents find jobs because the people they can connect to do not help them reflects this as well: default mutual trust and the altruism of others is an affordance in short supply in the inner city (cf. Sampson 2015). These are, then, examples of a world of affordances producing cognitive agents who are disadvantaged by the internal transformation that results from living in this world.

One other example might be useful. Popular discussion of the effects of the contraceptive pill routinely credit it as revolutionizing women's lives and roles, and changing culture. The conventional academic literature, in contrast, following the culture paradigm, argues that the pill itself did not have these consequences, but that cultural change was necessary (cf. Martin 1996); this is an "internal" explanation. The logic is impeccable: the culture of shaming and the values of abstinence and virginity, if they had not changed, would have made the availability of merely a new means of contraception irrelevant. The dichotomous choice, however, is misleading, and exposes the limitations of accounts of the effects of technology. One can schematically represent the change in terms of scaffolding and affordances as follows. Prior to the pill, sex, for women, was risky: not only was there the risk of pregnancy, there was also the risk of shaming. Thus the subclass of women who took these risks was distinctive, as a matter of empirical fact. Though obviously even "good girls" also took these risks, they carefully concealed it. Shaming was reinforced by the draconian response to pregnancy and the pressure to marry or give up babies for adoption. Bodily reactions to the fear of shaming were habitualized.

What changed? There were effective forms of contraception, notably the diaphragm combined with spermicidal jelly. This was an affordance. But it was also an affordance with certain limitations; it required planning and it, together with condoms, was unambiguous: these items were only for contraception – so even to acquire them involved a shameful admission. The pill, however, was somewhat ambiguous. It could be used to regulate the menstrual cycle, and thus did not automatically signal membership in the shamed classes of conscious risk-takers or pre-planners, and indeed removed the risk of pregnancy from unplanned sex.

Why did this matter? It meant that, empirically and in the actual experience of people, there was a new category of persons: women who were not risk takers or preplanners who were free to have sex without the older risks. This was a very different group than the women who were willing to risk shame or who calculated the risks and prepared for them. They were more "normal" and thus could serve as models and sources of information in a way that the others could not. The regime of shaming also broke down. The sexually active were no longer a distinctive group subject to social exclusion, but could be anyone. The "culture" changed because the shaming mechanisms and the practices of social exclusion, "had to" marriages, and the like lost their original target. Step by step, behavioral changes followed and the new "culture" adapted itself to it by providing new interpretations of sexual conduct consistent with the new empirical reality. This was a cultural change, but it was a change based on new realities of conduct. This kind of explanation does not require a prior cultural explanation for a cultural change: the "culture" is an adaptation to a novel external reality, in this case substitution of a convenient method of contraception for an inconvenient one of the past, namely abstinence. To be sure, the ideas that are part of this adaptation have their own consequences for behavior. And in this sense the cultural account is true. But, as Martin (1996) shows, the ideas long preceded the sexual revolution that corresponded to the introduction of the pill.

The model of scaffolding applies to many other controversies as well. The difference between labeling and differential association theories of delinquency is clarified if we recognize that labels are an affordance both for the authorities, who can use the label to invoke routines of legal discipline or treatment, and for the labeled, whose identity (however negative) nevertheless makes some things easier – including association with, and learning from, other delinquents. These associations, and living under these new affordances, transforms capacities in such a way that new things become affordances, such as criminal opportunities that previously would have been too risky or not understood. The new world of affordances produced by being labeled has its own transformative effect. The scaffolding process cannot be reduced to either labeling or differential association, but each allows for the transformative effect on capacities that allows for affordances higher up the scaffold.

Most of the phenomena of concern to sociology involve scaffolding, and include both conscious decision-making, such as the decisions and actions of political leaders and citizens along with many other players in a political order, and the tacit learned associations that have in the past been understood as part of political culture or tradition, which are part of the conditions of conscious thinking. And political orders, like other social phenomena, involve material means that substitute for "social" means – physical force in place of social sanctions, for example. The use of these means transforms the users through tacit learning as well as the kinds of overt doctrines and beliefs that are the stuff of folk psychology. The "objective," macro, and structural side of social life, and the material aspects, enter into explanation as affordances because it is the affordances that enter into cognition at the conscious as well as the tacit level. These considerations do not conflict; they fit together. Structures and routine, as well as other people, are affordances, and affordances make up the world of social experience and tacit learning.

Notes

1 These constraints are especially important for tacit learning because "some of the models – such as extremely computation-intensive Bayesian models of cognition … cannot be implemented by the human brain" (Miłkowski 2013: 123).
2 Exactly what the balance between tacit and explicit here is will likely vary from context to context. There is some evidence that some skills acquisition is best learned by rules, and that unconscious learning is limited (Tran and Pashler 2017). Cases like the "rules" governing an appropriate gift, mentioned earlier, have no "rules," and most of the relevant "social" contexts do not have rules of the sort that can easily be made explicit either.
3 The mirror neuron literature is relevant here: imitation is a means of speeding up the tacit learning process (cf. Sutton 2016).
4 Heidegger's picture is that *Dasein*, the life-world which is close to us, is a lie, in significant part because it is partly constituted for us by others socially, by our ordinary unreflective peers, which he calls *Das Man*. Departures from *Dasein*, such as the scientific point of view, still depend on it, and unconceal aspects of being but at the same time conceal other aspects (Mills and Polanowski 1997: 73). The concept of the *Verstehen* bubble is similar to this but, as we will see, can be specified in a different but cognitive science-friendly way.
5 Affordances, for Gibson, are objective facts in the world, as are individual capacities. But as the subsequent design literature showed, this was an overly limited conception, as it did not incorporate the role of long-term memory in making objects more or less convenient to employ. The lengthy debates over the use, overuse, and proper use of the term are discussed in Still (2009: 7–10). The issues here are much the same as those raised by Gallagher about the extended mind: the restrictions on the concept are largely arbitrary.
6 This is a point that has long been recognized in the science studies literature (Woolgar 1991).

References

Ackerman, P. (1988). "Determinants of Individual Differences during Skill Acquisition: Cognitive Abilities and Information Processing." *Journal of Experimental Psychology: General* 1117(3): 288–318.

Amodio, D. and S. A. Mendoza. (2010). "Implicit Intergroup Bias: Cognitive, Affective, and Motivational Underpinnings." In B. Gawronski and B. K. Payne (eds.) *Handbook of Implicit Social Cognition: Measurement, Theory, and Applications*, 353–374. New York: Guilford.

Anderson, J. (1983). *The Architecture of Cognition*. Cambridge, MA: Harvard University Press.

Arbib, Michael. (2012). *How the Brain Got Language: The Mirror System Hypothesis*. Oxford: Oxford University Press.

Aubin, Sean, Aaron R. Voelker, and Chris Eliasmith. (2016). "Improving With Practice: A Neural Model of Mathematical Development." *Topics in Cognitive Science*: 1–15. doi:10.1111/tops.12242.

Carruthers, Peter. (2013). "The Distinctively-Human Mind: The Many Pillars of Cumulative Culture." In Gary Hatfield and Holly Pittman (eds.) *Evolution of Mind, Brain, and Culture*, 345–365. Philadelphia, PA: University of Pennsylvania Press.

Chemero, Anthony. 2011. *Radical Embodied Cognitive Science*. Cambridge, MA: MIT Press.

Clark, Andy. (2008). *Supersizing the Mind: Embodiment, Action, and Cognitive Extension*. New York: Oxford University Press.

Clark, Andy. (1997). *Being There: Putting Brain, Body, and World Together Again*. Cambridge, MA: MIT Press.

Clark, Andy and David Chalmers. (1998). "The Extended Mind." *Analysis* 58(1) :7–19.

Damasio, A. R. (1994). *Descartes' Error: Emotion, Reason and the Human Brain*. London: Picador.

Dewey, John. (1922). *Human Nature and Conduct: An Introduction to Social Psychology*. New York: Holt.

Dimaggio, Paul. (1997). "Culture and Cognition." *Annual Review of Sociology* 23: 263–287.

Dubois, W. E. B. ([1903] 2007). *The Souls of Black Folk*, ed. Henry Louis Gates. Oxford: Oxford University Press.

Fiske, Susan T. and Patricia W. Linville. (1980). "What Does the Schema Concept Buy Us?" *Personality and Social Psychology Bulletin* 6: 543–557.

Gallagher, Shaun. (2013). "The Socially Extended Mind." *Cognitive Systems Research* 25–26: 4–12.

Gallistel, C. R. and Adam Philip King. (2009). *Memory and the Computational Brain: Why Cognitive Science Will Transform Neuroscience*. Malden, MA: Wiley-Blackwell.

Gendler, Tamar Szabó. (2008). "Alief and Belief." *Journal of Philosophy* 105(10):634–663.

Gershman, Samuel J., Eric J. Horvitz, and Joshua B. Tenenbaum. (2015). "Computational Rationality: A Converging Paradigm for Intelligence in Brains, Minds, and Machines." *Science* 6245(349): 273–278.

Gibson, James. J. 1977. "The Theory of Affordances." In Robert Shaw and John Bransford (eds.) *Perceiving, Acting, and Knowing: Toward an Ecological Psychology*, 67–82. Mahwah, NJ: Lawrence Erlbaum.

Goffman, Erving. (1959). *The Presentation of Self in Everyday Life*. New York: Anchor.

Gregory, Richard L. (1981). *Mind in Science: A History of Explanations of Psychology and Physics*. London: Weidenfeld & Nicolson.

Hackman, Daniel A. and Martha J. Farah. (2009). "Socioeconomic status and the Developing Brain." *Trends in Cognitive Sciences* 13(2): 65–73.

Kahneman, Daniel. (2011). *Thinking, Fast and Slow*. New York: Farrar, Strauss, Giroux.

Krupnik, Joseph C. and Christopher Winship. (2015). "Keeping Up the Front: How Disadvantaged Black Youths Avoid Street Violence in the Inner City." In Orlando Patterson and Ethan Fosse (eds.) *The Cultural Matrix: Understanding Black Youth*, 311–350. Cambridge, MA: Harvard University Press.

Lakoff, George. 1999. *"Philosophy in the Flesh: A talk with George Lakoff."* www.edge.org/ 3rd_culture/lakoff/lakoff_p2.html (accessed 30 May 2017).

LeDoux, J. (1992). "Brain Mechanisms of Emotion and Emotional Learning." *Current Opinion in Neurobiology* 2(2): 191–197.

Martin, John Levi. (1996). "Structuring the Sexual Revolution." *Theory and Society* 25(1): 105–151.

McIntosh, Peggy. (1988). *"White Privilege and Male Privilege: A Personal Account of Coming to See Correspondences through Work in Women's Studies."* Wellesley, MA: Center for Research on Women.

Meloni, Maurizio. (2012). "On the Growing Intellectual Authority of Neuroscience for Political and Moral Theory: Sketch for a Genealogy." In F. Vander Valk (ed.) *Essays on Neuroscience and Political Theory: Thinking the Body Politic*, 25–49. London and New York: Routledge.

Miłkowski, Marcin. (2013). *Explaining the Computational Mind*. Cambridge, MA: MIT Press.

Mills, Jon, and Januscz Polanowski. (1997). *The Ontology of Prejudice*. Amsterdam and Atlanta, GA: Rodopi.

Norman, Donald A. (1999). "Affordance, Conventions, and Design." *Interactions* 6(3): 38–42. www.jnd.org/dn.mss/affordance_conventi.html (accessed 12 August 2015).

Patterson, Orlando. (2015). "Overview." In Orlando Patterson and Ethan Fosse (eds.) *The Cultural Matrix: Understanding Black Youth*, 1–138. Cambridge, MA: Harvard University Press.

Reber, Arthur. (1989). "Implicit Learning and Tacit Knowledge." *Journal of Experimental Psychology: General* 118: 219–235.

Sampson, Robert J. (2015). "Continuity and Change in Neighborhood Culture: Toward a Structurally Embedded Theory of Social Altruism and Moral Cynicism." In Orlando Patterson and Ethan Fosse (eds.) *The Cultural Matrix: Understanding Black Youth*, 210–228. Cambridge, MA: Harvard University Press.

Scott-Philips, Thom. (2017). "A (Simple) Experimental Demonstration that Cultural Evolution Is Not Replicative, but Reconstructive – and an Explanation of Why This Difference Matters." *Journal of Cognition and Culture* 17(1–2): 1–11.

Searle, John. (1991). "Response: The Background of Intentionality and Action." In E. Lepore and R. Van Gulick (eds.) *John Searle and His Critics*, 289–299. Cambridge, MA: Blackwell.

Searle, John (1995). *The Construction of Social Reality*. New York: Free Press.

Smolensky, P., G. Legendre, and Y. Miyata. (1993). "Integrating Connectionist and Symbolic Computation for the Theory of Language." *Current Science* 64: 381–391.

Still, Jeremiah D. (2009). *Conceptualizing Design Affordances from a Cognitive Perspective*. Ph.D. diss., Iowa State University.

Still, Jeremiah D. and Veronica J. Dark. (2008). "An Empirical Investigation of Affordances and Conventions." In John S. Gero and Ashok K. Goel (eds.) *Design Computing and Cognition '08: Proceedings of the Third International Conference on Design Computing and Cognition*, 457–472. Amsterdam: Springer.

Sun, Ron. (1994). *Integrating Rules and Connectionism for Robust Commonsense Reasoning*. New York: Wiley.

Sun, Ron. (2012). "Prolegomena to Cognitive Social Sciences." In Ron Sun (ed.) *Grounding Social Sciences in Cognitive Sciences*, 3–32. Cambridge, MA: MIT Press.

Sun, Ron, ed. (2008). *The Cambridge Handbook of Computational Psychology*. Cambridge: Cambridge University Press.

Sun, Ron, Edward Merrill, and Todd Peterson. (2001). "From Implicit Skills to Explicit Knowledge: A Bottom-Up Model of Skill Learning." *Cognitive Science* 25: 203–244.

Sutton, John. (2012). "Exograms and Interdisciplinarity: History, the Extended Mind, and the Civilizing Process." In Richard Menary (ed.) *The Extended Mind*, 189–226. Cambridge, MA: MIT Press.

Sutton, John (2016). "Scaffolding Memory: Themes, Taxonomies, Puzzles." In Charles Stone and Lucas Bietti (eds.) *Contextualizing Human Memory: An Interdisciplinary Approach to Understanding How Individuals and Groups Remember the Past*, 187–206. New York and London: Routledge.

Sweller, J. (1988). "Cognitive Load during Problem Solving: Effects on Learning." *Cognitive Science* 12: 257–285.

Tomasello, Michael. (1999). *The Cultural Origins of Human Cognition*. Cambridge, MA: Harvard University Press.

Tran, Randy and Harold Pashler. (2017). "Learning to Exploit a Hidden Predictor in Skill Acquisition: Tight linkage to Conscious Awareness." *PLoS ONE* 12(6): e0179386. https://doi.org/10.1371/journal.pone.0179386.

Veblen, Thorstein. (1914). *The Instinct of Workmanship and the Industrial Arts*. New York: Macmillan.

Warwick, Andrew. (2003). *Masters of Theory: Cambridge and the Rise of Mathematical Physics*. Chicago: University Of Chicago Press.

Weber, Max. ([1927] 1961). *General Economic History*, trans. Frank H. Knight. New York: Collier.

Weber, Max (1958). *The Protestant Ethic and the Spirit of Capitalism*, trans. Talcott Parsons. New York: Scribner.

Weber, Max ([1968] 1978). *Economy and Society: An Outline of Interpretive Sociology* 3 vols, ed. Guenther Roth and Claus Wittich. Berkeley: University of California Press.

Wilson, William Julius. (2009). *More than Just Race: Being Black and Poor in the Inner City (Issues of Our Time)*. New York: Norton.

Woolgar, Steve. (1991). "Configuring the User: The Case of Usability Trials." In Keith Grint and Steve Woolgar (eds.) *The Machine at Work: Technology, Work and Organization*, 66–94. London: Polity.

6

SELVES, PERSONS, AND THE SOCIAL

It may seem that I have gone about this backwards: in the last chapter we considered the complex interweaving of tacit and explicit, their relation of mutual scaffolding, and the problems of conceptualizing the relations of internal to external facts. It might seem better to have done this in reverse: to make sense of the self as an organized, cognizing unit and to figure out how the self develops, how it engages with the external world, and also perhaps to figure out what kinds of selves there are. There is also a philosophical literature that figures in cognitive science, and occasionally in social science itself, which ascribes intentionality to groups, to a "we"; and this becomes another self that engages with the world, and the strategy of starting with the self might take us directly to it. But while starting with the self in this way would be a strategy that more or less fits with the standard computational approach, and also can be found in attempts to identify the self and consciousness with brain regions, it also takes sides in the issues that have run through the book so far.

What are the "sides" here? The big distinctions are between internal and external approaches, that is to say approaches that seek explanations in the world outside the traditional "mind" as described by the concepts of folk psychology: concepts such as affordances and those that build on folk psychology and extend and correct it, and use the corrected versions as explanations of the nature of the engagement with the world. The strategies discussed earlier, by, for example Gintis (2007), reflect the latter strategy: we clean up folk psychology by reducing it to its rational-choice core, and then explain adaptations as strategies for dealing with the world, and social life, and even animal ecological communities in terms of game-theoretic consequences that define the strategic situation. Or we construct a model of individual agents whose interactions can be modeled to produce aggregate patterns (Sun et al. 2001; Sun et al. 2014). But there are many other variants on the internal approach.

However, with the self, the person, the agent – however we describe the topic – we inevitably face problems which the internal approach seems incapable of solving. The concept is bound up with other problem concepts, including personality, personhood, consciousness, and "mind" itself. From the starting point of these concepts, getting an account of the self is a matter of understanding the cognitive, and preferably also neural, mechanisms by which self-awareness occurs, or that make for the individual experience of the world which belongs to and in a sense defines the self as something distinctive. But when we look at the anthropological (and philosophical) evidence about what we might call folk theories of the self and of personhood we get something very different, and very far from the kind of universal "self" that the internalist approach leads to.

What grounds the external approach? The starting point is the fact of diversity in overt, articulated concepts of the self. A famous and well-developed example is the Akan concept of the self – an African example which is part of a living, modern form of life. The Akan people have three self-related concepts forming "a tripartite conception of a person, considering a human being to be constituted by three elements: *okra, sunsum,* and *honam* (or *nipadua*: body)" (Gyekye 1978: 278).

> a human individual is regarded as an embodied *okra*. The body (*nipadua*, literally, "bodily tree") is the organic growth of a biological foundation that is jointly laid by man and woman when they unite in the mating process. In that process the mother contributes the *mogya*, literally, "the blood," and the father contributes *nloro*, literally, "semen." Both contributions have social significance. The *mogya* is the basis of lineage.
>
> *(Wiredu 1992: 111)*

Okra is "the life principle in a person, his vital force, the source of his energy, [and] is linked closely with another concept, namely *honhom* ... which means 'breath'", and is lodged in the head (Gyekye 1978: 278; italics in the original). As in the Western tradition with "pneuma," the term is ambiguous between its external meaning and its "spiritual" one as something like soul, which leaves the body with the last breath (Barfield [1928] 1964; Davidson 1978).

The *sunsum*, sometimes translated as "spirit," is the basis of the distinct personality and character of someone, and also has experiences: it is an analogue to "the mind" in that it acts on the brain (Gyekye 1978: 279). But "the word for person in Akan is *onipa*" (Wiredu 1992: 104), and this has other properties: the other terms are about that which is given at birth; one does not become a person until one has fulfilled certain obligations or, in effect, become a grown-up.

> A real *onipa* is a living being of human parentage who, through the biological, psychological, cognitive, and moral apprenticeship of a childhood

exposed to moral persuasion and correction, has come to develop moral sensibilities and rational habits conducive to a productive and edifying life in society.

(Wiredu 1992: 109)

It is a concept (unlike the English "person"), that is susceptible to degrees, and is not an all or nothing designation. And it is a strongly normative concept, bound up with social roles, lineage, and so on. This is reflected in ritual: when an infant dies it is not treated as a death of a person because, among other things that distinguishes it from a "person," it cannot be an ancestor (Wiredu 1992: 105–6).

So what do we do with this kind of concept of a person, or with this account of mind, body, and so forth? It is of course possible to dismiss these concepts as irrelevant to the true notion of self revealed by internal arguments, or to treat them as cognitive errors. But there are some reasons to be wary of this. The concepts, it should be clear, have important "external" elements – blood, semen, lineage, rituals, expectations, statuses, and so on – and are manifested physically. The division between person and not yet a person is manifested in rituals of death. Moreover, there is a telling clue: in all of these concepts, in their premodern form, there is an external (often physical) element, such as breath, bound up with the supposed internal element.

This strongly suggests, but only suggests, that the self as actually experienced is in some sense "socially constructed" or narrativized, based on external facts and incorporating external facts, rather than being a product and expression of purely internal processes. There is another set of considerations that follow from the discussion of the last chapter. The world is differentially accessible: some things that are part of the social and physical environment are, so to speak, taken care of and cognitively convenient, and even below the threshold of conscious experience – but serve to produce the normal life-world of the person. In any case, it is difficult to see how internal processes could produce culturally different experiences of self or personhood on their own.

This, then, is the big muddle: we have, in the standard approach, a strongly individualistic notion of the self. When we come to the problem of diversity, we are faced with a variety of concepts, which are matched up to activities or things and are not purely internal. Yet these external aspects of self have a strong influence on what people do, what they think about themselves, and on the way they experience the world and their social interactions. Indeed, it is the normal view in social psychology that "political ideologies and the position of one's group in the social structure create, sustain and influence people's personality traits through shaping their contemporary self-identities" (Turner 2004: xiii). So it looks like we have strong causal influences on the shaping and production of the self coming from opposite directions: the purely internal and developmental, and the social and communal. We have also, as seen in the last chapter, some possible tools for thinking about this, particularly the notion of scaffolding. But the use of these tools is subject to the same kinds of issues we have become familiar with in previous chapters, though in some novel and complex forms.

The Problems: A Guide

The problem of the self brings to the surface some basic issues that figure throughout the cognitive science literature. The phrase "create, sustain, and influence" takes us to the limits of social psychology. From a cognitive science point of view we want more: how exactly do these causal processes work? Is the path through "contemporary self-identities" the only, or even the most important, path? What about the external structures that make for the cognitively convenient life-world? The kinds of unexpected influences represented by the influence of verb tense forms on a vast range of behavior? The role of epigenetics? In the next few pages I will list and discuss briefly some of the key issues that vex this literature, some of which are forms of issues we have already encountered, some of which are new. The problems here are so complex, and the alternatives so closely linked to other issues, that there is no way to cut through them easily. The focus, however, will be on the ways these relate to the problem of "the social."

The Cause/Code Puzzle

The most basic issue for cognitive science is the problem of the shift from the causal world to the world of concepts, representations, or information. This is fundamental to the problem of the self, as it is to every other issue we have discussed. The external world, and much of the internal world of the body and the brain itself, is unmistakably causal: it consists of objects, chemistry, electrical impulses, and so forth. To make anything like the computer analogy of the standard approach work causes must somehow produce code. Indeed, because all the models of cognition are computational, it is taken as a given that this does in fact happen, even if we do not know how. As we have seen, the existence of DNA and RNA is a tantalizing basis for the faith that this problem will be solved: they show, or are taken to show, that there is no problem in something being both causal and coded, in being physical yet transmitting "information" (Gallistel forthcoming).

There is a small but persistent ambiguity here in that the code aspect of these processes is itself a kind of model, and there are different ways to model natural processes mathematically, so that it is not clear whether the arguments support anything beyond the claim that the model in question predicts or fits the process as distinct from saying this really is the code. The language of coding and encoding is nevertheless ubiquitous in this literature, and there are many reasons for thinking that something like coding has to be taking place. Memory, for example, needs to be stored; and it needs to be found, so it needs an "address" according to the conventional view of memory. To do either of these things, it is argued, it must be encoded in such a way to enable this.

There are influential proposals that attempt to solve a form of this problem: the transformation of external impulses into signals. The idea is that some mathematically describable quantity – such as wave properties or the distance between spikes in electronic frequencies in brain patterns – can be converted, by some as yet unknown brain process, into information-bearing code. There is a sense that something like this "has to" happen. We hear words (i.e. code), but what goes into our ears are vibratory waves with physical properties that have to be somehow converted into the words we "hear." But of course the words are not the same as the code, which is presumably a deep brain phenomenon that is universal and innate rather than learned or learnable, as the words are. So we need another transformation to actually turn the code into words that we understand. But that transformation needs to involve learning the language itself. And this sound-to-understood word transformation has to happen nearly instantaneously and not consciously.

This suggests a division of labor in brain processes between the innate and universal parts of the process and the learned and "cultural" or socially determined ones, which are incorporated into brain processes by becoming part of long-term memory. And this in turn suggests – though the exact linkages are very vague – that something built up out of the innate stuff amounts to a theory-like thing, an architecture, or a schema that arises in the developmental process universally and is not subject to the kinds of variation that learned things such as languages and distinctive socially distributed responses, the sorts of things designated as culture or habitus, have. These must be, so to speak, inserted into the architecture or over the schemas, and have a theory-like character with combinatorial, encoded, content that is not innate or based on innately given transformative processes, but is consistent with and combines with the encoded things that are innate.

Where this picture becomes problematic is with aspects of the developmental process and things that go on in the brain relating to social and emotional topics, such as trust, which do not seem to fit the code model and have a dose-response character. It is known that oxytocin levels influence trust, for example, and that changes these levels can be produced by such acts as touching a partner's hand. This does not seem like the sort of thing that is coded. But it does affect the kinds of things that are associated with the self, with self-other relations, and that wind up in memory, such as feelings and aversions.

The Homunculus Problem

There is a known problem with accounts of the self. The standard approach begins with a self-like thing – a scientist in the crib, for example – and accounts for the later self as a product, and version, of this self and its engagement with the world. There is a name for this self – the homunculus – and a "problem," even a "fallacy," associated with it. The issue appears in connection with the problem of mental imagery, which appears to produce a regress: we need, according to a standard way of thinking about perception, to have the elements of perception turned into a mental image or interpreted; this needs an interpreter, in our heads, constructing these images, like making a movie for us, so that we see, for example, a dog. We are not the interpreters: we see the dog, or the movie. The interpreting and constructing is done for us, off-stage, by a homunculus. But how does the homunculus that is doing the interpreting see the world? It needs a perceived world, a movie, so to speak, to start from as well. Where does it get this movie if not from another movie-maker, a homunculus inside the homunculus? And where does that one get its movie? The point of stating this as a fallacy is to show that by appealing to a homunculus we explain nothing; or, rather, we push the explanation back from one mystery to another mystery. Similarly for the self: explaining the self in terms of some more basic self just forces us to account for the more basic self, which we are no better equipped to account for by pushing it back one step.

The problem would be a philosophical curiosity if pushing things back a step in more or less the same way was not a common strategy. It points to a common problem with explanations that merely restate the problem being explained in different form. A simple example is this: there is a problem about norms which arises from the tacit character of many norms. Even social scientists have difficulty specifying what the norms are in a given situation. So how do the people who are supposedly acting in terms of these norms, as a kind of tacit theory, acquire this theory or internalize these norms? What powers do they have that the social scientist doesn't? We can say that there must be a norm-detection system which performs this task. We can even argue that because there are norms, and people need to be aware of them in some fashion to respond to them, there *has to be* a norm-detection system. But we still need an answer to the question of how such a system *could* perform this task. Imagining a little social scientist in our heads doing the detecting won't help unless we grant her quasi-magical powers that ordinary social scientists don't have. And we would need to know where she got those powers – which just continues the regress. There is a tempting use of "evolution" as an answer to such questions which absolves the user of any responsibility to say *how* it evolved: it is enough to say that because it is there it must have been the product of selection. But these are all "has to have been" arguments rather than explanations.

More generally, the problem is this: when does the self start? There are quite various answers to this question, such as by locating it in immunology in the development of the body's response to foreign cells. And there are commonplace usages of the term homunculus itself, not to specify a fallacy but to specify a solution. These come in various forms, from the thought that in the developmental process in embryo, neurons must get organized, make connections, and define their functions, and that to do this there must be some sort of organizer, or proto-self, that directs but also emerges from prior processes of self-organization, such as those that process immunological responses.

The term is also used in relation to the body and the sense of what one's body is. And this does seem like a good candidate for role of core of the self. The homunculus, in this context, means the part of the brain, together with some set of capacities of this part of the brain, which produces the activities and responds to the feedbacks that eventuate in self-consciousness, starting with body awareness. This requires two bodies, so to speak: the body as mapped in the somatosensory cortex, that enables one to move around in space; and what is called the body schema, meaning a sense of one's body that is the result of experience with it and its motions and place in physical space that goes beyond the static body, and amounts to something like a theory of what the body is and can do in space, but which is deeply rooted in the fundamental processes of the nervous system. There is a rare deficit associated with this distinction, involving "difficulties in identifying body parts and/or appreciating their relative relations to one another" (Mendoza 2011: 427), which indicates a failure with the body schema and therefore the body awareness that it makes possible: the person can still move, just not grasp the implicit theory of the body.

The Mirror Neuron Alternative

This problem cuts pretty deeply into accounts of the development of human social interaction. There is a large literature on infants' capacity to detect intentions. It turns out that they are pretty good at distinguishing accidents from intentional actions (Woodard 2009; Sakkalou and Gattis 2012; Baron-Cohen et al. 2013; Lee et al. 2015). This seems to warrant a certain picture: that there are real things called intentions that cause actions; that infants (and adults) have a homunculus with the special power of intention-detection which is doing the job that we might be doing when we reason out whether an action was intentional, but do this automatically, by different means. This is pure internalism: the explanation is in complicated internal mechanisms that in effect incorporate a theory of mind or something similar to it which is the basis of automatic inferences. But there is a problem with this picture: the infants have to do this with external data. We do use external data when we assess intentions overtly, for example in a court case, where the inferences are out in the open and debatable. But the model implies that the infants, and ordinary people as well, are doing something internal, and that this is being done by an internal inference-making homunculus.

There are, in fact, grounds for thinking that they, and we, are doing something different than "detecting" in this way. In the mirror neuron literature, "detecting" what someone is doing is part of perception, which activates the neurons for performing the same action of the detecting person. There is also evidence that in cases of intentional action we actually detect a subtle pre-act state, based on a "finding that the premotor system (where the mirror neurons are to be found) sometimes allows 'a brief prefix of the movement' to be exhibited, one which is recognizable by and can be responded to, involuntarily, by the other" (Reddy 2008: 56). But in either case, it is still something done entirely from external data. Can we get rid of the need for a homunculus here? There is a deep prejudice in cognitivism against behaviorism, and what are taken to be discredited behaviorist explanations that avoided reference to internal mental objects, which tried to deal with such things as one's knowledge of one's own intentions as an inference from external facts: I find myself wandering around looking and infer that I am looking for my glasses (Norman 1964; Skinner 1964). Mirror neuron explanations resemble this, with the difference that the "inferring" that is going on in reference to other people's intentions is a response not merely to external facts like noticing what they are doing, but also to noticing, or at least responding to, one's own involuntary response to what someone else is doing. But the involuntary mirroring response itself, which is internal, is based on external facts: in this respect, behaviorism was correct. We can hypothesize that this works through the mechanism of involuntary pattern recognition. If we combine external elements of a pattern with internal elements, such as subliminal awareness of a mirror neuron embodied response, we avoid the reduction of intention into a mysterious inner state that is also a causal force. We get instead something that allows for making the behavioral response, or at least the prefix to response, part of the pattern and part of the neuron activation pattern that includes mirror neuron-related perception.

The background to the discovery of mirror neurons – whose significance is still hotly debated, in large part because they are difficult to fit into the standard model (Hickock 2014: esp. 27–40) – needs a little explanation in order to see how they relate to the issue of the homunculus. The story is one we have already told. During a project involving measuring brain responses of a monkey with electrodes that monitored motor system activation, when an assistant working on the project returned from a break with ice-cream and began to eat it, he noticed that the monkey's brain was responding as though the monkey was itself making the motions of eating, and similarly to what the brain showed when the monkey was picking up a peanut (Reddy 2008: 55), led to the recognition that there was a fundamental link between the motor system and the perceptual system which involved the motor system being activated by perceptions of movements in others, and to the discovery of specialized neurons that connected the two: the mirror neurons. This also had implications for the self. It changed the way one had to think about "others" and therefore about the self–other relationship: at some level, the monkey was recognizing the lab worker as another like itself, with the same embodied capacities. Moreover, this now appeared to be a neuronal mechanism underlying the capacity to imitate.

Infant Imitation, Infant Social Selves?

Imitation, which we will see shortly is a high-stakes issue about the self, takes us back to the homunculus problem because it poses the question of what the monkey is doing when this mirror process is going on, and when it imitates, and what sort of self is involved. The problem of imitation thus seems to connect more or less directly to the problem of body schemas. The monkey could not respond without some sense of bodies in general, and the embodied character of what it was responding to. The same responses were not elicited in experiments with objects in motion rather than embodied action. So this seems as though there is some sort of proto-theory, a schema that allows the monkey to general-ize: the model of cognition as largely inferential, indeed, requires something like a theory to facilitate the inferences. The question becomes one of how this is acquired, and when. An equally startling result provides an important piece of data in relation to this question. Andrew Meltzoff and Keith Moore showed, and produced dramatic photographs as evidence, that neonates, immediately after birth, could imitate sticking a tongue out (Meltzoff and Moore 1977). On the theory-backed inference model this would appear to indicate that the infant had, before any post-utero experience to guide it or learn from, a capacity to recog-nize an embodied other as another, invoke their implicit theory of their own body, and act to mimic facial expressions. But where did this implicit theory come from? And how were the inferences that seem to be required possible for a newborn with no relevant experience or prompts to "activate" the theory?

No one – though in cognitive science this must be qualified because there are defenses of almost every possible thesis – wishes to defend the idea that infants have an implicit theory of self and other, mind, motivations to imitate, or any of the other things that might be thought to be implied by imitation understood as an act. But the reasoning that would lead to this conclusion is no different from the reasoning that leads to many other "must have been" conclusions about cognitive content. Nor did this kind of imitation fit with learning models, such as connectionism. There was no feedback, and there were no trials.

What is at stake here? The issue is this: where does the social life of an infant begin, and with what resources? More fundamentally, is there any such thing as a pre-social human? The act – if it is an act – of imitation clearly indicates that the social life of the child begins at the same time as its cognitive development, at least its development beyond some sort of innate endowment that is activated at birth or already activated *in utero*. The idea of a pre-social individual becomes, as a consequence, not an empirical phenomenon but a theoretical one – one in which the "pre-social" aspects of the individual need to be abstracted, on the basis of theoretical premises, from the actual empirical fact of active, apparently aware, social interaction from birth.

Not surprisingly, there were arguments to explain away Meltzoff and Moore's pictures, as not involving cognition, conscious effort, the self, recognition of the other, or action. The first claim was that these were reflexes. Many infant reflexes disappear quickly, and this one seemed to as well, suggesting they are sub-cortical phenomena – the cortical cingulate being the place of conscious effort. But many subsequent experiments weighed against this. Infant imitation was more variable, and often absent; it did not always appear immediately, but often much later in time – a day after the stimulus, for example (Reddy 2008: 53). The second argument was that whatever these imitative capacities were, they were irrelevant to cognitive development because they disappeared in a few months. This too turned out to be more complicated. People with certain kinds of frontal lesions imitate compulsively – it is thought they lack inhibitors; perhaps what appears in infants is inhibitory capacity. Infant imitation didn't look like something involuntary, but more like an intentional activity, perhaps of oral exploration. Moreover, unlike other reflexes, there was improvement in physical command, thus evidence of learning. And it was less clear that the capacity disappeared – it seemed instead that it was supplanted by better imitative capacities.

There were, however, many other forms of evidence for the significance of social interaction in infant development. The famous visual cliff experiments that were central to Gibson's thinking about how infants interacted competently with the world without learning worked like this: infants were placed on a glass bridge that covered a gap between tables, and the experiments showed that they did not go over the visual cliff, despite having no experience with cliffs or drop-offs (Gibson and Walk 1960). This was an important step toward the notion of affordances. But subsequent experiments showed something equally important and also "social." Babies could be coaxed across the cliff by the warm response to their doing so by their mothers, suggesting that emotional connection was equally fundamental to the infant's world. And the mother–child relation involved the same sorts of issues as the theory of the self: recognition of the other and conscious effort that signified cognition. This points to an early and pervasive role for interaction, but also one that is difficult to understand in conventional cognitive terms. Where do the relevant "representations" come from? What sort of inferences are being made? In what sense can anything, even self–world distinctions, be prior to the mother–infant bond and its emotional content?

So where does this leave us with the problem of the self? We have accounts that start with the development of antibodies that distinguish own cells from others, that start from motion and then move to bodies, to the firming up of self–world relations and self–object relations, to self-knowledge of bodies that is generalizable as body schemas, to various forms of self-consciousness – such as consciousness of experience, consciousness that experience is something belonging to one's self – to an articulable sense of one's self, a self–self relation that is itself conscious and open to conscious effort; and, finally, self–other relations which might, arguably, require all of these other self-related capacities in order to work, and particularly to apply the theory of mind to the job of inferring states of mind and beliefs, true or false, to others. We also have the interactively constructed self, the narrative self (indeed perhaps plural narrative selves), and the culturally defined self. Where do these fit in? Are they something that happens only once a proto-social self is established? Or are the influences we put under these headings – culture, interaction, and even narrative – there from the start, such as in the rhythms of life, or hearing Mozart, or hearing Mandarin inflections that the fetus is exposed to from the mother and her environment?

Personal Experience as the Core of the Self

One significant line of argument, taken especially in the philosophical literature, is that the central issue about the self is the connection of self and personal experience. In most of the discussion, there is a determinedly non-social focus: the issues have to do with such things as qualia, or the ways things seem to us; as Dennett (1988: 381) puts it, "an unfamiliar term for something that could not be more familiar to each of us: the ways things seem to us," especially in the case of visual experience of colors or such things as the way a particular glass of wine tastes to us. This experience is personal. Different creatures have different visual experiences. But explaining conscious experience, or even figuring out what an explanation of experience would look like, is a major stumbling block for conventional computational accounts, and indeed for the whole of cognitive science. It is bound up with the "hard problem" of explaining consciousness itself. But it is also critical for the socially relevant aspects of the concept of self: personal experience is the thing that distinguishes us from others, is our possession alone, and at the same time is the means by which we come to define and learn from self–world and self–other relations; and is the condition of self–self relations themselves in that we can only know ourselves through our personal experiences of our self. It is so central that thinkers who emphasize the centrality of personal experience typically ignore the social aspects of experience, perhaps because there is nothing to the social that is not filtered through personal experience. The rest of a fully phenomenological account follows from this thought (Ginev 2013).

The assumption here is that consciousness and conscious experience, and therefore conscious reflection or introspection, is not itself determined by the social environment, but fixed and universal. It is this presumed feature that makes it a viable starting point for approaching the social: we get a nice hierarchical image in which personal experience and the selfhood that corresponds to it are above the level of cognitive and brain processes, but produced by them; and social experience is above the level of the self, and explained by selves and their experiences. This neatly separates the "social" from the cognitive processes, and makes personal experience the gateway between them.

But there is good reason to reject this way of thinking. The issues are closely related to the problem of the limits of consciousness itself and the limits of self-reporting of mental processes. If we regard our access to our own mental processes as extremely limited, we can ask what "socially determined" aspects of mind lie beyond these limits, and whether the limits might also be, in part, determined by the social environment. Self-consciousness itself seems to be limited not only by intrinsic limitations of the brain but also by tacit, socially learned processes of inhibition. There are some obvious examples in studies of implicit bias such things as eye-blinks are measured as evidence of immediate response to stimuli of various kinds. The subjects routinely report no conscious bias in cases where the eye-blinks reveal bias. This suggests that what we are conscious of is partly determined by what is socially approved and disapproved of: the denials of bias represent conformity that is based on some form of tacit learning such that we repress or do not experience that which is socially proscribed.

There is a dramatic example of this: the discrepancy, for women, between sexual arousal as evidenced in brain patterns and physical changes and the conscious experience of arousal in the face of erotica. The stimulus of erotica – some male produced, some female produced – did not, for a large proportion of women, produce a subjective experience of arousal; and even, for some kinds of male-oriented erotica, produced self-reported feelings of shame and disgust. The brain scan evidence, and physical measures of genital arousal, however, told a different story: one of normal patterns of arousal and brain response (Laan et al. 1994; Laan and Everaerd, 1995; Rellini et al., 2005; Both et al., 2011; Laan and Both 2011). Personal experience did not correspond to the brain and physical manifestations. The neural correlates did not correlate. The disconnect is, plausibly enough, ascribable to social learning of inhibitions which work through inhibitory neurons. The discrepancies correspond to well-known social taboos. And it means that what we experience consciously is constrained and limited, in these cases very dramatically, by social learning, which is plausibly enough "tacit" social learning rather than the result of explicit instruction or direct messaging of some kind, and which is itself outside of conscious experience.

Is this merely one of the many oddities of cognitive science, marginal and irrelevant to anything important? The issue is a very large one: it is about the limits of the *Verstehen* bubble. Tacitly learned responses – which are called "automatic associations" in this literature and treated as following "from the direct activation of simple associations in memory," to distinguish them from "explicit cognitions" (Borg et al. 2010: 2150) – are the very stuff of "practice" and "culture." If they are among the things that are inaccessible or distorted we have a large part of "the social" which is also accessible to us only indirectly and with difficulty. Daniel Everett (2016) calls this "the dark matter of the mind" and attributes many definable qualities to it. In relation to the self and personal experience, it creates two large problems.

The first is that to explain this "social" material one needs to go outside the *Verstehen* bubble. This involves some problematic moves. One is to invoke processes that can only be understood in traditional mental language by problematic extensions, using terms like tacit knowledge or belief as tacit beliefs, or aliefs, as they are sometimes called. Do such things actually exist, or is this a case of the kind Weber mentioned in which one makes conduct meaningful by ascribing motives, when the conduct is actually caused, at least in part, by other, "meaningless" causal processes such as contagion or biological drives.

The second is even more problematic. What is the relation between behavior and brain processes? In the sexual stimulus case, the brain and even genital arousal processes are screened not only from consciousness but also from behavior. This suggests that there are powerful inhibitors also in the brain that intervene between other, reactive, responses, recordable in the brain, which would normally lead to action but do not. This, it would appear, provides a major mechanism for "social" influences. A common interpretation in the mirror neuron literature is that the default response to the physical actions of another is imitation, which would account for neurons devoted to the execution of actions being activated when an action is perceived. The response, observable in the neonate, is gradually overcome by learned inhibitions, and produced by an inhibitory system that shadows the mirror system and determines which responses lead to behavior. The learned inhibitions, however, fall into the category of tacit learning: they are not cases of verbal transfer of information, though they may be intertwined with verbalizations, but of something that happens largely or entirely outside of consciousness, which is also to say outside of the *Verstehen* bubble. This learning is at least partially "social," not only in the sense that it occurs in the course of interaction with other humans but also in the sense that it varies socially, so that what is learned in one social setting is different from what is learned in another. And this learning intervenes at one of the most fundamental levels: the causal sequences leading from neuron activation to action.[1] This means that whatever importance one attaches to personal experience and the explanation of personal experience, it is not the exclusive gateway between the cognitive and the social.

Some Not Very Good Answers: Selves and the Problem of Coherence

With these complexities in mind, we can finally turn to the question of the self, and the alternative accounts of the self. The range of research, theorizing, and problematizing of the concept of the self is exceptionally large and confusing. One can arrange, and conceive of, the problem of the self in many ways. As we have seen, it includes the somewhat better-defined problem of mind-reading in some accounts of the self, so the same issues arise, and even more issues arise: the nature of personal experience, the developing sense of having a body, and many more. We can consider the self to be the whole package, and make each aspect of the self something that a theory of the self must account for. We can arrange them, as I have, in order of commonly supposed basicness, where we claim that each prior step is a precondition for each subsequent step. Or we can omit (or ignore) one or another (or even many) of the self-relations in question, and construct a theory of what we take to be the real self which is more limited in what it attempts to explain.

Comprehensive coverage of the problem is thus hardly possible. But if we reproduce and vary somewhat our list of approaches to the theory of mind from Chapter 4, we can get a basic framework for distinguishing approaches to this problem, though one that will need significant supplementation. One supplement is this: there are accounts that deny there is a self, and hence a problem to be explained, on the grounds that the notion of the self adds nothing of explanatory value and there is nothing neural to which it corresponds. If we say that the self is real only if it corresponds to a neural process, we would dismiss it as a scientifically relevant concept. The reasoning is this:

> no single underlying neural process that can stand in a one-to-one relation to our everyday notion of the self. The ontological implication of the theory is that *no such things as selves exist in the world.* For all scientific and philosophical purposes, the notion of self – as a theoretical entity – can be safely eliminated (Metzinger 2003, p. 3).
>
> *(Beni 2016: 3730; emphasis in original)*

We can think of this account of the self, the eliminativist account (Beni 2016: 3727), as falling at the far end of the spectrum, beyond the four alternatives to be discussed here. At the other end of the spectrum, beyond the narrative self, one can find pluralist accounts of the self, which retain the concept but dispense with the idea of one self, as well as with the idea that there need be any neural correlate of the self. The four remaining options treat the self as a substantial object which requires a theoretical explanation. Where the four accounts differ, and the point to notice, is in the question of where they locate the coherence that is taken to be definitive of the self. We can modify the list from the theory of mind discussion as follows:

a   a purely internal account, in which awareness leading to self-awareness and other markers of self-consciousness and selfhood is pre-theoretical and partly learned, but as a kind of learning about one's self.

b   a universal theory-like conception of the self that is innate and needs only to be activated, perhaps based on a universal semantics but more likely based on a universal computational architecture or on specific module-like neural processes; alternatively, as more less universal body schemas which arise developmentally but are preconditions for bodily experience and the sense of self.

c   a cultural self, with a local semantic model and a local tacit theory of mind.

d   a narrative self, i.e., based on the publicly articulated forms of expression about the mind and the person, through which the self is discursively constituted and the discourse internalized. Here the substance of selfhood consists in the persistence of a master narrative which encompasses other narratives about the self, and which affects the brain from the outside, through habituation and similar processes, together with some propensity for narrativization which motivates the construct of such narratives, including narratives of the "true self."

As we have seen in the case of theory of mind, the extremes – the two beyond the spectrum extremes of eliminativism and pluralism, as well as a) and d) – can be made consistent with one another, and together provide an alternative to the middle two accounts.

Various examples could be given of each of these approaches, but I will limit the discussion to a few model cases. The a) category includes approaches that are aimed in part at minimizing the problem itself by taking the primary issue with the self to be minimal self-awareness, which can be limited further to bodily awareness. This then can be accounted for by a minimal self. The strategy can be nicely captured by the following:

> The existence of a coherent self-representatum for the first time introduces a **self–world border** into the system's model of reality. For the first time, system-related information now becomes globally available *as system-related* information, because the organism now has an internal image of itself as a whole, as a distinct entity possessing global features. On the other hand, environment related information can now be referred to as *non-self*. Objectivity emerges together with subjectivity. The functional relevance of this way of generating a very fundamental partitioning of representational content into two very general classes lies in the way in which it forms a necessary pre-condition for the activation of more complex forms of phenomenal content: *Relations* between the organism and varying objects in its environments can now for the first time be consciously represented. A system that does not possess a coherent, stable self-representatum is unable to internally represent all those aspects of reality associated with self-world, self-object, and, importantly, self-self and self-other relations.
>
> *(Metzinger 2005: 4; internal note omitted; emphases in original)*

Thomas Metzinger, the author of this formulation, adds a kind of scaffolding consideration to this: "complex information pertaining to dynamical subject-object relations can be extracted from reality and used for selective and flexible further processing only, if a conscious self-model is in existence" (Metzinger 2005: 4).

Cutting through the verbiage, the point is this: the infant, or the unborn, starts *without* a concept either of the self or the world. What gets developed is a boundary that emerges within a "system" – the system of the ecological setting of which the organism is a causal part. The boundary is not a causal one, but a conceptual one: the difference between the self and the world is a matter of an achieved representation of the "border" between the two, the "coherent self-representatum" which then allows the world outside the boundary to be represented, and for it to be represented as objective and the world inside as subjective.

The next two types are what is sometimes called substantialist, meaning that they take the self not to be discovered or constructed, but to be something with a definite structure that can be treated as a theoretical object. Ideally, a substantial notion of the self is grounded in something substantial, or structural, itself. Research directed at finding the place in the brain that is responsive to such things as images of the self are suggestive: they locate self-consciousness, or the capacity for self-consciousness, at a place in the brain that can be related to the characteristic functions of that part of the brain.

The problem to be solved by the computational approach, as Ron Sun and Nick Wilson put it, speaking here of personality, is this: "if it is a valid psychological construct, [it] should be accounted for by a cognitive architecture, without any significant additions or modifications of mechanisms or processes within the cognitive architecture" (Sun and Wilson 2014: 1). They explain the notion of cognitive architecture as follows:

> A computational "cognitive architecture" should, ideally, include all essential psychological entities, mechanisms, and processes of the human mind (Sun, 2004). The notion of a cognitive architecture should ideally be close to that of "personhood" (Pollock, 2008; Taylor, 1985). Within the cognitive architecture, the interaction among different subsystems (components and their mechanisms and processes) should be able to generate psychological phenomena of all kinds, which of course include personality-related phenomena (Sun and Wilson, 2011).
>
> *(Sun and Wilson 2014: 1)*

Here the point is to account for the self or personality, or whatever psychological phenomena one is interested in, as a computational outcome of the processes in the model of the person. The self is a product of these interacting processes. But the coherence is not in the self in the ordinary sense in which we talk about it, but in the architecturally organized processes that produce the self. This is a universalizing account, which posits some sort of computational content that corresponds with the self and generates the surface manifestations of selfhood.

One might not bother with centering the self in a computational architecture, but instead go directly to the idea of a universal theory-like thing, an innately given semantics for example, which included the concepts that are associated with the self. In this case the semantic markers would simply need to be instantiated by experience in order to be activated, and the self and its associated concepts would then be available for making inferences – about oneself and other selves. This is a much more limited account than the one suggested by Ron Sun. The standard he sets, the problem he thinks an account of the personality must solve, is more ambitious: it doesn't merely explain inferences about the self through a kind of tacit semantics; it also attempts to make sense of the idea of a coherent whole made up of a wide range of processes that are associated with the self – the emotions, the drives, and all the supposed psychological entities that together make a coherent self. This would include the kinds of representations that the semantic theory works with, or a surrogate for them. But it goes beyond being just an account of representations.

Sun's description of the problem takes over and updates the traditional behavioral science program and model for understanding what Talcott Parsons called the "personality system." That project was aspirational: it produced models, such as Parsons' own, which were long on arrows between hypothetical subsystems and short on answers to the question of what the arrows meant (Parsons 1965: 15–33). Sun's account is equally aspirational. But it at least proposes a way of answering the question of what the arrows or the supposed relations between the still hypothetical components – this time of the equally hypothetical architecture – might actually mean. The relations will be computational. This is an advance that comes at a price: it simply assumes that there will be, and will have to be, computational answers to these questions because the processes are computational. But at the same time it is an account consistent with the standard project, though Sun himself, as we have seen, has elaborated this project in a non-standard way.

There are, however, some puzzles revealed by this formulation. The personality system is different from what is ordinarily thought of as the self, especially the "self" of self-representation. It is the underlying causal and coded system that is largely inaccessible to consciousness, and therefore to self-conceptualization. We can simply take as given the fact that we do not have access to these processes, at least not fully. But we have access to *something* through introspection and reflection, and through the self that is reflected back to us from others. And we make up our self- conceptualization at least in part on the basis of what we have access to. But understanding how this works – how the real system and the one we think we have diverge – is tricky and will take a couple of asides.

One of the traditional motivators of discussions of introspection and language has been Wittgenstein's private language argument, which goes roughly like this: if we had an inner feeling (x), and we wrote down an x every time we had that feeling, we would, it seems, have a private language, or a piece of one. But Wittgenstein suggests otherwise: that to have a language, and to refer to something, requires something like a public standard, or what he called a criterion. It is only when others can assess the statements one makes (the x one marks, in this case – can a language do the usual things that language does) that we can talk about whether the statement is true, for example. This has been an argument that philosophers of cognitive science have wrestled with and disliked (Carruthers 2009: 164–76); it takes language out of the internal processes of the brain and into the realm of the social. And they have a point: a feeling of pain is personal. Nothing "social" is needed to recognize and respond to the feeling.

This is a place where the idea of the *Verstehen* bubble helps. If the bubble is limited to what we can understand about others – in the sense of understanding what their actions mean – and to understanding what their utterances mean, how do we understand utterances about pain? How do we know we are talking about the same thing they are when we talk about pain? Joint attention is not enough: there is nothing visible we can both attend to. But we nevertheless manage, though sometimes with difficulty, to talk about pain, as well as lots of other things that are not publicly accessible. But if we think of this in terms of the *Verstehen* bubble, we can also see that Wittgenstein had a point. We need some basis for attributing pain to others and matching these attributions to our own pain. There are behavioral manifestations of these inner things, and when we learn to use the language of pain and mental language generally, we learn the public aspects as well. Wittgenstein talked about "natural signs" in this context (see Rubinstein 2004), and that points to some other answers. We cannot be "sure" we are talking about the same thing in these cases, but we have a pretty good correlation between our public manifestations of our inner feelings and their public manifestations. And if we do not frequently go astray in thinking about these things we have some assurance, and as good an assurance as we need, that we are talking about the same thing.

This is a good model also for talking about the self and self-conceptions. We don't have "access" to the inner systemic processes of the personality system, if there even is such a thing. But we do have plenty of access to our own pain-like feelings of emotionally responding to situations; and there is a public, behavioral aspect to all of these inner things, at least to those things that we can form a self-conception out of. And a large part of our interactive experience in the world takes the form of validating or invalidating these self-conceptions. This is the process C. H. Cooley labeled the "looking-glass self" (Cooley 1902: 152), meaning the self we build up out of others' perceptions of us and of their explicit characterizations of us, as well as our tacitly learned, conditioned responses to their approval and disapproval of our actions, statements, and so forth. The learning goes on at the unconscious or tacit level, but our inner responses to this – shame or doubt, for example – are feelings that *are* accessible to us and that we can process in the course of developing a self-conception. What this process might be is a topic we will return to shortly.

An additional feature of the notion of the self is in the category of what we might call hermeneutic: we, in our *Verstehen* bubble, are both self-interpreting and interpreting the selves of others, and in ways that of course reflect the limitations of the *Verstehen* bubble – limitations imposed by the fact of our limited access to our own mental processes. But we also do this on limited data, and with a background history and heuristics that improve our capacity to recognize patterns, such as those of social situations, and fill them in. And we may operate with more elaborate, semi-permanent heuristics that make life manageable. What sort of heuristics? There is a tradition in psychology of studying these aspects of self-perception which suggests that we construct our self-conception and the conception we have of others' selves by positing a true self which has characteristics that go beyond and conflict with the data we have about people. The true self we attribute both to ourselves and others is a better self than the evidence would suggest. But it is through this true self in addition to "the data" that we interpret others' actions and our own (Strohminger et al. 2017). This is in itself a means of producing a kind of coherence: it goes beyond the data in a particular way, and in this respect is like a theory. What kind of a theory? We have all the options listed earlier to characterize it: tacit and cultural, innate and activated, or derived from narrative.

Terms like "construct" are of course misleading here. The usage is analogical. We do not "construct a self" consciously, and even if we attempted to, we would start from and employ materials that are taken from life. Even a novelist constructing a character works by using narrative forms to evoke a self: fully describing it would neither be possible nor desirable. As with pain, we need to respond with empathy to the descriptions in ways that involve our inner feelings, not just responses to marks on a page. But it is also worth asking if there are cognitive processes that produce the kind of coherence that we associate with the concept of the self.

Apparently, one important neural function of deep sleep is to enable the editing and consolidation of episodic memories – memories of events, which of course will normally arise from social/cultural interaction. This neural activity itself reshapes neural connectivity.

> Sleep benefits memory consolidation. The reviewed studies indicate that this consolidating effect is not revealed under all circumstances but is linked to specific psychological conditions. Specifically, we discuss to what extent memory consolidation during sleep depends on the type of learning materials, type of learning and retrieval test, different features of sleep and the subject population. Post-learning sleep enhances consolidation of declarative, procedural and emotional memories. The enhancement is greater for weakly than strongly encoded associations and more consistent for explicitly than implicitly encoded memories. Memories associated with expected reward gain preferentially access to sleep-dependent consolidation. For declarative memories, sleep benefits are more consistently revealed with recall than recognition procedures at retrieval testing. Slow wave sleep (SWS) particularly enhances declarative memories whereas rapid eye movement (REM) sleep preferentially supports procedural and emotional memory aspects. Declarative memory profits already from rather short sleep periods (1–2 h). Procedural memory profits seem more dose-dependent on the amount of sleep following the day after learning. Children's sleep with high amounts of

SWS distinctly enhances declarative memories whereas elderly and psychiatric patients with disturbed sleep show impaired sleep-associated consolidation often of declarative memories. Based on the constellation of psychological conditions identified we hypothesize that access to sleep-dependent consolidation requires memories to be encoded under control of prefrontal-hippocampal circuitry, with the same circuitry controlling subsequent consolidation during sleep.

(Diekelmann et al. 2009: 309)

So what is being consolidated about the Dinkelmann sequence – from self-world, self-object, and self-self (a conscious model of which is a condition of extracting complex and dynamic information from reality), to self-other relations – reflects a conventional view of the order of appearance, and perhaps the scaffolding, of the self. And it places self–other relations at the tail end and, implicitly, interpersonal emotion also towards this end. Different kinds of memories have different effects in the process of consolidation. While "post-learning sleep enhances consolidation of declarative, procedural and emotional memories," it seems that "enhancement is greater for weakly than strongly encoded associations and more consistent for explicitly than implicitly encoded memories. Memories associated with expected reward gain preferentially access to sleep-dependent consolidation" (Diekelmann et al. 2009: 309). So this is not a neutral process. But it produces a kind of coherence.

There is also another coherence-producing process which has more immediate effects, one which is associated with split brain research. Here the argument, based on studies of people with severed connections between the two halves of the brain, suggests that right brain perception is limited to more or less independent, dissociated but objective observational content which needs to be "interpreted" by the left brain to produce coherent thought. Michael Gazzaniga introduces the idea that the left brain serves as an "interpreter." He explains the findings thus:

The right cannot make inferences, and as a consequence is extremely limited in what it can have feelings about. It seems to deal mainly with raw experience in an unembellished way. The left hemisphere, on the other hand, is constantly, almost reflexively, labeling experiences, making inferences as to cause, and carrying out a host of other cognitive activities. In recent studies it has been observed that the left brain carries out visual search tasks in a "smart" way whereas the right hemisphere performs in a poor way (Kingstone [et al.], 1993). Everywhere we turn, we see these clues. The left hemisphere is busy differentiating the world whereas the right is simply monitoring the world (Mangun et al., 1993).

(Gazzaniga 1995: 1398)

This amounts to a distinction between coherent thought and "monitoring" that points to a potential answer to the problem of coherence of the self: part of the job of the left brain "interpreter," which Gazzaniga (1995: 1394) regards as a module, is "catching up with all this parallel and constant activity." And this has implications for selfhood because, although it is not "the system that provides the heat, the stuff, the feelings about our thoughts," it is "in many ways … the system that provides the story line or narrative of our lives" by turning what is monitored, the heat and the stuff, into something coherent.

This takes us to the verge of the narrative theory of the self. But there is another option between the narrative conception and the idea of a substantial self based on a universal architecture or universal theory-like endowment: the cultural approach. In a sense, the semantic approach is a stepping-stone to the cultural account of the self. If it is plausible to reduce the problem of the self to the problem of semantically universal concepts of the self in the language of thought or mentalese, which leaves us with the problem of explaining how mentalese relates to the actual highly diverse concepts of self in different cultures, it is more plausible to account for the self directly in terms of non-universal concepts, or culturally specific concepts. This too involves the idea of a theory-like shared endowment which is constitutive of the self and provides coherence to the self.

The passage quoted earlier about the Akan concept of the person should suffice to explain the attraction of the cultural approach: any concept of the self, or self-concept that goes beyond such things as a very minimal kind of body-awareness or brain circuit response to images of the self, is going to involve aspects of the self that are "culturally variable." Since Mauss's "Techniques of the Body" ([1934] 1973), we have been aware that the body itself, as it is lived in, is highly variable across cultures – not to mention the variation in folk biology and medical beliefs, in addition to folk theories of the soul, the person, and of the social meanings and implications of all of these things.

The difficulty, which cognitive science shares with social theory generally, is not with these facts but with the explanation. The older conception of culture on which this explanation relies runs like this: there is a set of presupposition-like or program-like cognitive elements, or, alternatively, embodied practices (a social habitus) that is shared between people in a culture or a social group that deter-mines their thinking, and therefore their behavior. The concept of culture itself has been subject to withering criticism (Lizardo 2015), and there has been a general acceptance of the idea that there is considerable individual variability within groups. This puts the focus on a variant of the same problem that we encountered with Chomsky: the question of how, if there are shared cognitive structures, they got where they need to be for the explanation to work. The cultural form of this problem is of course different, and in some ways even more per-plexing: what is it about group membership that produces the same "program" in the heads of its members? It is one thing to posit such a shared program as an explanation of common behavioral patterns in a group. It is another to account for the "programming."

Learning theory does not help here. Normal learning is based on experiences; experiences are highly variable. Tacit learning is no different. It is of course true that young students can learn basic arithmetic, or learn basic inferential patterns about making generalizations, inferences to subsets, and so forth. But this is the result of schooling, a particular form of discipline and an invented social technology. The famous experiments by the Russian cultural psychologist Alexander Luria ([1974] 1976: 112) showed that unschooled peasants, otherwise competent, did not make these inferences, or at least did not articulate them. And the difficulty in bringing about competence in these inferences shows that the capacity to make them does not come from mere universal experience. It is the product of scaffolding, involving overt interventions into cognitive development, as we have seen earlier in connection with Vygotsky (1978) (see Chapters 3 and 5).

If we substitute a different conception of culture, one in which the intertwining of tacit and explicit elements is basic, and allow for the consequences of individual variability in experiences and therefore learning, and assume that there is a great deal of tacit learning and empathic response in the mastery of the elements of a culture, we can avoid the problems of the "culture as shared program" model. But the cost of doing so for the standard model of cognition is significant. If we cannot simply extend it to cover culture, as commentators like Gintis supposed would be possible, we are forced to recognize that the formation of the self is causally influenced from a very basic level by socially variable experiences and by numerous external causes rather than internal developmental processes, causes which affect what is traditionally thought of as the self. This represents a shift from internal "architectural" explanation to explanations pointing to scaffolding, affordances, individual variability, and a shift to external explanations of coherence.

The narrative theory of the self preserves many of the advantages of the cultural theory without committing itself to the internal, programming, model. The cultural part of the narrative self is made up of no more than the various narrative accounts of ourselves and the conduct that we deploy in explaining ourselves to others and in reflection. These are, for the narrative account, two sides of the same coin: we do not have an inner self or true self that is accessible to us apart from the stories we can tell about it and the explanations we can give. They are external, interactional, other-oriented, and dependent on the fact that they have a role in social interaction and acceptance by others, as well as resonating in some sense with inner experience. The coherence of the self, at least the self in any but the most minimal physical or embodied sense, is ultimately itself a narrative achievement – a result of making a higher-level story out of the various narrations of the self that we have deployed in understanding ourselves and explaining ourselves, even in thought, to others. Shaun Gallagher (2000: 14) gives a version of this by distinguishing;

the "minimal self", a self devoid of temporal extension, and the "narrative self", which involves personal identity and continuity across time. The notion of a minimal self is first clarified by drawing a distinction between the sense of self-agency and the sense of self-ownership for actions.

It is a small step from this account to abandoning the idea of a coherent self entirely, to go past the narrative self on the spectrum. One can embrace the plural character of narratives, and accept the idea that the self is merely a transitory construction and one among many constructions available to the individual. This solves the problem of coherence by rejecting it. Narratives are still, on this account, "cultural," but not in the "programming" sense: they are simply narrative structures that are understood by other people. The plural view is well stated by John Mbiti ([1969] 1989: 106) in *African Religions and Philosophy*: "I am because we are, and since we are, therefore I am." As Abeba Birhane elaborates it:

> We know from everyday experience that a person is partly forged in the crucible of community. Relationships inform self-understanding. Who I am depends on many "others": my family, my friends, my culture, my work colleagues. The self I take grocery shopping, say, differs in her actions and behaviors from the self that talks to my PhD supervisor. Even my most private and personal reflections are entangled with the perspectives and voices of different people, be it those who agree with me, those who criticize, or those who praise me.
>
> (Birhane 2017: n.p.)

The apparent problem with pluralism, however, is this: the pluralist can't explain how the diverse aspects of the self are connected to each other in the absence of a well-defined unifying element (Beni 2016: 3736). But of course there may be connections, and therefore a minimal sort of coherence, without "unity." And, as we have seen in the preceding section, there are many available accounts of where this coherence might be found. To these we might add one more, consistent with pluralism: a purely external account, where coherence is given entirely through the responses of others so that what Cooley called the "looking-glass self" is itself the source both of the demand for coherence and the coherence itself, which gets internalized through habit or acceptance and becomes embodied. In its extreme form, the self is just an internalized social role, formed of the expectations of others, which the incumbent does not distinguish from the self. But this just raises another question: where do the others get the conception of the unified self that they attribute, and why do they have one at all?

The Self as a Problem

Each of these accounts works by taking something – culture, the body, computational architecture, the organization of memory, narrative – as given and
unproblematic, and attempts to build an account of the coherence of the self
around it. One might think that it would be possible to integrate the accounts
into a general theory of the self. But the elements are not only too diverse, they
also appear to be incompatible. The alternative would be reduction to one controlling consideration, or prioritizing one kind of coherence as representing the
core or true self. This does not seem plausible either. But without some attempt
at integration one would merely get a theory of plural selves: the social self, the
embodied self, the immunological self, the cultural self, the computational self,
and so on. There are, however, potential affinities between accounts of different
kinds. In what follows, I will list a series of considerations that relate to the
plausibility of these accounts of the self, which are of course highly programmatic,
and the obstacles to their integration.

The problem of the self *is* its irreducibility to either the material or spiritual
side of the subject, to use an older language. But we can replace the older language, or at least use the cognitive science data to improve it and specify the
issues: there is the self of the *Verstehen* bubble; the narrative and looking-glass self;
and the self understood in terms that include causal properties and processes that
are inaccessible to reflection and introspection. The self of the *Verstehen* bubble is
the self that is defined by our capacity to understand and distinguish ourselves
from others and to identify them as empathic subjects – capacities probably
rooted primitively in the embodied capacities to respond to others, to attend to
objects jointly with them, and to respond to the contagion of crying infants in
the crib (Ioannou et al. 2016). Then there is the body itself. The intractability of
the problem of the self is a result of two facts. First, that what happens inside the
Verstehen bubble and is accessible only within it has causal consequences for the
body, both in the simple sense of producing motion and in the sense of transforming its capacities through experience and action, habitualization, empathic
responses, and ingraining inhibitions. Second, that the body produces or is the
medium for the perceptions, feelings, and so forth that are experienced within the
Verstehen bubble in however limited ways by introspection and empathy, and that
these processes of production are influenced both by causes outside of the bubble
and things accessible only within it, through empathy or mirroring.

We can break these issues down by considering the relation between the self of
the *Verstehen* bubble and the self or person in the causal sense. The core of this
relation can be seen in an example. To be in love is to be in the grip of an
emotion. To say that one is in love is to articulate a feeling with behavioral and
perhaps physical manifestations, some of which are public, some of which are not.
These vary "culturally," that is to say with sets of interaction partners. Our
introspective access to these feelings is limited, as with all introspective access, but

it is made possible by our empathy for others in love, the behavioral cues we have learned to associate with it, and so forth. The "internal" part is accessible, and narrativizable, because of empathy and these external features. We stand in the same relation to the rest of our inner world.

This, however, is a description of a "mature" self with developed capacities to understand others. It assumes, as we will see shortly, some sort of core cognitive part. But even with this assumption there are major questions. Where in the developmental process does the external, caused part begin? Is it in utero, epige-netic, genetic, hormonal, or all of these and more? How do these causes interact over developmental time with the core cognitive part? How do the external causes interact with the internal ones? If we take the standard approach, we need a way of understanding how these external influences cross the cause–code barrier. This is a very abstract way of putting the problem, however.

A slightly less abstract way of putting it is to start with the cognitive core, which we might endow with self-like properties, as in the idea of a minimal self. The idea risks falling into the homunculus problem – but our account of the developmental process has to start somewhere, with some elementary pieces and processes that can produce the mature self we wish to account for. The homun-culus problem is typically a result of doing this backwards: taking some quality or capacity of the mature self, projecting it backwards in the developmental process, and explaining the process in terms of the employment of this capacity. And one can see why this is so tempting: if we explain the self in terms of the looking-glass self, for example, we seem to require a conscious subject, a self, to be doing the looking (a point made by G. H. Mead 1930). To explain the development of the self in terms of the acquisition of knowledge about the world, we need a scientist in the crib. Avoiding this requires some other device (such as a self-organizing principle) or a way of making some external fact, outside the putative self, do the crucial work: for example, by noting that the concept of the person, in its original Roman usage, was derived from the physical mask, which was not a "repre-sentation" of the person but the physical form of the abstract concept of the person (Mauss 1985), or a way of starting with some undifferentiated material that differentiates into the self and other.

The undifferentiated starting point might be unstructured experience. As Dan Hutto points out (quoting Tomasello 2003: 276):

> Yet it is hugely implausible that humans only enjoy temporally structured self-experience after they master narrative capacities – which they normally only get a firm grip on around the age of 5 years old ... Long before that children rely on their training and past experience to anticipate how things will generally unfold in their experience. They surely do not need to be a narratively competent adult to do this. Indeed there is every reason to sup-pose that the great bulk of our adult self-experience is temporally structured in innocent, child-like ways, it has its basis in embodied habits, routines and

repertoires for engaging with the world formed early in our development and in later life. These ways of experiencing the world owe nothing to narrativizing and they do not cease when narrative capacities for reflecting upon and understanding the wider significance of my doings and actions are acquired.

(Hutto 2016: 38)

This is at least a way of stating the problem: there is a period before we talk about things, and before we talk narratively about them (an obscure and perhaps meaningless distinction), which is nevertheless one in which we have experiences, memories, and manage to act and interact with others.

Narrative forms, however, come from without: they are learned in "external" social interaction. As with the case of pain and love language, the forms of narration – which are local, or specific to sets of interaction partners – have to hook into something "internal." But these internal things are rarely if ever entirely internal, and that is true also of the abstract concepts we have been discussing. The mask that is the original meaning of "person," the breath that is also the soul are cases where something public and physical corresponds to an object of empathy. And for love and pain there are behavioral manifestations.

We can equip our cognitive core with very simple, precognitive, physical processes – such as mirror neuron responses, visual responses to stimuli, and so forth – and try to build up from them to more complex cognitive processes. But there is still a gap between these measurable brain processes and the stuff inside the *Verstehen* bubble. The gap is filled by or can be designated in terms of "awareness." We are aware of some things and not others, but we do not have a physical account of it. Nor is an exclusively physical one possible: as we have seen, there are socially produced sources of inhibition that affect awareness of one's own responses.

As we have seen in the case of theory of mind, the extremes – both the two beyond the spectrum, eliminativism and pluralism, as well as a) and d) – can be made consistent with one another and provide an alternative to the middle two accounts. The pluralist can accept a very minimal notion of the self, perhaps consisting of no more than the "awareness" that is shared (though this too is controversial) with lower animals, perhaps together with some basic memory capacity (also shared with lower animals), and account for the more elaborated but socially and individually variable aspects of the self in narrative and interactional terms.

The standard approach is most congenial to b) and c): in these, the external influences on the self are limited. In b), the only role of external causes is to activate an innate concept of the self or to add variation within a standard and universal "architecture." But in this case the self then becomes identified not with the conceptualized self or the self which has habitualized or internalized the local language of the self, but with a more limited abstract, hypothesized, universal self.

In c), the external influence, however it is understood to overcome the cause–code barrier, is restricted to the insertion of a cultural "program" or theory-like content into a culture-ready brain. Both have a problem, namely explaining how the tacit theory or "program" get inserted: they can't come from normal interaction, except through some hitherto unknown means of transmission.

Note

1 There is a dispute over whether perception itself is influenced by conditioning and learning (see Firestone and Scholl 2016, which includes extensive peer commentary).

References

Barfield, Owen. ([1928] 1964). *Poetic Diction: A Study in Meaning.* Middletown, CT: Wesleyan University Press.

Baron-Cohen, S., H. Tager-Flusberg, and M. V. Lombardo, eds. (2013). *Understanding Other Minds: Perspectives from Developmental Social Neuroscience.* Oxford: Oxford University Press.

Beni, Majid Davoody. (2016). "Structural Realist Account of the Self." *Synthese* 193: 3727–3740.

Birhane, Abeba. (2017). "Descartes Was Wrong: 'A Person Is a Person through Other Persons'." *Aeon*, 7 April. https://aeon.co/ideas/descartes-was-wrong-a-person-is-a-person-through-other-persons (accessed 25 April 2017).

Borg C., P. J. de Jong, and W. Weijmar Schultz. (2010). "Vaginismus and Dyspareunia: Automatic vs. Deliberate Disgust Responsivity." *Journal of Sexual Medicine* 7: 2149–2157.

Both S., E. Laan, and W. Everaerd. (2011). "Focusing 'Hot' or Focusing 'Cool': Attentional Mechanisms in Sexual Arousal in Men and Women." *Journal of Sexual Medicine* 8: 167–179.

Carruthers, P. (2009). "How We Know Our Own Minds: The Relationship between Mindreading and Metacognition." *Behavioral and Brain Sciences* 32(2): 121–182.

Cooley, Charles H. (1902). *Human Nature and the Social Order.* New York: Scribner.

Davidson, Donald. (1978). "What Metaphors Mean." *Critical Inquiry*, 5(1): 31–47.

Dennett, Daniel C. (1988). "Quining Qualia." In A. Marcel and E. Bisiach (eds.) *Consciousness in Modern Science*, 381–415. Oxford: Oxford University Press.

Diekelmann, S., I. Wilhelm, and J. Born. (2009). "The Whats and Whens of Sleep-Dependent Memory." *Sleep Medicine Reviews* 13(5): 309–321.

Everett, Daniel. (2016). *Dark Matter of the Mind: The Culturally Articulated Unconscious.* Chicago, IL: University of Chicago Press.

Firestone, Chaz and Brian Scholl. (2016). "Cognition Does Not Affect Perception: Evaluating the Evidence for 'Top-Down' Effects." *Behavioral and Brain Sciences* 39: 1–77.

Gallagher, Shaun. (2000). "Philosophical Conceptions of the Self: Implications for Cognitive Science." *Trends in Cognitive Sciences* 4(1): 14–21.

Gallistel, C. R. (forthcoming). "The Neurobiological Bases for the Computational Theory of Mind." In Lila Gleitman and Roberto G. De Almeida (eds.) *Festschrift in Honor of Jerry Fodor.*

Gazzaniga, Michael. (1995). "Consciousness and the Cerebral Hemispheres." In M. Gazzaniga (ed.) *The Cognitive Neurosciences*, 1391–1400. Cambridge, MA: MIT Press.

Gibson, E. J. and R. D. Walk. (1960). "The 'Visual Cliff.'" *Scientific American* 202: 67–71.

Ginev, Dimitri. (2013). "Ethnomethodological and Hermeneutic-Phenomenological Perspectives on Scientific Practices." *Human Studies* 36: 277–305.

Gintis, Herbert. (2007). "A Framework for the Unification of the Behavioral Sciences." *Behavioral and Brain Sciences* 30: 1–61.

Gyekye, Kwame. (1978). "Akan Concept of a Person." *International Philosophical Quarterly* 18(3): 277–287.

Hickock, Gregory. (2014). *The Myth of Motor Neurons: The Real Neuroscience of Communication and Cognition.* New York: Norton.

Hutto, Daniel. (2016). "Narrative Self-Shaping: A Modest Proposal." *Phenomenology and the Cognitive Sciences* 15(1): 21–41.

Ioannou, Stephanos, Paul Morris, Samantha Terry, Marc Baker, Vittorio Gallese, and Vasudevi Reddy. (2016). "Sympathy Crying: Insights from Infrared Thermal Imaging on a Female Sample." *PLoS ONE* 11(10): e0162749. www.ncbi.nlm.nih.gov/pmc/articles/PMC5055358/ (accessed 27 April 2017).

Kingstone, Alan, James T. Enns, and M. S. Gazzaniga. (1995). "Guided Visual Search Is a Left Hemisphere Process in Split-Brain Patients." *Psychological Science* 6(2): 118–121.

Laan, E. and S. Both. (2011). "Sexual Desire and Arousal Disorders in Women." *Advances in Psychosomatic Medicine* 31: 16–34.

Laan, E. and W. Everaerd. (1995). "Determinants of Female Sexual Arousal: Psychophysiological Theory and Data." *Annual Review of Sex Research* 6: 32–76.

Laan E., W. Everaerd, G. van Bellen, and G. Hanewald. (1994). "Women's Sexual and Emotional Responses to Male- and Female-Produced Erotica." *Archives of Sexual Behavior* 23: 153–170.

Lee, Young-eun, Jung-eun Ellie Yun, Eun Young Kim, and Hyun-joo Song. (2015). "The Development of Infants' Sensitivity to Behavioral Intentions when Inferring Others' Social Preferences." *PLoS ONE* 10(9): 1–16. doi:10.1371/journal.pone.01355.

Lizardo, Omar. (2015). "Culture, Cognition, and Embodiment." In James D. Wright (editor-in-chief). *International Encyclopedia of the Social & Behavioral Sciences*, 2nd edn., 576–581. Dordrecht: Elsevier.

Luria, Alexander. ([1974] 1976). *Cognitive Development: Its Cultural and Social Foundations.* Cambridge, MA: Harvard University Press.

Mangun, G. R., R. Plager, W. Loftus, S. A. Hillyard, S. J. Luck, T. Handy, V. Clark, and M. S. Gazzaniga. (1994). "Monitoring the Visual World: Hemispheric Asymmetries and Subcortical Processes in Attention." *Journal of Cognitive Neuroscience* 6(3): 267–275.

Mauss, Marcel. ([1934] 1973). "Techniques of the Body." *Economy and Society* 2: 70–88.

Mauss, Marcel (1985) "A Category of the Human Mind: The Notion of Person, the Notion of Self." In Michael Carrithers, Steven Collins, Steven Lukes (eds.) *The Category of the Person*, 1–25. Cambridge: Cambridge University Press.

Mbiti, John. ([1969] 1989). *African Religions and Philosophy*2nd edn. Oxford: Heinemann.

Mead, George H. (1930). "Cooley's Contribution to American Social Thought." *American Journal of Sociology* 36(5): 693–706.

Meltzoff, Andrew N. and M. Keith Moore. (1977). "Imitation of Facial and Manual Gestures by Human Neonates." *Science* 198: 75–78.

Mendoza, John E. (2011). "Body Schema." In Jeffrey Kreutzer, John DeLuca, and Bruce Caplan (eds.) *Encyclopedia of Clinical Neuropsychology*, 427–428. New York: Springer.

Metzinger, T. (2003). *Being No One: The Self-Model Theory of Subjectivity*. Cambridge, MA: MIT Press.

Metzinger, T. (2005). "Précis of Being No One." *PSYCHE: An Interdisciplinary Journal of Research on Consciousness* 11(5): 1–35.

Norman, Malcolm. (1964). "Behaviorism as a Philosophy of Psychology." In T. W. Wann (ed.) *Behaviorism and Phenomenology: Contrasting Bases for Modern Psychology*, 141–155. Chicago: University of Chicago Press.

Parsons, Talcott. (1965). *Social Structure and Personality*. New York: Free Press.

Pollock, J. (2008). *How to Build a Person: A Prolegomenon*. Cambridge, MA: MIT Press.

Reddy, Vasudevi. (2008). *How Infants Know Minds*. Cambridge, MA: Harvard University Press.

Rellini, H. A., M. K. McCall, K. P. Randall, and M. C. Meston. (2005). "The Relationship between Women's Subjective and Physiological Sexual Arousal." *Psychophysiology* 42: 116–124.

Sakkalou, Elena and Merideth Gattis (2012). "Infants Infer Intentions from Prosody." *Cognitive Development* 27: 1–16.

Skinner, B. F. (1964). "Behaviorism at Fifty." In T. W. Wann (ed.) *Behaviorism and Phenomenology: Contrasting Bases for Modern Psychology*, 79–97. Chicago, IL: University of Chicago Press.

StrohmingerN., G. Newman, and J. Knobe. (2017). "The True Self: A Psychological Concept Distinct From the Self." *Perspectives on Psychological Science* 12(4): 551–560.

Sun, Ron. (2004). "Desiderata for Cognitive Architectures." *Philosophical Psychology* 17: 341–373.

Sun, Ron and Nick Wilson. (2011). "Motivational Processes within the Perception–Action Cycle." In V. Cutsuridis, A. Hussain, and J. G. Taylor (eds.) *Perception–Action Cycle: Models, Architectures, and Hardware*, 449–472. Berlin: Springer.

Sun, Ron and Nick Wilson. (2014). "A Model of Personality Should Be a Cognitive Architecture Itself." *Cognitive Systems Research* 29–30: 1–30.

Sun, Ron, Edward Merrill, and Todd Peterson. (2001). "From Implicit Skills to Explicit Knowledge: A Bottom-Up Model of Skill Learning." *Cognitive Science* 25: 203–244.

Taylor, Charles. (1985). "The Concept of a Person." In *Philosophical Papers 1: Human Agency and Language*, 97–114. Cambridge: Cambridge University Press.

Tomasello, M. (2003). *Constructing a Language: A Usage-Based Theory of Language Acquistion*. Cambridge, MA: Harvard University Press.

Turner, John C. (2004). "Foreword." In Bernd Simon, *Identity in Modern Society: A Social Psychological Perspective*, x–xv. Malden, MA: Blackwell.

Vygotsky, L. S. (1978). *Mind in Society: The Development of Higher Psychological Processes*. Cambridge, MA: Harvard University Press.

Wiredu, Kwasi. (1992). "The African Concept of Personhood." In Harley E. Flack and Edmund D. Pellegrino (eds.) *African-American Perspectives on Biomedical Ethics*, 104–117. Washington, DC: Georgetown University Press.

Woodard, Amanda L. (2009). "Infants' Grasp of Others' Intentions." *Current Directions in Psychological Science* 18(1): 53–57.

7

SOCIAL THEORY AND COGNITIVE SCIENCE

The impact on social theory of cognitive science, social neuroscience, and research on cognitive development has been limited by a mismatch or disconnection between the ground-up, mechanism-driven perspectives developed in these areas and the top-down perspective of social science, which begins with descriptions of social phenomena that need explanation – such as the fact of the state or the behavior of prices in markets, or "culture" – and looks for lower-level mechanisms that can be aggregated or combined to account for them. But there are issues galore with the things to be explained, as well as with the explanations. On the side of cognitive science, as already discussed, there has been a limited but occasionally active attempt to address at least some generic issues about "the social." What is needed is to think through this gap, and perhaps diminish it, despite the very different intellectual cultures of the two fields, which are themselves complex and supra-disciplinary.

In this chapter I will try to break the issues down into their elements, and to distinguish what I take to be two fundamental ways of thinking about "the social" in cognitive science terms. The first is the dominant one in the traditions of social and political theory, and fits, roughly, with the standard approach; the second fits with another loosely connected strand of social theory that can be called "interactionist," and points to the ubiquity of "social" determinants of cognition. I will proceed by considering the elements of the standard view one by one and discussing the issues with them and the alternatives.

Starting from the Top

Social science works (largely and perhaps necessarily) within the *Verstehen* bubble to account for such things as markets, institutions, organizations, movements, cultures, states and political orders, and so forth. These are not, so to speak, natural objects: they are either defined, initially, by the people who are involved with them, or are constructed by the observer on the basis of an understanding, a second-order understanding, of what the people involved understand themselves to be doing. This is not always obvious, and the long history of appropriating such scientistic terms as "operational definition," which even its creator, Percy Bridgman (1927), thought was inapplicable to the social sciences, obscures their dependence on *Verstehen*.

As Gordon and Theiner put it (citing Dennett 1978; Bechtel and Richardson 1993; Cummins 2000; Machamer et al. 2000), describing the problem of accounting for organizations, a basic institutional form at the "top" that needs explanation: "A micro-foundations approach asks ... of a particular capacity or property that is attributed to an organization, what are the resources, processes and mechanisms that underwrite this capacity or property?" (2015: 156). They add that:

> Adopting a micro-foundations approach is thus an inquiry into how things work that seeks to open up the "black box" of organizational learning in order to see how the organizational-level properties and capacities are enabled by the interactions of more basic elements and processes.
>
> *(Gordon and Theiner 2015: 156)*

The question, however, is this: what *are* the more basic elements? Are they individuals? Subsystems? Individuals characterized as subsystems? Or individuals in the sense of what a person can access through reflection and the understanding of others? Do they include physical objects such as the computers and desks in the organization's offices, the products, and so forth? Do the interactions consist of network relations, such that the autonomy of the big collective facts is illusory,[1] or of relations between more or less autonomous units that interact to aggregate into larger units with their own more or less autonomous characteristics? What is the glue that holds individuals together? What are their basic drives and dispositions, and what is culturally variable? How is cultural variation produced? How do these dispositions get harnessed or aggregated into a unified system?

There is no "standard view" of this set of problems, but there is a robust tradition in which the problems are restated in different forms. Thomas Hobbes is the progenitor of this tradition, and one can start with the famous frontispiece of his *Leviathan*, the image of the state and the elements of sovereign authority, a concept which is later transposed in various ways but for our purposes can be understood as the power of "society." Thus the image is an image of "the social." It consists of the sovereign, who is made up of the individual bodies of his subjects or citizens. "A multitude of men, are made one person, when they are by one man, or one person, represented; so that it be done with the consent of every one of that multitude in particular" (Hobbes ([1651] 1965: I.16.13). This is key:

in this view, the "social" is "society," and society is an arrangement of members. This arrangement involves something like authority or causal superiority over its members, but at the same time is sustained by nothing more than its members. The arrangement, however, is dependent on two kinds of glue or authority: for Hobbes, this was ecclesiastic and temporal authority, represented in the image by a torch for the ecclesiastical and a sword for the temporal, each held in a hand of the sovereign.

The usual way to connect the two is through a characterization of the individual. But this is not quite enough to explain the state. As Carl Schmitt ([1938] 2008: 31) depicted the creation of the mortal God, the state: "The terror of the state of nature drives anguished individuals to come together; their fear rises to an extreme; a spark of reason (*ratio*) flashes, and suddenly there stands in front of them a new god." The spark of reason is not the spark of individual interests, but another kind of reason – one that allows the anguished individuals to give up their freedom and become subjects. Hobbes' argument, much simplified, works like this: he constructs a model of the individual, complete with certain dispositions and motivations. He sees what he wants to explain: the authority of the state. His bridge is a kind of contract, the contract that creates sovereignty and the sovereign. So he needs to motivate the individuals to accept this contract and to account for its availability as an idea. This is where things get tricky. Motivating it is not so hard: one points to the anguish of a nasty, brutish, and short life. Getting the idea to come about and be understood and accepted is more difficult to explain. This is why Schmitt introduces the spark of reason – a bit of explanatory magic. Hobbes' successors, in the tradition of social and political theory, introduced their own bits of magic: German state metaphysics, in which the "state" was itself an autonomous being; and Parsons' convoluted argument that because society did not fly apart there must have been a shared normative force (Parsons 1937: 89–94), among many other accounts.

The updated cognitive science versions of this problem can be understood by starting with Herbert Gintis (2004; Gintis 2007). For him, the fact that human and animal populations have relations between their members that produce a kind of stability means that they have attained some sort of game-theoretic equilibrium. Identifying this equilibrium, and explaining what is balanced with what, is the goal of the explanation, and the collective fact to be explained. And it serves to identify the characteristics, the right dispositions and motivations, that the individual members must have in order for them to be partners in this equilibrium. This is a complex form of reasoning, however, with many pitfalls, and with potential alternatives.

The Standard Model, Agency, and Social Theory

The relevant cognitive science background to these arguments can be summarized in the following manner. As we have already seen, the original and core approach to modeling the mind in terms of the brain brought together a set of basic ideas, more or less organized around a common strategy: to identify the functional conditions necessary for the production of particular mental processes, and to reconstruct these as elements of a process that could be represented by flowcharts. These elements included reasoning understood as concept manipulation, memory, perception, motor skills, representation, pattern recognition, language, the ability to orient in space; and, over time, added such things as facial recognition and, notably, the understanding of other minds, the understanding encoded in folk psychology – that is to say the ideas behind the ordinary way in which people speak and think about the beliefs and intentions of others.

The standard model, as we have seen repeatedly in previous chapters, is biased towards a conception of the self and the cognitive agent in which the mental life of the agent is accounted for by internal processes acting on perceptual data to transform it into coded strings that can be transformed, combined, stored in the brain, accessed, and combined again and again. The processes themselves are not influenced by external causes, and it would not make sense if they were: the main tasks of the brain involve coding and transformations of coded chunks, complex processes that in themselves do not allow for variation. Memories may differ, that is to say content may differ, but the memory process will be universal and uniform. Moreover, these processes develop according to an internal logic that leads to a more or less uniform, universal, cognitive agent. This agent then acts in the world. At earlier stages of development (infancy and childhood) there may be other processes, but these are replaced as higher-level processes, such as semantic-like inference, are activated. The effects of interaction vary at each developmental stage, depending on what processes have been activated, but they do not alter fundamental processes. The self and self-concepts are incidental products of this developmental process. Content may vary and beliefs about the self may vary, and these variations may be the result of external causes, such as cultural experience; but the core processes of the self, such as the attaining of self-awareness, do not vary.

This is a model that fits very well with a picture of society, and therefore "the social," as a product of interacting agents with developed cognitive processes, such as rational decision-making, together with a collection of innate dispositions that are familiar character traits. A current form of this way of constructing the issues is "agent-based modeling (ABM)," which is a characteristic top-down method. The aim is to account for some aggregate fact, such as financial market instability. The approach is to find a model that predicts the facts about financial market instability we already know, but by building up from micro-foundations consisting of models of agents. The models require a large number of agents who can be configured in various ways to produce different aggregate outcomes, and agent-like powers such as a decision-making procedure and a learning procedure. The agents are then set in a model of interaction with other agents and an environment, and the model is tested by seeing what happens as a result of the interactions. In the case of financial instability, the model varied the agents' imitation behavior between three different types, which led to a good approximation of actual market behavior (Farmer and Foley 2009; Stefan and Atman 2015).

The details of this case need not concern us here; the key is the method, which is to take a top-down topic and explain it by a bottom-up method. The reasoning is reciprocal. We hypothesize agents that can produce the effects at the top level, and allow their interactions to produce the effects. But we also establish facts about the agents by showing that the model works at the aggregate level. This is the same approach as that of Hobbes and Parsons: we start from an aggregate fact and infer the properties of the agent that need to be there for the fact to have developed as it did, whether it is the sovereign state (in Hobbes) or the stable social system (as in Parsons). In an even more general sense, we are talking about equilibria: these are cases in which there is equilibrium in the game-theoretic sense with a set of participants whose properties we infer from the fact of the equilibrium.

The elements of these arguments vary: one can change the motivators and dispositions for the agents in the models to include altruism, an innate desire for transcendence or a religion gene, norm-sensitivity, and so forth; and one can identify multiple cognitive mechanisms. As the founding American sociologist Franklin Giddings put it nearly a century ago:

> there was a plethora of other mechanisms equally plausible and easily illustrated: habit, instinct, herd habit, sympathy, empathy, and impression. Darwin himself, in *The Descent of Man* (1874), supplied a list of his own which fit this list closely: group cohesion, sympathy as a basis for group cohesion, the importance of fidelity and unselfish courage, and the importance of praise and blame in bringing these about.
>
> *(Giddings 1922: 7)*

But the basic problem remains of getting from individual facts, bottom-up facts about members, to collective facts – the top in the top-down explanatory model. But what sorts of individual facts are we working with? This problem divides into two: one is the problem of the nature of the relevant "individuals" or subunits that are being aggregated; the other is with the type of fact. These turn out to be mixed up in complex ways.

What type of fact is "the importance of fidelity and unselfish courage"? Despite coming from Darwin, it is plainly a fact within the *Verstehen* bubble, and moreover a fact stated in terms of the language we use to express our understanding of one another. But the *Verstehen* bubble is highly constraining: our understanding is limited, our own grasp of our own minds is limited, and the expression of this knowledge takes culturally specific forms. Our own version of this form of expression is so basic to us that we find it difficult to think beyond it or relativize it to our own culture. Nevertheless, the folk psychology of belief and desire, which is at the core of the usual picture of human agency, is also not free of the limitations that result from its connection to Western culture and from the limitations of the *Verstehen* bubble in which it applies. It can be argued that these are only surface manifestations of a true human nature which also has this form: we explored some of these arguments in the last chapter.

What does this mean for "the social"? What is the status of the idea that equilibria, or more generally social relations, are structured by beliefs, desires, constraints, and the actions they produce, and by the rational choices that are implied by the combinations of beliefs and desires? The top-down approach implies that if these micro-foundations or bottom-up explanations are sufficient for explaining or producing the relevant equilibria or structures, we are done: we have explained what we need to explain, and hit the explanatory rock bottom. There may be general facts, like those of biology or neuroscience, which can explain folk psychology and general human conditions for action. But this doesn't help much in the construction of agent-based models, which typically need more content to produce the aggregate results one wishes to explain; so, they are essentially irrelevant to the explanation of the equilibria or structures. And this means they are irrelevant to the social, if what we mean by "the social" is simply the interactions of people acting in accordance with their beliefs and desires, the sources of which we take to be exogenous to the model.

This is, so to speak, social theory within the *Verstehen* bubble: it works with notions that are familiar or close to everyday language. But there are some large red flags here. The first is the cultural relativity of the terms of folk psychology and the belief-desire model of action itself. We can hope, with Jerry Fodor, that these closely match what goes on in the brain; but what if they don't? The second red flag comes from within social theory itself. There are some contexts in which this form of explanation is insufficient, including the one at the very core of Hobbes – the leap from the individual to the collective fact of sovereignty, enabled by the lightning flash of "reason." One of the traditional problems with game-theoretic accounts of moral orders is that while it is possible to define various equilibria – that is to say socially beneficial arrangements involving, for example, rules of conduct – it is also beneficial for individuals to ignore these rules for personal gain. Therefore one needs some additional element – a variant of the flash of reason – to get the individual to obey the rule. There are many easy solutions to this problem: one might obey because one believes that one will go to hell for violating the rule, for example; or, in the most basic of moral systems, believe that violating a tabu will bring an automatic harm to the violator. But these are false, or at least only semi-rational beliefs, and the very existence of such beliefs conflicts with the information-processing model of the brain.

The difficulty of this problem is signaled by the fact that there are so many awkward attempted solutions to it. The aim of the solutions generally is to somehow make the relevant collective belief arise naturally or rationally from the social situation. An irrational belief does not solve this problem without departing from the limits of folk psychology, though odd beliefs are certainly in some sense understandable and thus within the *Verstehen* bubble. One needs instead something outside the model of rational action. Parsons introduced the *deus ex machina* of the normative order; Hobbes the paradoxical social contract story – paradoxical because the rule that one should obey one's contractual promises needs to be grounded on the same sovereign power that it is supposed to explain. Compared to these, lightning flashes of reason seem plausible.

Is there a solution within the standard model of cognitive science? As it turns out there is, but it is equally awkward. But the awkwardness is concealed by some standard practices of explanation. The standard computational model of the mind is quite elastic: it can be expanded to account for any functional capacity. One could, for example, take something described in symbolic interactionist terms, such as significant gesturing, redescribe it in functional capacity terms, and then break it down into the modular components necessary for the exercise of this capacity. Or one might enhance this model by giving a functional account of joint action or collective action and positing the necessary modules for these capacities. Or one can take a Parsonian account of norms, and endow the mind with a functional capacity for norm-detection and responsiveness to norms that fits with this account of norms.

In this sense, the computationalist model of mind does not come into direct conflict with the various conventional accounts of "the social," and indeed fits them very well. It works, however, simply by assuming that there are such things as norms (and, as we will later see, intentions) to be detected, and concocting a capacity to detect them. And in one sense this seems legitimate. It is not the job, one might say, of cognitive science to challenge the conventional terminology of social science, but to provide micro-foundations for its explanations. The awkwardness comes in when we try to break into the circular reasoning this involves, and look more carefully at the moving parts of the explanation.

A prominent example of the extension of the standard model to account for institutions comes from John Searle (1995). He undertakes to explain the institution of money. He argues that the physical fact of money doesn't make something money. It needs something more, and that something is ultimately to be found in the cognitive capacities of the mind. Other social institutions can be explained by reference to the same cognitive capacity. So what does the explaining? The mind's capacity to have intentions that are "collective," at least collective in form. The magic ingredient that makes pieces of paper into money, then, is our collective will to make it so; and this collective will is grounded in an added on, made up, cognitive capacity. From the point of view of social theory, this is not very satisfying. There is a long history of "will" theories of law and of society, and they all look like short-cuts to avoid the basic problem: people obey for various reasons, including convenience and habit, and don't actually share a common will – though there may be some common legitimating beliefs to which a large portion of them subscribe. Legitimating beliefs, however, do not do the trick; they are just facts about individuals, and no number of individual facts adds up to a collective fact.[2]

But these collective forms of intentionality – which of course lack the possibility of authoritative "declaration" because the declarer of the intention is always speaking for another person, or the collectivity – display the circular character of intentional explanations as explanations generally: all they are or can be are arguments that the ends, such as law, are intended because they actually happen. When we speak about detecting intention, for example by infants, we are plausibly speaking only about detecting patterns of action with typical outcomes. And the dubiousness of the idea that we do in fact "detect" something called intentions is shown by the fact that we also routinely ascribe intentions to geometrical objects in motion, as Heider and Simmel (1944) showed in an experiment which found that subjects normally described random movements in intentional terms, such as "the circle avoids the triangle." This testifies to the fact that people over-discern patterns, not that they have magical cognitive powers that confirm folk psychology terms.

Other contexts are by definition impervious to being accounted for in terms of the belief-desire model: those involving the tacit, embodiment, the frames in terms of which beliefs become intelligible and taken to be true, and the causes of desire. Norms, to the extent that they are not explicit and encapsulated in beliefs but are tacit, are not part of the model. And consequently much of what we would call "culture," that which operates at the level of perceptual structuring, is also excluded. These topics, however, can be, and are, normally accounted for by extensions of the belief-desire model to "tacit" forms of the same thing. A "culture," for example, is understood as a set of presuppositions, that is to say a set of tacit beliefs. A norm is understood to be a tacit rule. Values are tacit values. And so on.

Are these extensions of the language that is appropriate to the *Verstehen* bubble to these other domains of fact problematic? There are two views on this: one is the Dennett (1978) view that ascribing ordinary mental terms to things that are not ordinary, such as the modules that go into functional boxology constructions, is benign, and justified by the successes of cognitive science when using these terms. This also fits with Fodor's claim that it would be a great tragedy, and something of a mystery, if fundamental brain processes were not more or less like the picture of the mind found in folk psychology. The alternative view is this: the picture given by folk psychology is false, limited in the same way that the mind is limited in its own self-understanding. The *Verstehen* bubble, the domain in which we understand each other and ourselves, is limited and potentially fundamentally misleading about mental processes because we are limited in understanding our own mental processes. Our understandings of ourselves and others are limited and biased: just as introspection is systematically faulty and limited, so our knowledge of other minds is also limited, and is limited in the same ways. We are not aware of the sources of our implicit biases, for example, or for that matter much of what is tacit, which is a result of adaptation at the level of fast thinking, not learning that resembles conscious reasoning. We can say when we learned that Kennedy was dead; we cannot say when we learned our implicit biases. And this implies that extensions of the language appropriate to the *Verstehen* bubble are also potentially misleading about the processes they are applied to, such as "culture" understood as "assumptions."

Rethinking the Social and the "Collective"

The sheer elasticity of the standard model, especially its tendency to add hypothetical cognitive capacities to account for anything that is in need of explanation, seems to make it impervious to empirical refutation, and potentially consistent with any possible social theory. And the free use of extended senses of the language appropriate to the *Verstehen* bubble to things like modules understood as not very smart but very fast units is crucial to this elasticity. There is no such thing as "detection" of norms in reality; no little sociologist homunculus inside the brain doing what actual sociologists cannot, namely determine what the norms actually are. This is simply a *Verstehen* bubble label for a hypothesized capacity. But the strategy has an effect: it puts such things as norms inside the brain, to be accounted for in accordance with the standard approach, and deflects us from what is "outside."

Begin with the apparently benign practice of using language from within the *Verstehen* bubble to describe facts that are not in the bubble. What would happen if we were strict, à la Weber, about limiting our social explanations to what he called meaningful social action (Weber [1968] 1978: 4)? He took the view that the problems of social science were constituted within the *Verstehen* bubble, and also within particular historical and cultural outlooks – we explain and interpret for an audience within our own historical horizon, in his view. This gets us an important result: it allows us to treat the belief-desire model not only as our cultural artifact, but also as a normal, legitimate, and easy way to describe and explain things in the bubble. The explanations, however, come with a big warning label: they are culturally relative and reflect our limited capacity to understand and articulate our own mental processes.

Weber was even more careful than this. He was so wary of metaphysical commitments that he excluded not only collective concepts (such as the state) but also, as much as possible, the notion of purposeful behavior. He avoided this usage in favor of meaningful behavior in order to avoid the possibility of construing "purpose" as the basis of a teleological metaphysics. We should take his use of "meaningful" in the same way. He did not intend to posit a metaphysics of "meanings," such as the idea of a language of thought containing the semantics of thought or of a symbolic realm, as Cassirer ([1925] 1946) did in this time. Weber's focus was on understanding actions, such as the woodcutter chopping down a tree, that could be understood unambiguously; and on systems of thought, such as mathematics and law, about which one could also attain clarity. This notion of meaning can be restated in cognitive science terms, more or less as follows: meaning, and the boundaries of the *Verstehen* bubble as the term has been used here, is the property of objects of joint attention. Joint attention makes the action "social" in Weber's sense because joint attention is inherently other-regarding. Moreover it directly links to neuronal processes – joint attention in primates involves mirror neurons.

This might seem to make everything meaningful, and inside the *Verstehen* bubble. But making something meaningful as an object of scientific investigation – the processes of perception, for example – is not to make it directly accessible to joint attention. It is to make squiggles by a scientific instrument or a theoretical concept the object of joint attention. The squiggles and the facts underlying them are facts in the causal world: we do not respond to them at the neural level as we respond to the woodchopper or to the person we are interacting with. We can't introspect them. Attributing intention, belief, and so forth to the causal facts in the brain underlying these squiggles is a different matter from attributing intentions to the woodchopper or the interactional partner: it is akin to attributing intentions to triangles and squares in motion. This is the difference Weber wished to capture with the notion of *Verstehen* aspiring to *Evidenz*. Much of his "theoretical" (a word he normally did not use) work took the form of constructing "ideal-types" which were meant as a means of enabling the analyst to get to the point of understanding the superficially mysterious actions of others in different eras and cultures. But Weber conceded that some human activity was perhaps beyond the reach of understanding, and could be addressed only in biological terms.

This long excursion in the history of thought was necessary to get to the following question: how, in cognitive science terms, might an alternative to the top-down model, which depends on the assumption that states, societies, sovereign power, and so forth are real, actually work? What it would need to explain is the ubiquitous fact of belief in these collective objects and their apparent causal efficacy in the social world, as well as their apparently "collective" character. Weber gives an answer within the *Verstehen* bubble: that the state and its powers are a conceptual construction that is convenient for certain purposes, but can be broken down into its components in the understandable actions of individuals. People have, for example, beliefs in the legitimacy of the state; they believe that the agents of the state have a right to command and speak for the state, and they obey. But this is all the state amounts to – there is no "power" or efficacy, and hence no "real existence," beyond the aggregated facts of these individual acts of obedience and consent.

This answer keeps the question within the *Verstehen* bubble. But from a cognitive science point of view this is not enough: we want to know, for example, not just what people believe or to understand the belief, but why people believe these things. And we also want to know something about the affordances that facilitate not only the beliefs but also the tacit cognitive conditions for the beliefs, such as the habit of deference to authority, the recognition of authority, and so on. The standard approach would look for a corresponding module or cognitive capacity, as Searle did, and in this case perhaps find something: that certain areas of the brain activate during responses to authority, which could then be called an authority module. But this has the same whiff of circularity we found earlier.

What is an alternative? One answer, available from a long tradition prior to cognitive science, is itself cognitive: the claim that the belief in the reality of collectives and their mysterious powers is the result of an intelligible cognitive error (Kelsen [1922, 1943]; see also García-Salmones 2011). And we can provide a similar answer in more contemporary terms, and as it happens an answer that applies to other puzzling social phenomena. We can also provide an account of the "collective" aspects of these phenomena in terms that do not involve collective minds, intentions, and special "collective" mental processes. The two answers go together.

We can use the example of religion, traditionally considered (for example by Durkheim) as the core of "society," to illustrate the relation between the two answers. The first part is the external aspect: religion is a game played with objects. The current reformers of religion recognize this. Mitchell McLaughlin (2017: 12), the prophet of "religion without religion," describes it as "the overcoming of all outward forms of the practice of organized religion," so that "the only outward element remaining would be the hearts of other people." The explanatory question, however, is "why has religion always involved objects, places, and physical things?" We can go back to the notion of affordances, and the recognition that cognition occurs in a world of physical objects which individuals use or respond to, and to which uses they become habituated.

The fact that this is also a shared world – a common object of experience and joint attention – and that it is formative for "mental contents," however these are ultimately to be understood, is an important starting point for understanding the problem of the collective character of institutions. We already have, in the form of the objects – in this case ritual objects, places, and so forth – something non-mental that is "collective" and "shared." And indeed the physical environment, including the invented and sacralized environment of religion, is a pervasive part of and shaper of our experience. And there are of course other shared objects – texts, documents, works of art, and so forth.

If we start with these "shared" objects, we can ask the question "what is collective" in a different way: we can ask what mental stuff needs to be added to these "collective" but physical facts in order to account for whatever it is that ideas of collective will, group mind, and the rest of it were supposed to be needed to explain. The argument for these mysterious mental collective facts was always an argument from explanatory necessity: that one could not explain the institution of money merely be reference to the objects called "money" and that, as Searle (1995: 142–3) argued, a collective intention to treat the objects as money was needed. But one can also claim quite plausibly that the physical objects, together with our dispositions and the dispositions of others to treat them as valuable objects and use them for exchange, is all there is to money. Nothing "collective" is needed. All the relevant dispositions are individual, though it may be that we can readily predict what others will do with these objects. There is thus no need for anything "collective" and "mental."

Religion, however, seems to present another problem, beyond money: it involves mysterious powers, beings, forces, and so forth. These do not seem to be reducible to objects and habituated dispositions in the same way. And it also seems that despite the radical diversity of religious beliefs across cultures, there are some common, or at least frequent, elements of the belief systems that make the objects "sacred." And it also seems like this is a problem akin to the problem of the mystery of the state and political authority. These are the kinds of considerations that originally drove Émile Durkheim to claim that religion was the *fons et origo* of all collective phenomena, and to invent the notion of the collective consciousness (Durkheim [1912] 1995). So there does seem to be a "cognitive" question that is not resolved by the recognition of the role of shared objects. Is there a cognitive answer?

Mercier and Sperber give a useful account which supplies the framework for an answer to this problem. They make a larger argument about the relation of conscious thought to what they call "intuitions," and suggest that dedicated modules produce intuitions, a relationship they understand as follows:

> Intuitions … are produced neither by a general faculty of intuition nor by distinct types of inferential process. They are, rather, the output of a great variety of inferential modules, the output of which is to some degree conscious while their operations remain unconscious.
>
> (Mercier and Sperber 2017: 133)

There is a hierarchy of these modules in which higher-level modules use the output of lower-level ones, which produce outputs that are conscious through unconscious operations. Reasons are for them meta-cognitions. But the job of the meta-cognition module:

> is not to provide a psychologically accurate account of the reasons that motivate people. In fact, the implicit psychology – the presumption that people's beliefs and actions are motivated by reasons – is empirically wrong. Giving reasons to justify oneself and reacting to the reasons given by others are, first and foremost, a way to establish reputations and coordinate expectations.
>
> (Mercier and Sperber 2017: 143)

Reasons are for social consumption: the point made earlier about the primacy and developmental priority of declarations as learned instrumental speech acts.

The point that is relevant to religion follows from Mercier and Sperber's account of the operation of these lower-level modules, which generate many outputs, many of which are erroneous.

> Inputs that trigger the operation of a module are imperfect. They do not pick out all and only cases at hand that fall within the proper domain of the module. ... Often, the trigger is oversensitive-think of the trigger of jealousy or of danger detection – but this oversensitivity may well be adaptive.
>
> (Mercier and Sperber 2017: 289)

This leads to an account of culture itself. "Many aspects of culture," they suggest, are based on the "mismatch between the proper and the actual domain of cognitive modules." People need to think, using their limited modules, outside of the limited domains that the modules are primarily suited for, in part because the cost in cognitive effort that figuring out whether the actual domain is a correct match is very large. And this has direct relevance to religion:

> Belief in supernatural agents, for instance, may be rooted in a disposition to overdetect agency and intentionality to the point of attributing mental states to non-agents such as the sun or a mountain, and to seeing in natural patterns the effect of the actions of an imaginary agent. Mismatches between the actual and proper domains of modules are a bonanza for the development of cultural ideas, practices, and artifacts.
>
> (Mercier and Sperber 2017: 289).

We think money, the state, or a ritual object has a special power because of our hyperactive agency-detection module – which we have seen before producing an intentionalizing bias. And we erroneously ascribe agency to various actions (prayer, for example), and find it difficult – costly, as Mercier and Sperber say – to root out our errors. To the extent that the errors are shared with others, they are "valuable": they form the basis of the kinds of social prediction that are central to social interaction. They need not even rise to the level of consciousness, or may do so as intuitions that we eventually construct and accept declarations about.

In all of this there is nothing that is both "collective" and "mental." The cognitive processes are private and personal. They result in and respond to interaction with others, but the "content" is the external fact of the behavior of others. That this behavior employs objects and is shaped by objects that are shared is sufficient to account for the "collective" aspect of the phenomenon in question. The objects are external and not "mental," so they explain the collective aspect of such things as religion without reference to collective intentions, collective consciousness, or any sort of group mind. To be sure, interacting with these objects, using them and becoming accustomed to them, has mental effects – but they are individual facts, not some new form of collective mentation.

Models of Thought: Redundant Variation vs. Computation

Error, pattern over-recognition, mismatches between proper domain of modules and actual domains of application fit with some of the alternatives to the standard approach to cognition. And these ideas raise the question of whether there is an alternative to the standard model at its core: calculative rationality. As it happens, however, there is a result from artificial intelligence (AI) mentioned earlier in relation to pattern recognition and chunking which sheds a great deal of light on the issue: the long struggle between computerized chess playing and human chess grandmasters. As noted earlier, the idea was to explain how chess masters are able to see the board strategically and to perform many feats, such as playing a large number of games simultaneously and very quickly. The issue, as it developed, came down to the role of calculation. Computers used massive processing power to calculate the outcomes of multiple possible moves and pick the most beneficial one following explicit rules programmed into them, along with massive numbers of previous games and outcomes, among other things. Chess grandmasters, according to the theory developed by Gobet and Simon (1998), operated by pattern recognition and "chunking," that is to say the agglomeration of patterns into even larger bodies of connected patterns. As Garry Kasparov, the world champion victim of the Deep Blue computer explains:

> Computers are very good at chess calculation, which is the part humans have the most trouble with. Computers are poor at recognizing patterns and making analogical connections [n.b. such as those discussed by Mercier and Sperber as applications outside the "proper domain" of a module], a human strength.
>
> *(Kasparov 2017: 54)*

Eventually the computers won, but not easily. And this carries an important lesson: other cognitive processes can produce similar results to the ones that are normally modeled as computational rule-following. This undermines the "must have been" arguments that are central to the case for the standard model.

The thing that made the standard model attractive was its flexibility, and it was assumed that this flexibility was based on the fact that simple codes (such as the 0,1 code of computers) and the simple combinatorial rules governing them could be the basis of higher-order sets of rules and combinations, such as those involved in language. This begged the question of where the higher-order rules came from, as we have seen, but it did demonstrate the power of code. Gobet and Simon's model provides flexibility in a different way: by using the human pattern-recognition capacity, and indeed its propensity to over-recognize patterns which allows humans to provide multiple pattern solutions to such things as chess problems. This is an error-prone capacity, but also a creative one; and, as the chess example shows, it can produce results that mimic the model of the programmed computer without having a program. Moreover, it can avoid some of the mysteries of the standard model about the origin of the rules and programs.

It is well known that actual speech is not grammatical and involves fragments of sentences and utterances not in sentence form – which would be a deadly obstacle for a logic-like system which requires well-formed formulas. Chomsky claimed that humans have a special mental capacity to interpret these fragments as expressing complete sentences. But the pattern model would point to the capacity to recognize and complete patterns that need not be in sentence form or require the positing of special grammatical capacities, but depend only on ordinary learning. Michael Tomasello explains this in relation to the early language use of children:

> It is quite widely believed that young children begin their linguistic careers by learning words, which they then combine together by means of rules. But this is not exactly accurate. Children hear and attempt to learn whole adult utterances, instantiating various types of constructions used for various communicative purposes. Sometimes children only learn parts of these complex wholes, and so their first productions may correspond to adult words. But these are always packaged in conventional intonational patterns indicating such things as requests, comments, or questions – which correspond to the general communicative functions for which adults use more complex constructions. And so from the beginning children are attempting to learn not isolated words, but rather communicatively effective speech act forms corresponding to whole adult constructions.
>
> (Tomasello 2011: 259)

There is no reason to think that anything special happens differently in adult speech. And adult speech can then be understood in terms of patterns.

> As opposed to linguistic rules conceived of as algebraic procedures for combining words and morphemes but that do not themselves contribute to meaning, linguistic constructions are themselves meaningful linguistic symbols – since they are nothing other than the patterns in which meaningful linguistic symbols are used in communication ... In this approach, mature linguistic competence is conceived as a structured inventory of meaningful linguistic constructions – including both the more regular and the more idiomatic structures in a given language (and all structures in between).
>
> (Tomasello 2011: 258)

As with chess, this gets the results of "linguistic competence" without the need to posit mysterious innate structures governing codes.

Why is this an issue? The motivation for getting rid of "codes," either a multiplicity of codes or some sort of underlying supercode, is clear enough. Think of it this way: suppose the way the brain works as Mercier and Sperber (2017: 133) describe it, as consisting "of a great variety of inferential modules, the output of which is to some degree conscious while their operations remain unconscious." The problem is to get these parallel modules, each of which has a specific output, to aggregate – to get the various relevant modules to produce complex cognitive responses employing these inputs together. Otherwise one would be limited to reflex actions. But this raises questions about the code model.

The key question is this: do they all operate with the same coding system or is there a kind of central processor that translates all the different codes into one meta-code that enables thought and action? First, there is no physical evidence for such a processor. Second, if they all operated with the same code, how would it perform the myriad of specialized tasks of the different modules? And third, if it is not the same code, and there is no central translator, how do the outputs of the modules add up to coherent thought? Fourth, is this the same code that all life uses? And if different species have different codes, or different modules have different codes, how did they come to differ, and why didn't the interspecies processes that made them differ also operate within species to produce differentiation (like other evolutionary processes) rather than producing a uniform code for all members of the species? If one resolves these questions by narrowing the role of code, say to underlying linguistic and semantic code, one still needs a story of how it connects to other codes, as well as an answer to this question.

The necessity for codes is also obvious enough – one needs a combination of inputs, or "content," to produce new outputs such as thoughts and actions, and perhaps also for memory, though this is more controversial: memory simply does not work this way, and is prone to all sorts of errors that are inconsistent with its working in this way.[3]

But if this can be accounted for in another way, one can avoid these difficult questions. The issue is with the has-to-be character of these arguments: the standard model of memory, for example, has to involve, as Gallistel argues, addresses and whatnot. But this is true only if we think memories are encoded and stored – for example as what are known as engrams, in some kind of neural storehouse.

So Is There an Alternative?

The various "E" approaches to cognitive science point in the direction of what is at least an alternative strategy for approaching these problems. But the implications for the social are not especially clear. We can, however, draw some of them out by describing the general strategy. The standard approach builds from the bottom up in the sense that it is concerned with figuring out the conditions for each "higher" level of cognition and finding these in the internal structure of cognition itself, leading to the cognitive agent capable of facing and acting in the world. The basic level is the information-processing brain itself, realized, though it is not clear how, in the physical brain. This brain does all the information-processing tasks necessary for agency – perception, memory, specialized capacities such as facial recognition, and so forth – and generates appropriate outputs from the inputs. Learning occurs at early developmental stages as well as for adults, but differs at different stages of development. Development itself is taken to be the addition or activation of different capacities, which take the form of module-like input-output units themselves, and the integration of these units marks the next stage of development. At the higher levels these are theory-like, such as the theory of mind. At each level the operations become more theory-like, more amenable to reconstruction in familiar semantic terms as a kind of implicit theory. And at the "highest" level development takes the form of explicit theory – principles, intentional structures with theory-like qualities – or the form of adding information and revising the theory.

The alternative of radical enactivism, grounding it in the "body" or sensor-imotor processes, is also clearly motivated. This gets us an evolutionary-friendly, non-discontinuous answer to the question of where this capacity came from, as well as one that fits with the fact that higher processes "use" the neuronal groupings of lower processes. It coheres with the fact that these processes occur throughout the animal kingdom, and are not specifically human. The code story, as we have seen with Chomsky, requires a mystery of radically discontinuous development. Enactivism, along with predictive processing (which nevertheless preserves the code story) works by shifting the image of the mind from a passive information processor to an active and engaged kind of cognition which creates its place in the world and adjusts to it in the course of engagement. Enactivism is the paradigmatic "constantly rewiring brain" approach which emphasizes neural plasticity. This image conflicts with some influential computationalist accounts of memory. Gallistel (2017), for example, calls for the idea of the rewiring brain to be finally abandoned because there is evidence that information is stored, not in synaptic networks as normally assumed, but inside single cells – so that learning and remembering "may involve putting something like bit strings into molecular switches found inside individual neurons – rather than rewiring the neural circuits."

Memory looks like an invincible citadel for the storehouse view of memory. But it is yet another topic that can be understood in terms of the strategy of starting with the anomalies. Selectivity, confabulation, influence by others and reliance on others to remember and affirm memories, and memory enhancing and selective and confabulating external things like objects, photographs, and public commemorations of events are all major features of actual memory (Heersmink 2017). The storehouse model of memory has to explain these features away or incorporate them through auxiliary hypotheses; if we make them central, we get a better fit with the rewiring the brain model, and a range of causal processes that affect this rewiring.

Stability, for enactivism, is something that is a result of a stable relation with the environment with which the individual is engaged. And this points to some other E's. The individual doing the engaging is not the information-processing mind, engaged with operating the body, but with the body itself, which is not a passive sensorium but one which is physically and pragmatically generating novel kinds of inputs in the course of its engagement with the world. It may be noted, and will be discussed further in the concluding chapter, that many of the arguments for embodiment, which point to the importance of interaction with the world in constituting cognition, apply as well to social interaction, the world of other people. This can be applied to the paradigmatic problem of memory itself. The influences of other people, what can be called "social remembering" (Barnier at al. 2008: 41), are persuasive – something that can be accounted for within the 4E approaches but is puzzling from an encoding perspective.

The two E's of embedding and ecology point to external facts as well: ecological psychology stresses the relational character of perception, and its special relation to the niches the organisms occupy.

> Classical ecological psychology regards perceiving as an active, relational phenomenon, where organisms are taken to be defined by sets of abilities and it is assumed that they occupy niches understood "as the set of situations in which one or more of [an organism's] abilities can be exercised" (Chemero 2009, 147–148).
>
> *(Hutto and Myin 2017: 84)*

Embedding is concerned with the situated character of cognition, the fact that cognition always occurs in circumstances that constrain it and which are a large part of the explanation both of the cognitive outcomes in action and thought.

There is, however a large downside to these "E" approaches. It is difficult to model the complex relations on which they depend. This is a matter of academic fashion and scientific values, in large part: mathematical modeling is an achievement and provides a standard of success. The modeling that fits the "E" approaches is "dynamical systems modeling," which uses covariances to generate predictions about the internal development or self-organization of systems.

> Dynamical systems theory is the perfect partner for the Gibsonian conception of perceiving as an embodied activity. This is because it employs differential equations to explain and predict how the states of nonlinear systems evolve over time. It begins by taking stock of a number of variables that describe the state of a system at a particular point in time. It then makes use of its special mathematical tools to chart the trajectory of changes in the states of such systems as they move through a space of possibilities.
>
> *(Hutto and Myin 2017: 23)*

But this method is more difficult to use to generate testable results, and remains largely speculative. It is one thing to show how these systems might produce observed results, another to show that they actually do.

The dilemma of the "E" approaches is this: as critiques and alternatives to the standard approaches, they are effective and powerful; as a source of computational models that can simulate observed processes they are weak. And this mirrors the dilemma of the standard approach: it can generate testable predictions and explain them within a properly limited universe or domain; but the very strengths that enable it to do so, the internal, intellectualist or cognitivist form of its explanations, prevent it from dealing with the pervasive role of external facts of the kind the "E" approaches focus on. Yet there is no denying the importance of these facts and the need to deal with them – something that is especially apparently in dealing with complex phenomena such as social life and social institutions.

The Problem of Morals as Social Theory

The standard approach does not imply, but is congenial to, a certain basic picture of social life and its relation to morality. The goal of social life, or the thing to be explained, is the fact of coordination. The "social" problem is to obtain some sort of equilibrium. This needs to be done under two major constraints: it must accommodate the interests, rationally pursued, of the individuals in the arrangement; and it must overcome and constrain the pursuit of these interests in ways that produce the benefits of coordination, which are assumed to be greater than the benefits of individual, non-coordinated, unsocial pursuit of aims. Primate studies show the existence of various forms of coordination, or monkey politics, and it is assumed that humans have evolved propensities for coordination involving self-sacrifice or other-regarding action that produce similar results. This fundamentally Hobbesian model also implies a particular view of the social, sociality, and the explanatory necessities to which an account of the social must respond.

The neuroscience of morals points directly at one major issue: the parts of the brain involved in moral responses indicate that the process differs from ordinary cognition but at the same time is often connected to it. The issue is the role of emotion, which figures into ordinary reasoning but plays a larger role in moral reasoning (see Prinz 2007). That there is a role of emotion in reasoning at all is a problem for the code and computational model. But understanding the relation of emotion to morals is a larger problem. Emotions are often considered to be universal, and for there to be quite a short list of basic universal emotions.[4] Moralities are diverse. So there is an intrinsic problem of relating the two, which provides us with another explanatory necessity: much of what is normally understood as moral behavior involves things that bear little relation to these generic moral impulses, but are nevertheless powerful. The relation in the brain is undeniable: understanding the relation between the universal and the local aspects of morality is the puzzle (Stich 2006; Doris and Stich 2007; Kelly et al. 2007).

This puzzle is routinely evaded, and the means of doing so serve to immunize the extension of the standard model to morality from empirical refutation. The major means is the idea that morality is universal but that convention is not, and that the things that pass as examples of the diversity of morals fall into the category of convention. There is, however, no neural basis for this distinction (Kelly et al. 2007). And this amounts, or can amount, to a kind of circular argument in which one separates the universal elements from the diverse ones, and calls the universal ones "moral" and the diverse ones "conventional." But there are other problems with the distinction, and also other ways of making it.

One way of making the distinction work as a genuinely empirical matter is to consider morality developmentally, and look at the emergence of moral responses in children who are not yet encultured. This allows one to separate the conventional elements from the "seemingly hardwired tendencies and intuitions emerge [that] very early in ontogeny, and as a result are assumed to be the outcomes of selection pressures due to their adaptive value in promoting group living" (Decety and Cowell 2017: 1).

Decety and Cowell (2017: 1), pointing to a developing literature, pointing to a developing literature, focus on one of these elements: that physically harming others and violating considerations of fairness are central to the moral domain (Gray et al. 2012; Hauser 2006).

> When shown events depicting fair and unfair distributions of goods (such as milk or cookies), 15-month-old infants looked longer at the unfair situation. This suggests that even infants expect equality and are surprised by violations of distributive justice (e.g., Schmidt and Sommerville 2011; Sloane [et al.] 2012). Preverbal infants as young as 10 months old manifest sympathetic responses to victims of antisocial behavior, represented only by moving geometrical objects.
>
> *(Decety and Cowell 2017: 4)*

The notion of interpersonal harm is quite broad, and context dependent – and therefore dependent on other cognitive capacities, such as empathy; but we can construct a plausible path, with these additional capacities, to higher forms of moral consciousness:

> Noticing interpersonal harm alongside the development of empathic concern, theory of mind, and socialization can lead to an understanding that harmful actions cause suffering and an appreciation that complex moral rules and norms depend on contexts within cultures.
>
> *(Decety and Cowell 2017: 1)*

Fully mature moral reasoning and response involves even more cognitive capacities: knowledge, values, reputation, and relevant behaviors. It involves both unconscious and deliberate processes such as harm aversion, empathic concern, and social emotions (e.g., guilt, remorse, and shame). These change in the course of development:

Taken together, findings from these neurodevelopmental investigations of the perception and evaluation of third-party intentional harm, using both electrophysiology and functional imaging, highlight the importance of the dynamic integration of several interconnected neural networks implicated in processing distress cues, intentionality of the agent, consequences for the victim, valuation, and social decision making. In infancy, the valence of the observed action is readily coded, as reflected by early ERP [event-related potential] responses distinguishing antisocial from prosocial interpersonal behaviors. However, when viewing visual scenarios later in development, intentionality of the agent seems to be processed first, which is then followed by an affective reaction, valuation, and reasoning.

(Decety and Cowell 2017: 8)

And this conclusion is driven by a particular view of moral decisions as other-regarding in the following way:

Human moral decisions are governed by both statistical expectations (based on observed frequencies) about what others will do and normative beliefs about what others should do. These vary across different cultures and historical contexts, forming a continuum from social conventions to moral norms typically concerning harm to others (Tomasello and Vaish 2013).

(Decety and Cowell 2017: 1)

This gets us to a kind of core-periphery model in which apparently harmful moral actions, such as honor killings, make sense as "moral." In this case it is plausible to say that the harm in question is the harm to the family reputation, and therefore to its members. So it can plausibly be said to have a core of harm prevention, and perhaps even fairness, as these are retributive acts as well as restorative ones.

With each step into the periphery, and toward mature moral reasoning – with its wider array of cognitive elements, however – one also moves toward content that is itself more overtly social. And here we run into the usual difficulty: how pervasively social are the relevant processes? A few quotes can set this problem up. The first comes from participatory sense-making: if regulation of social coupling takes place through coordination of movements, and if

movements – including utterances – are the tools of sense-making, then our proposal is: social agents can coordinate their sense-making in social encounters. This means that the sense-making of interactors acquires a coherence through their interaction and not just in their physical manifestation, but also in their significance. This is what we call participatory sense-making.

(De Jaegher and Di Paolo 2007: 13)

Mercier and Sperber make a similar point, emphasizing the retrospective role of normative reason-giving in social interaction:

> Reducing the mechanisms of social coordination to norm abiding, mind-reading, or a combination of these two mechanisms misses how much of human interaction aims at justifying oneself, evaluating the reasons of others (either those they give or those we attribute to them), criticizing past or current interactions, and anticipating future ones. In these interactions about interactions, reasons are central.
>
> *(Mercier and Sperber 2017: 186)*

The conflict between the two approaches is evident in the Decety and Cowell conclusion:

> that while the evidence for the role of the sensitivity to interpersonal harm in moral cognition appears convincing, further research is necessary to fully characterize whether this information and its underlying neural computations are domain specific (specialized for a circumscribed class of stimuli), process specific (specialized for a particular type of computation), or rather should be seen as a general reaction to negative emotion akin to the negativity bias.
>
> *(Decety and Cowell 2017: 10)*

This allows for two possibilities. We could have a process governed largely by public justification, interaction, and arguing over reasons, or "participative sense-making" which begins at a very early stage in development and involves a general reaction to negative emotion; or we could have a largely internal process in which the child matures by the more or less independent development of modules which eventually get employed in a mature, moral reasoning process, which spans multiple capacities, by an autonomous moral agent.

If the moral is not reducible to its own module, as these accounts imply, we can also take other directions from these findings. Decety and Cowell suggest one direction – that mature morality is the result of a developmental process that results in reductions of interference among systems:

> Across ontogeny, these task-level control networks show significant developmental change in functional connectivity, particularly between the amygdala, vmPFC, and pSTS. While neural network modules emerge very early in life (Fair et al. 2008), these functional modules are refined during toddlerhood, childhood, and adolescence, and become more distinct, characterized by changes in connectivity both within information processing modules and between modules. Such development allows for functional

specialization, reducing interference among systems and facilitating cognitive performance to support adaptive behavior [Fornito et al. 2012].

(Decety and Cowell 2017: 9)

This assumes that mature morality is marked by moral coherence at the level of individual brain function, and that interference is a lower stage to be overcome. This is a purely internal notion of moral development. But we might take this in a direction in which conflicts between systems is central to morality, and perhaps the spur to conscious morality. We can imagine a less coherent moral world in which we have various "moral" impulses, drives, or module-like capacities that are universal, such as for fairness and harm avoidance, but which do not necessarily cohere, and indeed often conflict – as they do in the case of honor killings, which require doing harm to a close relative. The lesson of the neuroscience of the trolley problem is that we have a resistance to directly harming someone and a potentially conflicting impulse to harm fewer people (Greene 2016). This can be generalized to a broader view of morality and its role: to a picture in which internal conflict is normal and productive.

The evidence of neuroscience and evolutionary studies suggests: that people are averse to harming others or having them harmed; altruistic, meaning that they experience altruistic behavior as rewarding; that they experience rewards for punishing free-riders; that they have a sense of justice and equity; that they respond reciprocally; that they think rationally in terms of self-interest; and that they have a strong capacity for empathy and mind-reading, among many other things, including a propensity to prefer people like themselves. The list could be greatly extended, but its obvious feature is that these human moral cognitive propensities not only do not add up to an ethic, they also conflict. And this suggests that we are routinely forced to think through, or rely on the thinking through of others, or participate in the kind of negotiation described by Mercier and Sperber to resolve, however temporarily and contextually, the conflicts between these propensities.

However, we resolve them not simply by an internal process, but by believing certain things about the world and categorizing people in certain ways – things that come from social learning. Marcello Truzzi (1973: 242–4) made the point about cognitive dissonance theory that one needed to know what relevance people's beliefs had to one another, as they understood those ideas, in order to know whether they would experience them as conflicting. The same kind of point holds for ethical beliefs. The most extreme violation of a sense of justice might be regarded by the perpetrator as perfectly just if the person being treated unjustly was regarded as less than human, as undeserving (and hence a free-rider), and so forth. Much of what we know from the very revealing research about basic human morality that comes from observations of small children in partly structured social settings with other children is largely un-illuminating when it is applied to the kinds of complex belief situations that arise in adult social life. Are bankers free-riders or deserving? Are unionized government employees with good contracts free-riders, bullies, or deserving? Does labor produce all value, or does risk taking count as well? These are the kind of questions whose answers depend on a large set of complex beliefs. But the moral responses and mechanisms that the evolutionary/neuroscience universalist appeals to, such as the pleasure we get from punishing free-riders, depends on the beliefs we use to categorize people as free-riders in the first place.

Where does this leave us? Evolution and neuroscience do not deliver a universal morality: they help identify a set of mechanisms that potentially conflict. Situations arise that bring these conflicts out into the open and make them a problem for participants. In some cases the conflicts may be internal, cognitive conflicts. In others they may represent ideological conflicts between different groups with different interests. These conflicts can sometimes be resolved or at least managed by beliefs which enable the relevant feelings to be directed in ways that do not conflict. Indeed, the origin of public doctrinal morality is in ideas about the external world. Notions like tabu, such things as fetishes – which represent the magical creation of a compact invoking the threat of misfortune for violating it – as well as the appeal to the afterlife, the wrath of God, and so forth are all claims about "facts." These beliefs, however, are about the external world and are beliefs in the sense of public beliefs – things that have been affirmed by others or are patterns closely associated with public beliefs.

These beliefs – which may include articulated moral theories, beliefs about categories of persons, beliefs about the causal world, particularly about consequences in the social world – may resolve the conflicts for a time, but new situations may arise which compel their revision. Diversity itself may be the cause of conflicts. Normal human variation with respect to the relevant mechanism (such as altruism or self-interest), diversity in belief, and so forth may need to be accounted for by the beliefs, and cause changes in the beliefs. There are of course interactional, "social," mechanisms for the standardization of belief and the production and enforcement of conformity. It is often inconvenient to believe in or follow conventions that your peers and persons you interact with do not also adhere to. So, "solutions" in the realm of moral belief tend to be shared through public affirmation, though there will also be variation – if only because of variation in experience and in make-up between individuals in the setting. But this shifts the issue to the problem of culture and cultural transmission.

Notes

1 See Callon and Latour 1981; Epstein 2015.
2 This is a subject with a large literature, but I recommend Hägerström's essay "Is Positive Law an Expression of Will?" (1916 [1953]: 17–55) as one of the best, and certainly the funniest, texts on the topic.
3 For a popular discussion, see Sloman and Fernbach (2017). They cite considerations that imply that memory is much more limited than is assumed in the standard approach,

which in turn implies that memory and knowledge rely on a combination of other people, through a social distribution of knowledge, on embodied knowledge, and on technology which has knowledge built into it. For a discussion of memory and self-deception, as well as a discussion of deception and self-deception generally, see Trivers (2011: 143–4). This book also discusses such topics as biased encoding, the cognitive load of lying, and many other issues from an evolutionary and anthropologically sophisticated perspective.

4 There is a vast literature on this general topic. An accessible account is Bloom (2013).

References

Barnier, Amanda J., John Sutton, Celia B. Harris, and Robert A. Wilson. (2008). "A Conceptual and Empirical Framework for the Social Distribution of Cognition: The Case of Memory." *Cognitive Systems Research* 9: 33–51

Bechtel, W. and R. C. Richardson. (1993). *Discovering Complexity: Decomposition and Localization as Strategies in Scientific Research*. Princeton, NJ: Princeton University Press.

Bloom, Paul. (2013). *Just Babies: The Origins of Good and Evil*. New York: Crown.

Bridgman, Percy William. (1927). *The Logic of Modern Physics*. New York: Macmillan.

Callon, Michel and Bruno Latour. (1981). "Unscrewing the Big Leviathan: How Actors Macro-Structure Reality and How Sociologists Help Them Do So." In K. Knorr-Cen-tina and A. V. Cicourel (eds.) *Advances in Social Theory and Methodology: Toward an Integration of Micro- and Macro-Sociologies*. Boston MA and London: Routledge & Kegan Paul, 275–303.

Cassirer, Ernst. ([1925] 1946). *Language and Myth*, trans. Susanne Langer. New York: Harper Brothers.

Chemero, Anthony. (2009). *Radical Embodied Cognitive Science*. Cambridge, MA: MIT Press.

Cummins, R. (2000). "'How Does It Work?' vs. 'What Are the Laws?' Two Conceptions of Psychological Explanation." In F. Keil and R. Wilson (eds.) *Explanation and Cognition*, 117–145. Cambridge, MA: MIT Press.

De Jaegher, H. and E. Di Paolo. (2007). "Participatory Sense-Making: An Enactive Approach to Social Cognition." *Phenomenology and the Cognitive Sciences*, 6(4): 485–507.

Decety, Jean and Jason M. Cowell. (2017). "Interpersonal Harm Aversion as a Necessary Foundation for Morality: A Developmental Neuroscience Perspective." *Development and Psychopathology*. Online 19 April: 1–12. doi:10.1017/S0954579417000530.

Dennett, D. C. (1978). "Artificial Intelligence as Philosophy and Psychology." In *Brainstorms: Philosophical Essays on Mind and Psychology*, 109–128. Cambridge, MA: MIT Press.

Doris, John M. and Stephen Stitch. (2007). "As a Matter of Fact: Empirical Perspectives on Ethics." In Frank Jackson and Michael Smith (eds.). *The Oxford Handbook of Contemporary Philosophy*, 114–152. Oxford: Oxford University Press.

Durkheim, Émile. ([1912] 1995). *The Elementary Forms of Religious Life*, trans. Karen E. Fields. New York: Free Press.

Epstein, Brian. (2015). *The Ant Trap: Rebuilding the Foundations of the Social Sciences*. Oxford: Oxford University Press.

Fair, D. A., A. L. Cohen, N. U. Dosenbach, J. A. Church, F. M. Miezin, D. M. Barch, and B. L. Schlaggar. (2008). "The Maturing Architecture of the Brain's Default Network." *Proceedings of the National Academy of Sciences* 105: 4028–4032.

Farmer, J. Doyne and Duncan Foley. (2009). "Nature." *Nature* 460 (7256): 685–686.

Fornito, A., B. J. Harrison, A. Zalesky, and J. S. Simons. (2012). "Competitive and Cooperative Dynamics of Large-Scale Brain Functional Networks Supporting Recollection." *Proceedings of the National Academy of Sciences* 109: 12788–12793.

Gallistel, C. R. (2017). "Stop Saying the Brain Learns By Rewiring Itself." *Nautilus* 5 May. http://nautil.us/blog/stop-saying-the-brain-learns-by-rewiring-itself (accessed 19 June 2017).

García-Salmones, Mónica. (2011). "On Kelsen's Sein: An Approach to Kelsenian Sociological Themes." *No Foundations: Journal of Extreme Legal Positivism* 8: 41–70.

Giddings, F. H. (1922). *Studies in the Theory of Human Society.* New York: Macmillan. https://archive.org/details/studiesintheory01giddgoog (accessed 31 August 2015).

Gintis, Herbert. (2004). "Towards a Unity of the Human Behavioral Sciences." *Politics, Philosophy, and Economics* 3(1): 37–57.

Gintis, Herbert (2007). "A Framework for the Unification of the Behavioral Sciences." *Behavioral and Brain Sciences* 30: 1–61.

Gobet, Fernand and Herbert A. Simon. (1998). "Pattern Recognition Makes Search Possible: Comments on Holding (1992)." *Psychological Research* 61: 204–208.

Gordon, Brian and Georg Theiner. (2015). "Scaffolded Joint Action as a Micro–Foundation of Organizational Learning." In Charles B. Stone and Lucas Bietti (eds.), *Contextualizing Human Memory: An Interdisciplinary Approach to Understanding How Individuals and Groups Remember the Past,* 154–186. Abingdon: Psychology Press.

Gray, K., L. Young, and A. Watz. (2012). "Mind Perception Is the Essence of Morality." *Psychological Inquiry* 23: 101–124.

Greene, Joshua D. (2016). "Solving the Trolley Problem." In Justin Sytsma and Wesley Buckwalter (eds.) *A Companion to Experimental Philosophy,* 175–189. Hoboken, NJ: Wiley.

Hägerström, Axel. (1916 [1953]). *Inquiries into the Nature of Law and Morals.* Uppsala: Almqvist & Wiksells.

Hauser, M. (2006). *Moral Minds.* New York: HarperCollins.

Heersmink, Richard. (2017). "The Narrative Self, Distributed Memory, and Evocative Objects." *Philosophical Studies.* Online 24 May. doi:10.1007/s11098–11017–0935–0.

Heider, F., and Simmel, M. (1944). "An Experimental Study of Apparent Behavior." *American Journal of Psychology* 57: 243–259.

Hobbes, Thomas. ([1651] 1965). *Leviathan.* London: Dent. www.gutenberg.org/files/3207/3207-h/3207-h.htm (accessed 31 May 2017).

Hutto, Daniel and Erik Myin. (2017). *Evolving Enactivism: Basic Minds Meet Content.* Cambridge, MA: MIT Press.

Kasparov, Garry. (2017). *Deep Thinking: Where Machine Intelligence Ends and Human Creativity Begins.* New York: Public Affairs.

Kelly, Daniel, Stephen Stich, Kevin J. Haley, Serena J. Eng, and Daniel M. T. Fessler. (2007). "Harm, Affect, and the Moral/Conventional Distinction." *Mind and Language* 22(2): 117–131.

Kelsen, Hans. (1922). "Der Begriff des Staates und die Sozialpsychologie." *Imago* 8: 97–111.

Kelsen, Hans. (1943). *Society and Nature: A Sociological Inquiry.* London: Kegan Paul, Trench, Trubner & Co.

Machamer, P.K., Darden, L., and Craver, C.F. (2000). "Thinking about Mechanisms." *Philosophy of Science,* 67(1): 1–25.

McLaughlin, Mitchell. (2017). *Post-Traditionalism and Religion without Religion: A Brief Introduction.* N.p.: Createspace Independent Pub.

Mercier, Hugo and Dan Sperber. (2017). *The Enigma of Reason.* Cambridge, MA: Harvard University Press.

Parsons, Talcott. (1937). *The Structure of Social Action*. New York: Free Press.

Prinz, Jesse J. (2007). *The Emotional Construction of Morals*. Oxford: Oxford University Press.

Schmidt, M. F. H. and J. A. Sommerville. (2011). "Fairness Expectations and Altruistic Sharing in 15-Month-Old Human Infants." *Plos ONE* 6: e23223. doi:10.1371/journal.pone.0023223.

Schmitt, Carl. ([1938] 2008). *The Leviathan in the State Theory of Thomas Hobbes: Meaning and Failure of a Political Symbol*, trans. G. Schwab and E. Hilfstein. Chicago, IL: University of Chicago Press.

Searle, John. (1995). *The Construction of Social Reality*. New York and London: Free Press.

Sloane, S., R. Baillargeon, and D. Premack. (2012). "Do Infants Have a Sense of Fairness?" *Psychological Science* 232: 196–204.

Sloman, Steven and Fernbach, Philip. (2017). *The Knowledge Illusion: Why We Never Think Alone*. New York: Riverhead.

Stefan, F. and A. Atman. (2015). "Is There Any Connection between the Network Morphology and the Fluctuations of the Stock Market Index?" *Physica A: Statistical Mechanics and Its Applications* 419: 630–641.

Stich, Stephen. (2006). "Is Orality an Elegant Machine or a Kludge?" *Journal of Cognition and Culture* 6(1–2): 181–189.

Tomasello, Michael. (2011). "Acquiring Linguistic Constructions." In Usha Goswami (ed.) *The Wiley-Blackwell Handbook of Childhood Cognitive Development*, 255–298. Malden, MA: Blackwell.

Trivers, Robert. (2011). *The Folly of Fools: The Logic of Deceit and Self-Deception in Human Life*. New York: Basic.

Truzzi, Marcello. (1973). "The Problem of Relevance between Orientations for Cognitive Dissonance Theory." *Journal for the Theory of Social Behaviour* 3: 239–247.

Weber, Max. ([1968] 1978). *Economy and Society: An Outline of Interpretive Sociology* 3 vols, ed. Guenther Roth and Claus Wittich. Berkeley: University of California Press.

8

THE TWO SOCIALS AND THE *VERSTEHEN* BUBBLE

We can distinguish, as has been done implicitly throughout this book, two conceptions of the social. Now is the time to make this distinction explicit, and compare them. But in doing so we inevitably need to go beyond the existing literature. The standard approach to cognitive science has close affinities with positions in social theory that have deep roots in the history of social thought, so it will be convenient to simply point out the basic elements of this family of ideas and explain its relation to the standard approaches to cognition. The alternative, however, will require more explanation, and will also require adding in some elements that are not developed in the alternative approaches to cognitive science but which fit with and enhance them.

The issues here concern the problems of linkage and levels, and this requires some discussion. The standard approach, especially what Mark Bickhard (2001) calls encodingism, has made repeated advances. Efforts have been made to figure out how sounds get encoded into internal brain code, and therefore words, for example; and a vast new effort at constructing the human brain has produced controversy, especially in relation to the very expensive European project to model the brain, as well as patents on algorithms that "are designed to intelligently map internal events, such as neural spiking activity, to external physiological, linguistic and behavioral expression" (Nuffield Department of Surgical Sciences 2017, n.p.). These models go beyond encoding to deal with brain chemistry and other issues, but rest on the basic ideas of the standard approach.

The European Union (EU) has created a vast project to provide a full simulation of the brain using supercomputers which has drawn criticism, and there are parallel efforts in the US and Japan. The vast sums invested in these projects will produce results. Yet, in the case of each of these projects, there is still a vast gap between actual human behavior, thinking, and interaction and the mechanisms being identified or simulated. And in this gap there is still a great deal of room for speculation and for reconceptualizations of the problem. There is also the sense that methods that go a long way to simulate and even interface with brain processes, for example by directly feeding stimulation into the brain in advanced coded form, will fall short of, and indeed prevent, understanding cognition as a whole. Why might this be so? Simulations require targets. If the basic model is the brain as understood by the standard approach – as an information processor which needs to be augmented by some learning capacities and capacities for development – and the target of the simulation is the autonomous agent, one will perhaps get results, and even an account that can scale up to societies made up of these autonomous agents. But if the target is something different, this approach may not work.

The standard approach has been called internalist and intellectualist; the rivals, as we have seen, place more emphasis on external facts. This fundamental difference carries over to the domain of social theory. But we have added an important qualification to this contrast by the idea – vaguely developed so far – of the *Verstehen* bubble and the special significance of the neuroscience validation of the phenomenon of empathy. The idea of the bubble is largely irrelevant to the standard approach, as is the phenomenon of empathy. But it is crucial to understanding the alternative as well as to understanding the limitations of the standard approach.

We can give names to these two conceptions of the social. The standard approach depends on the idea of autonomous agents, and conceives of "society" as the product of an arrangement between autonomous agents: call this "the autonomous agent social" or the "Hobbesian social." In this conception effects of "society" on the individual and on cognition are effects of the social arrangements created by autonomous agents. The alternative I will call "the pervasive social." This will require some explanation, but the explanation can begin with an example given at the beginning of the book: the apparent causal relation between tense systems in different languages and overt behavior in relation to planning, saving, and future-oriented behavior generally.

This is a kind of fact that plays no role in the autonomous agent social, or in the *Verstehen* bubble. Yet it is "social" both in the sense that the use of the relevant language is socially distributed and in the consequences of the fact, which are also socially distributed and have effects on important social outcomes, such as life chances. It is also not "cognitive" in the sense of being part of the information-processing apparatus of the brain. Yet clearly it involves the brain, cognition, choice, and thinking. And this is not the only kind of case in which socially distributed facts produce socially distributed outcomes by way of what would have to be regarded as mental processes, yet do not fit either within the *Verstehen* bubble or with the standard model of cognition.

The case of epigenetic inheritance presents the same problems. Epigenetics is concerned generally with the variation that occurs in the expression of genes, which is to say with the gap between genotype and phenotype. Recent, but still controversial, research on animals has shown evidence of inheritance of differences in expression resulting from differences in experiences, and there is indirect evidence in some cases of similar inheritance in humans, involving starvation in prior generations. Needless to say these causal conditions are socially distributed, raising the question of whether there is a significant role of this kind of social inheritance elsewhere. If cognition was affected by the experiences of previous generations, which has been suggested, for example with reference to the heirs of holocaust survivors, we would be admitting a form of causality that undermines not only the autonomous agent model but also the assumptions about the social irrelevance or neutral character of genetic inheritance on which the usual uses of evolutionary considerations, which place the fixation of the human cognitive endowment in the environment of the African Savannah, rely (Antón et al. 2014).

These causes come from outside the *Verstehen* bubble – they are not "intelligible" in the way that human action and conduct is intelligible to other humans. In Weber's terms, they are not "meaningful." These examples, moreover, merely scratch the surface. There are reported findings in neuroscience-related research daily – not surprisingly in a field with 100,000 publications a year – that point to relations between causes which are socially distributed and various kinds of neuroscientifically related outcomes that do not easily fit into the standard model, and certainly not in the narrow form of the code model. And this raises a large question about the limits and nature of "the social." We can address this by thinking through the relations between different kinds of social explanation, in cognitive science terms, and provide some more precise definitions.

The Bubble, the Tacit, and the Causal

I have used the term "*Verstehen* bubble" without defining it, and there is a reason for this: the term is best understood in the narrow sense that Weber had in mind – the realm of the meaningful or intelligible, to which he added, for sociology, the qualifier of social, or oriented to other people. This is a definition within the *Verstehen* bubble: it uses more or less ordinary language of the sort we use in normal human communication. But we can reformulate this qualifier in cognitive science terms by reference to the concept of joint attention: something is in the *Verstehen* bubble if it is the object of joint attention, and potentially in the bubble if it is a potential object of joint attention. Joint attention can be defined as it is for monkeys – it involves the mirror neurons or the equivalent human system. But it is also accessible to consciousness: to be jointly attentive is to be conscious of the attention of the other.

But this definition introduces a problem: before the discovery of mirror neurons, they were not themselves a subject of joint attention; and without the scientific instruments that enabled us to make them the subject of joint attention, they were not even potential objects of joint attention. So the category is an elastic one, defined only by our capacities for making something an object of joint attention. Moreover, it is not limited to "real" things or objects. Consider the concept of tabu. Tabu is a quality of things, places, and persons – but not a "real" one. It is nevertheless very real in the sense of W. I. Thomas, that a "definition of the situation is real if it is real in its consequences" (see Thomas and Thomas 1929: 572). It is also intelligible, though perhaps with the help of some anthropological explanation.

What can we say about this case? Ghosts, fairies, gods – all these sorts of things are the object of joint attention. But we can tell a story about how they emerge as cognitive realities to become the subject of joint attention, and how they are connected to deep emotions. Tabu, to take the example most discussed in the history of anthropology, is rooted in the reality of danger. There are strong emotions associated with it, and the objects of joint attention are socially learned (for example by imitation), and the nature of the danger is beyond normal empirical testing: to be told something is tabu, meaning that bad outcomes will befall the violator of the tabu through an automatic mechanism, precludes this. And a violator will be subject to fear and loathing as well as the expectation of automatic punishment – hardly a desirable position.

Gilles Fauconnier and Mark Turner (2008) argue that there is a process they call "conceptual blending" which is perhaps at work here: we begin with something like danger, a vague concept, which is then associated with and treated through imitation and social learning as dangerous. It then becomes, for cognitive purposes, dangerous. It can be associated with binary oppositions – a typical cognitive economy. How this all might work will be discussed below; but the basic elements, the thingness of the original object of joint attention, the epistemic uncertainty and social certainty surrounding it, are sufficient to account for the cognitive response. And the fact that tabu is about not theological theory but about dangerous people, places, and things serves to externalize the explanation, or rather to see the tabu object as itself a product of cognitive operations, joint attention, and the world that is cognized.

What does this have to do with social theory? More will be said about this shortly, in relation to concepts like "socio-cultural practices," but there is an important answer that can be given immediately. Tabu was a basic organizing principle of the Polynesian societies in which it was found: it was a morality, world-view, set of physical practices, and something learned – for example by imitation, but also by explicit teaching and verbalization, thus exhibiting the mix of explicit and tacit characteristic of practices. At the same time it served as a means of coordination within societies: by adhering to tabus, behavior could be predicted and aligned, and patterns of behavior stabilized so that long-term projects could be pursued: these things are the basics of organized society.

How does this relate to the "autonomous agent social"? A key to the scaling up of autonomous agents to societies is coordination, and it is normally modeled by game theory. But in these models the agents are normally equipped with beliefs, desires, and rationality, and the beliefs and desires are varied to produce different outcomes: different stable game-theoretic bargains. The object is to explain the equilibrium that is arrived at. But it is also possible to arrive at game-theoretic equilibria much more simply. Francesco Guala (2016: 90–91) has shown how a simple physical marker which has become the subject of joint attention between two groups – what he calls a "focal point" – can produce a border-like equilibrium even without communication or "agreement." We can think of actual societies as made up of multiple focal points which are the subject of joint attention by different overlapping groups, as the distributed rather than centralized source of multiple modes of coordination.

What might these focal points be? There are obvious candidates, all of which, like religion, have physical manifestations: rituals, dangerous things, shared spaces and technologies, and people who are taken to have a certain status, such as the Polynesian chief who is himself tabu and can pronounce something tabu. But if this sort of thing is the basis of society, it seems to be beyond the reach of any internalist program. What becomes a focal point, or object of joint attention, is the product of human activity, but activity that is social in the sense of joint in joint attention, and also incorporates things in the world – things, as we have seen, that are also affordances and which can be created. These focal points obviate the need for agreement (tacit or otherwise), for a central value system, for a field and habitus, and so forth. They do the job of coordination to the extent it needs to be done to explain social stability or equilibrium – to the extent that these things need to be explained and are not figments of the imaginary of the ideologically motivated theorist.

Focal points can be understood in neuroscience terms: the act of jointly focusing on something, imitating, and so forth are all familiar neuroscience processes. But the act itself, which is within the *Verstehen* bubble, is not determined in any strict way by these processes; the sheer range of possible focal points or objects of joint attention, the potentially relevant external facts, is so great that "deriving" social institutions from neuroscience facts is impossible. One is tempted to call this human creativity. But, like all forms of creativity, it is constrained in various ways, and neuroscience can potentially say a great deal about these constraints – not so much about the explicit, but about the conditions for the explicit, and about that which is tacit and causal which is bound up together in the form of practices which are partly tacit and partly explicit.

We can now construct a kind of geography of the relevant domains. First there is the *Verstehen* bubble. Beyond the *Verstehen* bubble, beyond joint attention, is the tacit, or what Searle calls "the Background" – that is to say the operations of the mind that are not accessible to consciousness. It is true that some of this domain can be talked of indirectly, using terms like "assumptions"; but there is no reason to think that these articulations conform to or represent anything in the brain itself. Mercier and Sperber (2107: 126) note that: "When we attribute to ourselves an implicit reason, we are just interpreting our thoughts or actions in terms of newly constructed conscious reasons that we fictitiously represent as having been implicit before."

Most of what is tacit, such as the operations behind facial recognition, which can be modeled by an algorithm, is not even semantic. Nevertheless, like the causal processes discussed above, what is in the tacit is socially distributed, and indeed, in part, the product of social learning, practice, and social processes themselves.

Here we come to a conundrum. It would be convenient if the tacit was all universal, as we might assume the capacity for facial recognition is. We could then think that the algorithm we have constructed, which does a good job of actually predicting faces from brain states, is also universal. We could assume variation away. We could assume that there was no effect of learning or inputs, of the kinds of faces a person would have seen and would come to be able to distinguish and recognize. But we know that this is not true – that the faces of people of different ethnicities from one's own, for example, are more difficult to distinguish. So even in this case we must grant variation.

This points to a conceptual problem with algorithms. In the literature algorithms are used to represent total processes – processes like facial recognition. A procedure or object that produces the same result is said to have the same algorithm, even if it is physically different. Here the term "same" and the designation of the functional process represented by the "algorithm" itself are not well defined, and the results are different depending on how fine-grained the descriptions of the processes are (Miłkowski 2013: 67). They can be readily extended from very simple perceptual processes to large action sequences, such as a human being going home from work, which can be performed in a large variety of ways, using a large variety of devices, but getting the "same" result. These may include such mental content as the memory of what bus to take, knowledge of the routines of public transport, map-like memory, and much more. Different content, analogous to different computer code for the "same" algorithm, would be involved if the person walked home or drove a car. But the result, at a high enough level of abstraction, would be "the same." So what is the same at one level is not the same at another.

This may seem to be an exotic issue. But it becomes a pressing issue when we are talking about tacit processes that are subject to substantial variation. Facial recognition may be relatively unique in its isolation from other cognitive processes, but it too is subject to variation. The variation in processes that are somewhat similar, but not "the same," is a much bigger problem. Here the fact of variation makes access to, or even thinking about, the tacit conditions a stone wall. Any algorithm would be only a vague approximation of what is actually going on. And what holds for algorithms holds for "theoretical" constructs of these things, such as "culture," generally. "Culture" is an abstract concept constructed with materials from within the *Verstehen* bubble – what Weber would have called an ideal-type. Getting an algorithm to mimic some idealized cultural phenomenon would tell us little about the highly variable underlying processes such as the tacit basis of each individual's cultural cognition.

Diversity and variation produce problems for the idea of culture as code and for the idea that this code has something to do with the "code" in the brain, if there is such a thing. If the relevant operating code for a culture is the fantastically complex thing it needs to be to fit computationalist models other than connectionism, it has to be transmitted by some other method than learning – the underlying code is too involved to transmit on the mother's knee. This is why the followers of Fodor, correctly, infer that the relevant innately given code, which they take to be semantic, would itself have to be fantastically complex. Building "concepts" up from a simpler list of semantic units would never get us to the nuanced distinctions found within the *Verstehen* bubble. The code story, in short, true or not, is not much help in the face of the fact of variation.

Is there an alternative to the code story, at the level of culture and action if not at the level of basic brain processes? As we have seen, what can be modeled by a theory, or a program, can in fact be produced by the recognition of multiple smaller patterns: the paradigmatic case of chess. And this result has highly general implications: what looks like "economic rationality" when modeled at the level of the market, for example, may in fact be, and more plausibly is, the result of decisions made on the basis of multiple smaller patterns – the choice to buy a particular vegetable when the price difference with another seems too high, rather than a choice made with perfect knowledge and a full range of transitive preferences. Similarly for Daniel Kahneman's (2011) model of decision-making and error: what may be occurring is one process of pattern-fitting which the decision-theory model misrepresents by dividing it into the parts that conform and the parts that do not, and thus need an explanation of a different kind, such as a theory of heuristics. For culture the point is even clearer. The idea that culture as a complex theory-like code transmitted to each member of the culture is implausible. The multiple, redundant pattern recognition one is not.

Reasons, Desires, and the Autonomous Agent

The strength of the autonomous agency approach to the social is the fact that it appears to be rooted in the most secure of all models of the individual – in folk psychology, the belief-desire or belief-desire reason model of action. The question that needs to be asked about this model is whether it belongs within the *Verstehen* bubble, as a human product, or whether it is, so to speak, a picture of human nature that belongs in the scientific image of humanity and cognition. To say it belongs in the *Verstehen* bubble implies this: that the model is a cultural artifact, a way in which humans can think and talk about the limited set of things that appear within the bubble – namely the kind of knowledge we have of ourselves that we can recognize and apply to others. The subject matter of the model, in short, is the domain that is accessible to us through the limited and biased operations of our own self-consciousness. The language we apply is one of many. The alternative, favored by the standard approach, is to say that the language is not subject to these qualifications, and is rooted in the reality of the mind itself, in our fundamental human capacities to read other minds, and that the cultural and linguistic variation in expressions of the knowledge produced by these universal capacities is superficial – and, crucially, there is no alternative.

We can address the issue of alternatives and what it would mean for this model to be a "cultural artifact" at the same time. Rüdiger Bittner (2001), in his *Doing Things for Reasons*, which I will briefly summarize here, provides an argument against the model and provides an alternative. He argues that desires and beliefs cannot be the reason for anything. A genuine reason is a state or event, an external fact. When we give reasons accounts we construct narratives in which the act is a response to the event or state, and which may contain a series of such responses, including of course responses to acts of others. What goes on inside need not consist of desires, rational calculations, and beliefs. Instead, as he puts it, people select the reasons for their actions by being disposed in a way that makes that event or state salient and response-producing. Although Bittner stops at this point, we can add that if we have a sufficiently broad view of "dispositions," to include learned dispositions, and reinterpret "beliefs" in terms of learned dispositions, for example, we can dispense with the belief-desire model. We can replace it with an account of action consisting of the external facts and dispositions to respond to them – including dispositions to respond to requests for declarations of belief.

Bittner's version of doing things for reasons thus completely dispenses with the language of belief and desire. This actually fits with our quite limited understanding of how the brain produces action. Something like dispositions are activated by external facts to produce actions – this is the sensorimotor model. We can understand the acquisition of dispositions in terms of models like predictive processing and the idea that the brain is constantly rewiring itself. Going beyond this to ascribe *Verstehen* bubble language to units of mental processing is justified neither by what we know about what happens in the brain in the course of action nor by the demands of understanding action within the *Verstehen* bubble. Mind-reading operates, by necessity, with external states and external manifestations of dispositions. We can find patterns, learn patterns, and respond to patterns, but we have no way of accessing thoughts other than through the externals. This part of "behaviorism" is inescapable.

Mercier and Sperber have recently developed an argument that speaks to these concerns, and that is congenial also to the denial of the claim that mental processes closely mimic the language of reasons, beliefs, and desires. They argue that:

> Reasons are social constructs. They are constructed by distorting and simplifying our understanding of mental states and of their causal role and by

injecting into it a strong dose of normativity. Invocations and evaluations of reasons are contributions to a negotiated record of individuals' ideas, actions, responsibilities, and commitments. This partly consensual, partly contested social record of who thinks what and who did what for which reasons plays a central role in guiding cooperative or antagonistic interactions, in influencing reputations, and in stabilizing social norms. Reasons are primarily for social consumption.

(Mercier and Sperber 2017: 127)

This is similar to what was said earlier about declarations: their first life is as instrumental speech acts, not as means of surfacing mental content or reporting on it. This leaves the issue of reasons behind: they are narratives with a particular set of social purposes. We can of course recognize patterns and be conscious of them, such as patterns of "intentional behavior," and these patterns can correspond to narratives. And narratives, like any explicit practice, can become habitualized. But to habitualize narratives about souls does not mean that there are such things as souls.

Practices

Frequently in the cognitive science literature one finds a reference to "sociocultural practices" as an explanatory resource. And one finds this both in the standard approach and in the autonomous agent social, as well as in the alternatives. Practices are the differentiators between "societies" or social contexts. In the case of narrative practices, for example, we are concerned with something that is both cognitive, even a cognitive instrument which shapes cognition, and in some sense external. But what, in cognitive terms, is a practice? In answering this we can come to a kind of end to the book as well, for practices, in some sense, epitomize the problem of the relation between internal and external.

The case of tabu has already been outlined: it is a classic example of a practice, as well as the foundational case of a "norm" and the most rudimentary political order. But we can expand on this outline to clarify the cognitive science issues with social practices generally. We can begin with the fact that humans recognize patterns even in random arrays. Pattern seeking and finding is simply characteristic if human cognition, at the most basic level. Patterns and many other things can be learned unconsciously (Reber 1989). But pattern finding is promiscuous, allows for redundancy, in the sense that multiple patterns can be found in the same material – that they can overlap. If pattern finding is linked to predictive processing, as it plausibly is, we have a mechanism for filtering patterns to select for the most predictive ones; and with feedback that affects memory and the reinforcement of these pattern recognitions we have a filter that selects for the most predictive ones.

Whatever the exact nature of the transformative effect of pattern recognition is on the neural level, whether it is in memory as storage or as a kind of rewiring that disposes to recall, it is clear that memories cross and combine various modes, so that an olfactory stimulus can recall a physical place, or emotion, for example. This means that the pattern recognition involved in such cases is not purely formal or factual, but contains context along with what is focal, regardless of the source of the pattern-recognition experience. Whether it is a seeing ghosts error of the kind discussed by Mercier and Sperber (2017) or the kind of social *mise en scène* discussed by Barsalou (2013), it will contain multiple elements, engaging multiple parts of the brain. They will also typically engage in action production: the model, perhaps, is the response of a cat running into the underbrush when the shadow of a hawk passes over it. This is an innate pattern-recognition response: no room for learning here. But learned or filtered for patterns also produce action responses, because action is going to be a part of the pattern available through joint attention: one is typically attending to something that the other agent is acting on, and one attends to their actions, their emotions, and the rest of it, most of which will be unconscious even in the case of conscious pattern recognition.

Here the "pervasive social" shows its power. The inputs include social ones: the promptings of others to recognize patterns where they are attending to something. This raises the question of whether their attending leads us to recognize the "same" pattern. This requires two answers: on the neural level, our recognitions – and especially our response to feedback, our filtering and selective memorizing – will be affected by our learning history, and this learning history will be, on the neural level, unique. At the *Verstehen* bubble level, the answer will be different. For the purpose of explaining how a patterned response becomes entrenched in the behavior of socially related individuals, individuals who are part of the joint of joint attention, of getting the practice going, we do not have to worry about whether we are recognizing the "same" pattern: they need to be the *same* to sustain joint attention; and of course joint attention is itself subject to error about the other, or at least a degree of mismatching, and therefore variation. But the "criterion" of sameness in the *Verstehen* bubble is pragmatic and predictive: does it work and continue to work in cases of joint attention, or does it break down in miscommunication and misunderstanding?

Given the promiscuity of pattern recognition or attribution, it would facilitate social learning and joint attention itself if these pattern-recognition and filtering processes were constrained by some more general parameter. One parameter is given by the limits of mind-reading. But there is also a long but persuasive tradition of more or less speculative thinking based on anthropological data and philosophy to the effect that there are some common basics of human cognition that bear on joint attention and promote particular kinds of pattern entrenchment. Wittgenstein spoke of natural symbols (see Rubinstein 2004). Durkheim considered all thought to derive ultimately from the sacred–profane distinction

(Durkheim [1912] 1995). Lévi-Strauss discussed a wide range of mythogenic binary oppositions, characteristically those in which some physical fact stood in for a more fundamental distinction, such as the raw and the cooked to signify culture vs. nature, or the spatial organization of a village for its kinship structure. He coined the phrase "animals are good to think [with]" (Lévi-Strauss [1962] 1964: 89). Lakoff and Johnson (2003) on metaphor, in the same tradition, point to the physical things and bodily processes that are used metaphorically, as does (Lakoff 1987) in *Women, Fire and Dangerous Things*. Mary Douglas (1966) identifies some of the most prevalent distinctions ordering the moral order, notably purity and danger. Whether these are in some sense innate or take the form they do because they are grounded in some physical fact that is easier to learn socially in the form of binary oppositions is an open question. However, the sheer diversity of norms (Henrich et al. 2004) and the resilience of moral disagreement (Machery et al. 2005) suggest that fundamental conflicts, not unanimity, are at the core of morality.

Much of the literature on norms is focused not on norms like tabu, but on such general norms as fairness. There are even animal studies that indicate that ravens will not accept an unfair distribution of treats, and that even in these animal contexts there are interfering effects of hierarchy on these responses (Wascher and Bugnyar 2013). Another study suggests that people learn to respond both to hierarchy and egalitarian considerations, but that hierarchy is the more fundamental (Vendantam 2016; see also Thomsen et al. 2011: 477). We can assimilate the hierarchy–equality distinction to the ones we have listed above: it is a binary opposition that is in some sense unable to be resolved in actual social life, and is therefore "mythogenic" – that is, to the repeated attempt to resolve it by an explicit narrative, theory, category-distinction, or some similar means. What might the cognitive mechanisms for this kind of genesis be? One might think of it as follows: as in such cases as the trolley problem, we as individuals have two sets of conflicting dispositions, each of which is invoked by recognizing a known pattern. One is egalitarian, the other hierarchical. One leads to fair distribution and perhaps to joint attention to cheaters, and thus to punishing free-riders or other advantage takers who violate fairness; the other leads to obedience. We can amalgamate the notions of ideology, myth, and narrative here and note that it is precisely these kinds of conflicts that are "resolved" discursively or partly discursively through these means.

Tabu, in the form of the tabu and tabu-pronouncing character of the "chief" of these societies, provides such a resolution: "authority" is assimilated to danger, and there is no longer a question of "fairness" when the tabu person is excluded by being placed in a different category. Similarly for such institutions as caste: hierarchy is assimilated or conceptually blended with purity in such a way that considerations of fairness do not arise. In each of these cases one finds a kind of explicit theory, founding myth, or ideology justifying and explaining the solution which is a solution to the cognitive dissonance or conflict between dispositions that would otherwise routinely arise, as a kind of daily trolley problem. In this way basic but undirected emotions are cognitively hijacked by ideologies, but in a way that is cognitively advantageous for the user. It is then reinforced by the social learning that comes with joint attention. The ideologies are also "normative," but in the sense of tabu: they are external, and relate to persons, places, and things, and the supposed properties of these things that require a particular kind of response. Social learning hardens the response into a wired-in neural disposition.

With these elements, we have a full-blown "socio-cultural practice": it is "normative" because there is one or another explicit doctrine or normative assertion within the *Verstehen* bubble that makes it so – traditionally, in Christian contexts, that God demands it; it is rooted in the basic emotions that it hijacks; and at the core is the process of pattern finding and joint attention, including attention to and learning from action responses, that links the neural and *Verstehen* bubble levels. Such a practice is both "external" and "internal" to the individual. It is internal because it becomes wired into basic emotions and dispositions through the process of pattern recognition and feedback, including the feedback of imitation and social learning. It is external in two senses: it is about external things to which we develop dispositions to respond; and it is entrenched in the many events of joint attention that are presented by social interaction, as well as by the explicit and public aspects of the practice, the declarations, and reason-givings that are intertwined with the learning and execution of the practice, as well as the physical objects and places used in connection with them.

Plausibility and the Social: A Short Afterword

All these external social things, physical and social, produce inputs that feed back to the brain, and transform it. Experience, conscious or not, together with neural plasticity, transforms physical brains (Losin et al. 2010; Lende and Downey 2012). And experience is socially distributed and itself produced in interacting with others, with all the complexities this implies. So there is no escaping the need to fit this kind of topic into an integrative cognitive science. And this leaves us with the unanswered question of the book. Can the standard approach account for practices, social institutions, ideologies, and the like? Are the alternative approaches adequate to the task? Or is the problem of the social the place where the place where challenges became overwhelming? From the narrower point of view of social science, the question can be reversed. Largely taken for granted social concepts – such as rational choice, the belief-desire model, and concepts of norms and institutions – are cognitively involved. To the extent that they depend on cognitively implausible ideas about the relevant cognitive processes, they are strictly speaking unscientific. There may be good reasons for remaining outside the circle of consilience that is science. But to do so would be to abandon the project of social science as science itself.

As has been noted repeatedly in this book, the approaches to cognitive neuroscience that presently exist are highly incomplete, and consequently depend very heavily on considerations of plausibility, particularly the plausibility of the idea that they can be extended to cover new facts and domains. The social is the great unexplained domain. Is it the place where plausibility goes to die? It is of course absurdly premature to dismiss an approach because of difficulties which may be solved. But the social, however it is understood, does provide a set of constraints on explanation the significance of which may be unclear but which cannot be denied.

References

Antón, Susan C., Richard Potts, and Leslie Aiello. (2014). "Evolution of Early Homo: An Integrated Biological Perspective." *Science* 345 (6192): 1–14.

Barsalou, Lawrence W. (2013). "Mirroring as Pattern Completion Inferences within Situated Conceptualizations." *Cortex* 49: 2951–2953.

Bickhard, Mark. (2001). "Why Children Don't Have to Solve the Frame Problems: Cognitive Representations Are Not Encodings." *Developmental Review* 21: 224–262.

Bittner, Rüdiger. (2001). *Doing Things for Reasons*. Oxford: Oxford University Press.

Douglas, Mary. (1966). *Purity and Danger: An Analysis of Concepts of Pollution and Taboo*. London: Routledge & Kegan Paul.

Durkheim, Emile. ([1912] 1995) *The Elementary Forms of Religious Life*, trans. Karen E. Fields. New York: Free Press.

Fauconnier, Gilles and Mark Turner. (2008). *The Way We Think: Conceptual Blending and the Mind's Hidden Complexities*. New York: Basic Books.

Guala, Francesco. (2016). *Understanding Institutions: The Science and Philosophy of Living Together*. Princeton, NJ: Princeton University Press.

Henrich, J., R. Boyd, S. Bowles, C. Camerer, E. Fehr, and H. Gintis. (2004). *Foundations of Human Sociality*. New York: Oxford University Press.

Kahnemann, Daniel. (2011). *Thinking Fast and Slow*. New York: Farrar, Strauss, Giroux.

Lakoff, George. (1987). *Women Fire and Dangerous Things*. Chicago, IL: University of Chicago Press.

Lakoff, George and Mark Johnson. (2003). *Metaphors We Live By*. Chicago, IL: University of Chicago Press.

Lende, Daniel and Greg Downey. (2012). *The Encultured Brain: An Introduction to Neuroanthropology*. Cambridge, MA: MIT Press.

Lévi-Strauss, Claude. ([1962] 1964). *Totemism*, trans. Rodney Needham. New York: Penguin.

Losin, Elizabeth Reynolds, Mirella Dapretto, and Mark Iacoboni. (2010). "Culture and Neuroscience: Additive or Synergistic?" *Social Cognitive and Affective Neuroscience* 5(2–3): 148–158.

Machery, Edouard, Dan Kelly, and Stephen Stich. (2005). "Moral Realism and Cross-Cultural Normative Diversity, Comment on Henrich et al." *Behavioral and Brain Sciences* 28(6): 830.

Mercier, Hugo and Dan Sperber. (2017). *The Enigma of Reason*. Cambridge, MA: Harvard University Press.

Miłkowski, Marcin. (2013). *Explaining the Computational Mind*. Cambridge, MA: MIT Press.

Nuffield Department of Surgical Sciences. (2017). *"Researchers Take Major Step Forward in Artificial Intelligence."* Oxford: University of Oxford Medical Sciences Division, John Radcliffe Hospital. www.nds.ox.ac.uk/news/researchers-take-major-step-forward-in-artificial-intelligence (accessed 12 June 2017).

Reber, Arthur. (1989). "Implicit Learning and Tacit Knowledge." *Journal of Experimental Psychology: General* 118: 219–235.

Rubinstein, David. (2004). "Language Games and Natural Reactions." *Journal for the Social Theory of Behavior* 34(1): 55–71.

Thomas, William I. and Dorothy Thomas. (1929). *The Child in America*, 2nd ed. New York: Knopf.

Thomsen, Lotte, William E. Frankenhuis, McCaila Ingold-Smith, and Susan Carey. (2011). "Big and Mighty: Preverbal Infants Mentally Represent Social Dominance." *Science* 331(28): 477–480.

Vendantam, Shankar. (2016). "Hidden Factors in Your Brain Help to Shape Beliefs on Income Inequality." *Hidden Brain.* NPR, 5 January. www.npr.org/2016/01/05/461997711/hidden-factors-in-brain-help-to-shape-beliefs-on-income-inequality (accessed 20 June 2017).

Wascher, Claudia A. F., and Thomas Bugnyar. (2013). "Behavioral Responses to Inequity in Reward Distribution and Working Effort in Crows and Ravens." *PLoS ONE* 8(2): e56885. http://journals.plos.org/plosone/article?id=10.1371/journal.pone.0056885 (accessed 19 June 2017).

INDEX